The Freedom to Be Tragic

Also by David Lindley

POETRY
Poems
The Night Outside
Five, Seven, Five
Something & Nothing: Selected Poems

PROSE
Ideas of Order

THE FREEDOM TO BE TRAGIC

David Lindley

Verborum Editions

First published 2013 by Verborum Editions

Verborum Editions
5 Lauds Road
Crick
Northamptonshire
England
NN6 7TJ

www.verborumeditions.com

Set in Janson

Book designed by Sarah Rock

978-1-907100-02-4

CONTENTS

Suppose I put it to you in abandoned words, and you listen with the same abandon. Chuang-tzu

Preface
The Facts in the Case

*So the universe has always appeared to the natural mind
as a kind of enigma, of which the key must be sought in the
shape of some illuminating or power-bringing word or name.
That word names the universe's principle, and to possess it is
after a fashion to possess the universe itself. 'God', 'Matter',
'Reason', 'the Absolute', 'Energy', are so many solving names.
You can rest when you have them. You are at the end of your
metaphysical quest.* William James, *Pragmatism*

*It would be enough for me to know
who is writing this
and sleep knowing it...*
W S Merwin, *Envoy from D'Aubigne*

Think less and live more. J G Hamann

I am the creative nothing... Max Stirner

This book is both a quest and a confession. The quest is not for truth, since I already know with startling clarity that there is no truth. The quest is rather to reconcile the contradictions of a mind that desires what it has already ruled to be impossible. What I find myself doing, in consequence, is resolving on definitive statements about what I believe to be, and anxiously desire to be, incapable of being confined by such assertions. By ardently wishing to be done with it, I hope to rescue from the futility of certainty the endlessly renewable possibilities of astonishment.

Once having begun, realising that the end result will add nothing of value to the hopeful beginning, and may even be viewed as a crime against the innocent hopefulness that inheres in beginnings, one has a moral obligation to the world not to allow it to expect too much. It is not given to everyone, as Hamann says, to be a system-building spider, for how could I bear to lose the world's and my own imperfections?

This is not an argument in my defence. One should try to say as little as possible. Since I am not concerned with the truth, I can hardly concern myself with doubt. Ideas, in any case, don't come all at once, marshalled into blocks of prose looking for a fight. Ideas that turn up like this, so full of themselves, are like uninvited guests who stay too long and talk too much. Ideas should be more like birds that come and go, leaving the day quiet and undisturbed, just as it was, a continuum of the merely observable that lacks the weight of rhetoric but is not immune to thought. I prefer statements that may be true or untrue depending on the weather or the state of one's bowels, to be read and recognised or passed over and not.

Since one cannot begin with objectivity but must always start from a point of view, whatever I say can never be more than a personal confession about matters to which there are no corroborative witnesses, who no doubt would have their own motives in claiming to be somewhere else. No statement can add to the fact of the world or confer on it any qualities it does not already possess. All that is possible is to assert some personal relationship between what I know and what may be known. So if an argument does not stand up to cross-examination, that is because it was never intended to convince but merely to propose how I came to be brought here against my will and to consider what should be done about it.

For that is certainly the first fact in the case. My only certainty is that something other than myself preceded me, that I am an unwitting accessory to another fact, having suddenly become a subject of some interest when, until now, I had been a complete nonentity, nothing. In addition, I have to say that whatever lends itself to reason does so only as an afterthought, since nothing was founded on reason but simply became subject to it arbitrarily. It follows (such is the way one is allowed to proceed under this arbitrary regime) that there can be no finality of judgment that appeals to universal principles, since these confessions are after all nothing more than the self-absorbed abstractions of a mind confined to a bonehead, permitted to speak but by no means authorised to pronounce on matters outside its jurisdiction, which naturally must be limited to its own selfish interests.

Other facts have since come to light. Although I wish to remain a reasonable man, I can't count on reason to reveal definitively a first cause or principle that created something out of nothing only to reserve judgment on its true nature for millions of years until it could become the subject of various mental abstractions that rise up and subside with each birth, with each generation, and that remain true only as a sort of rumour among us for a short time. Even though the world can't be dependent on my reason for its justification just because I happen to be wandering through it with my head in the air, the fact is that order does prevail, and my ideas of order define the relations that subsist between myself as the subject and everything else as the object, even though both can only have been given contingently. One must, in the light of these facts, proceed with caution and not be too dogmatic. I am, after all, only talking to myself, not (as I might have been tempted to say) writing to pass the time, but writing of time passing. Nothing else can come of it.

In the course of time (and time is another fact in the case largely responsible for the situation under review) what may have begun innocently enough as not very much seems, by the very fact of having become something more than itself, to have been unable to return to its former state of complete and utter emptiness and to have organised itself into ever more complex algorithmic knots until it has arrived at this strangely unnecessary condition of being able to talk to itself in this manner. One can hardly pass the fact by without notice, or pass on to other things without first acknowledging that everyone owes to this singular fact a debt of gratitude or ingratitude.

The question of how I myself came to be, in the guise of this mental construct of an actual person, is in every respect but one a very minor matter. I came to be because the species came to be, which is a matter of some interest, not least as evidence of how the self-organising regulation of objects naturally gets out of hand. The story that is myself is obviously a fiction that serves to bind together the facts in the case as though there were nothing more reasonable in the world. Such an eventuality would be of no significance whatsoever were it not for the important singularity that this fictionalised persona decides *everything*, including all the facts in the case, and treats the entire universe as peripheral to this one point at which its invisible threads happen to have become entangled in consciousness.

For this also is relevant to the facts in the case that must be given at the outset before one can begin to make sense of it: that

I should be under no obligation to bear witness, particularly to be a witness of my own fate. I should not have to know anything. Knowledge has crept into the scheme of things, along with guilt, and has proved a troublesome intrusion (a 'scandal in biology', Cioran says) into the indifference of the natural order of the world by demanding that it have a heart and that it should state its intentions once and for all. I was not permitted a choice. Once I had been cast ashore on the other side of silence by that very same wave of indifference, I was beset by anxiety and apprehension, knowing that I bore a great weight of responsibility to account for everything in words, while all along recognising that everything that lies outside my knowledge continues its own objective round without the least concern for the passing of time, the limits of space, or the fabrications of reason which are to be my burden alone.

I say alone, for though I have the companionship of the species and its memories, only I myself am at this fulcrum of experience in which everyone else bears a marginal relationship to the centre that is the grand illusion of being. To be the centre, as Pessoa says, is a fact we owe to nothing more than a certain geometry of the abyss. We each, certainly, are companions in adversity, and exchange terms of endearment, sympathy and consolation, but there is only meagre comfort in that. One's life, like one's death, is essentially endured alone.

To say that one is happy or unhappy about this state of affairs is nothing more than a trite observation. I don't care one way or the other. They both seem to me to be anaesthetised states of mind that refuse to face the true facts, facts that are not to be remedied by any sweet or bitter pill.

I set out to consider what it might be like to live without any attachment to anything, without an opinion or any interest in the varieties of experience. But I found that I was permanently attached to everything by the very nature of being, which is a form of material existence that differs from that of a stone or a tree or a frog by never knowing what it is like not to know anything. I might remain unattached to experience if experience could just pass by as the sunlight passes through leaves or the moon floats over the head of the night-watching owl. I might remain unattached if I were unaware of myself as someone to whom experience happens, and fall through the world like the cry of a bird.

To fall through the world without falling out of it, to live constantly aware only of the lyrical flow of experience manifesting itself in my consciousness, seemed to me to hold out the possibility of redemption, of justification for having to bear the weight of the knowledge of being in the fact of knowledge itself, in the pure condition of knowing without knowing for any purpose or out of any necessity to know. I can only occasionally glimpse, in momentarily imagined breaks in the clouds of another darkness, what it must be to be otherwise and to awake to pure knowing free from the forms of knowledge.

I am not without hope. I have inherited my mind courtesy of a primate legacy that has been heavily invested over time, and if some extraneous and incidental thoughts arise in it not fundamental to its main purpose, then I ought to be able to put them to rest on their own terms. Hope and despair are not the essence of mind. What arises in the mind goes to rest in the mind.

I am not without hope, because the privileges of mind are all that matter to me. The fact that they are emanations from a cerebral whirlpool that is itself dependent on a heartbeat and are therefore temporal and not eternal only serves to make them more delightful and indispensable to a life worth living.

The whole world exists to itself, and in a state of mindlessness I should exist to myself integrally with it, undying but unborn. The condition of being born is given as an unfathomable fatality that will always and forever remain undisclosed. The architecture of being, the biological organism and its nervous system and brain, is given and, without any reason for it to do so, strives to preserve itself and reproduce itself even in cases where it has no idea that the privilege of living has been conferred on it.

The instrumentality of mind that has emerged as a finial to this architecture of the will to live does not change the essential condition given at the outset. It serves it. The essence of mind is to serve the otherwise blind will of the living organism. But this essential mind accomplishes nothing more than was the case before it appeared on the scene, and so long as it continues to serve the will of the organism just so long will the condition given at the beginning continue until the end. Yet it quite incidentally, in consequence, imposes on me the entire burden of consciousness and the anxiety of being. Since I am born to this condition I am fatally bound by it, but if I accept my bondage the round of my life can only proceed like that of a worm or a cockroach illumined by the knowledge of its fate.

My life is of no importance. How can it be? It is already given and already taken away. Only my mind holds out any hope because only my mind places any value on it. If my essential mind is actually a collaborator in my fate, it has made a serious error by allowing me the freedom to deny it.

What actually matters to me is not the essential, which is conditional, but the inessential and the unconditional, what I know unattached to the need to know, my life freed from the need to live. What matters is not living but knowing that I live, that is to say, what matters is the subjective fact of being, not the undisclosed fact of living. One is given by the other but, once having been given, life is subordinate to knowledge.

I will lose my life, as creatures do, but no other creature anticipates its loss. Life does not mourn its own passing. What we mourn is the absence of knowing, for when I cease to know I cease to be. Living is one thing, being is another and, let it be known, something that is inessential to life itself. Life itself has no intrinsic worth. I bestow value on it by being, and for so long as I hold the knowledge of the world and myself in the nexus of consciousness it presents itself as something of value about which I may speak.

This is my relationship to the world, outside of which nothing is and nothing is known. While I acknowledge the objectivity of the world, and my self as an illusory object belonging to it, just the same all I can ever know is my subjective experience of it, and all it can ever be is the object of my experience. And so this is how one must proceed, on the ground of a subjective order, that is, on the basis of a personal aesthetic. For what else is there? The blind impulse of life that goes on without me, the orbiting detritus of a readymade world to which it clings, the great silence of eternal absence. What are the true facts in the case? Where on earth will they be found? Where in the universe can they possibly come to rest? There is no final judge or mediator. There are no arguments to be concluded, no settlement to be reached, no harbour in which to take refuge, and no other place to be where I may be myself except here as something sprung from nothing, whose truths are the few private contemplations with which I am satisfied.

Why I Am Allowed to Be

so here's a world of given
things already sorted out
Cid Corman, *Of*

As your mind is so clear, and as you consider so carefully the meaning
of words, I wish you would take some incidental occasion to consider
when a thing may properly be said to be effected by the will of man.
Charles Darwin *in a letter to Chauncey Wright*

Life is an unpleasant business; I have resolved to spend it reflecting
upon it. Arthur Schopenhauer, *Conversations*

I

...the basic problem has come to be how a mere state of consciousness can be the vehicle of a system of truth... John Dewey, *Consciousness and Experience*

I know nothing directly of how I came to be here. I can only begin, each day, from the singular point of the awareness of my own being. Even in sleep, watching the incoherent parade of my dreams, like a visitor at a carnival, I know this is my own experience. I know death is not like sleep, that death is the absence of both the real and the unreal worlds of my experience. Whether in fact I am myself one of those phantasmagorical carnival figures will forever remain unknown, for who is it that can know such a thing? The Cartesian paradox of proving the certainty of one's own existence as a first principle through the logical mental processes of a mind already given to us from God knows where, is reason's little joke with itself. I have nothing else to play this game on but the checkerboard of my own thoughts.

I accept my existence first, as the one certainty upon which my experience depends. Whatever I conclude about the reality of my experience, I am only permitted to arrive at that conclusion within experience itself. I have nowhere else to stand, only some place I can imagine standing, but to imagine such a place I have to be here, in this place. Wherever my mind leaps to – to the future or to the past – I myself may not move. I am stuck, with this body and its mind, in this place, tethered to the present and the incontrovertible fact of my experience. All that I know of the past is a present knowledge. I have no knowledge in the past. Even my own history, my past experience, exists only as present knowledge and my experience now. I believe without any doubt that I am the subject which experiences and that the world is the object of my experience.

Of course, among the objects that fill the world of my experience is the object that is myself, the body with its mind. In fact, since I spend so much time thinking, feeling, remembering, deciding, talking, acting, I am the single most apparent and important object of my experience. While I do not doubt my own existence as the subject and experiencer, I equally have no doubt as to my objective existence as a 'thing' in a world of other things.

Yet, when I think of myself as an object, a creature, a complex organisation of physical material made of the same substances as other objects in the world, an object that somehow has acquired this odd capacity for subjective experience, my idea of myself as the subject of my experiences begins to look fragile. Might I after all simply *be* that object, with some peculiar attributes of organisational complexity that permit me to accumulate sensations as experiences and experiences as knowledge by which means, as an object, I misrepresent myself as the subject? I am sure in fact that I must be that object, that this 'I' does not exist, only the object that calls itself 'I' exists and that it goes about with my name simply as a way of subordinating the whole of existence to its own interests.

I become convinced of this when I reflect on a further fact, that this 'I' who is the subject of experience and the one now reflecting on things he calls facts, had no part in his coming into existence. It is not even true to say that at least his mother and father 'wished' him to be and that therefore he had some sort of imaginative existence prior to his sudden appearance. What they wished for was something, to be sure, but something else. This grown up, self-willed, and ungrateful person that is myself, this tangle of tissue and cartilage and bone, blood cells and brain cells, this demi-octavo reader of books loafing about the world with his hands in his pockets, came into being not for any familial or social reasons as the disappointing fulfilment of a preconceived idea, but because of an unavoidable rupturing of the membrane of an egg. I have no elective life. I did not choose, nor was I chosen. The physical processes at work in the world in which I make this brief appearance decide everything. And they must, in some way or another, have decided on that very subjectivity of being that permits me my thoughts.

I begin with myself because there is nowhere else to begin. I look out with these eyes. The window is open. I am inside and the world is outside. Subject and object. Everyone understands everything this way: experience, history, memory, time. I may doubt the truth of my observations, I may question the soundness of my judgment, I may deceive and delude myself. But among all these uncertainties I am sure of myself as the subject of my experiences, doubts and illusions. It is the objective world about which I can say nothing with any certainty. I can make no assertions about the world outside my experience of it or my representation of it. What I think it is depends on what and how I think, on the cognitive architecture given to me, on the nature of the understanding itself and how it works. I can't bypass any of this to find another form of objective understanding that could possibly make any sense to me, one that has no idea of space or time, of cause and effect, of reason or language. My mind functions in a particular way because my body does and my brain does. I can't speculate on who or what I am except through the medium of who and what I am already.

The world is my representation. But idealism itself is only an idea. In practice we are all pragmatists, and we are not too surprised to find that the world continues to appear to be pretty much what it always seemed to be regardless of any abstract ideas we form about it. My daily encounters with the resistance of the physical world are sufficient proof of its existence, and incidentally of my own as that which meets that resistance. The planets must indeed orbit the sun the way we think they do because, with some help, I can predict the next appearance of Halley's comet or the transit of Venus (2117). But then the amoeba, too, and the ant and the mole and the woodlouse possess in various degrees of development a cognitive architecture of the senses and the nervous system sufficient for all their practical needs. I must infer that they inhabit a primitive cognitive sphere of experience bounded by their particular interests. Their experience will venture outward towards but never beyond the immediate needs of sustainable organic economy – they will live and not die, thrive and not perish, by virtue of their capacity to accommodate their inner needs to outer conditions. I cannot, though, further infer that, because their experience of the world is perfect for all practical purposes and can never be contradicted by anything outside their experience, the world of their experience is exactly equal in all respects to the world itself. The truth of the world never expands beyond the limits of the experience of the organism that has grown up in it, of the sensible and mental faculties that have evolved to cope with it.

Even some of the simplest organisms know the difference between earth and air, rain and shine, up and down, and know the perimeters of safety and danger. They know when the sun is in the sky and when the moon has risen, they navigate by the magnetic pole and even the dung beetle holds its course towards the Milky Way. If they needed to they might predict the course of the planets. For worms, astronomers and philosophers alike, if they are not to make serious errors of judgment, the seamlessness of the truth of the world with their experience of it is a necessary illusion.

The worm's view of the universe is, from my own larger conscious perspective, clearly an insufficient ground on which to base the objective reality of the world itself. Increased cognitive complexity in the brain does not make for another case. It is only the same case writ more eloquently, and we can't make a case that the rise to this level of cognitive sophistication came about in order to corroborate the truth of the world rather than to extend the usefulness of the worm's eye view by getting a better understanding of causality and the relationship of the world to ourselves in our experience of the world as object and our self as the subject of experience.

The world is the 'it' and 'I' am only 'it' acting in some manner on the self-sustaining organism that needs to know something of the world in order to get by. If the subject is the channel through which experience is filtered and condensed, the subject is also, and firstly, the object that is doing the filtering. It is like a setup of laboratory equipment someone is using for the purpose of experimental proof, condensing in one receptacle something previously diffused in another – something that then afterwards might again be dispersed into the atmosphere and never seen again. What if I am not this solid subjective certainty comfortably seated at the window looking out on the world of the objective as though it had been laid out just for my benefit, like a Dutch landscape painting in the Rijksmuseum? What if this self of mine, with all the synaptic exchanges of chemical and electrical signals between my brain cells that are the cause of it, is more like an image created by fragments of a shattered mirror floating free in space, a temporary concatenation of matter and energy framed momentarily in coherent patterns, the reflection of a world only partially connected, with here and there a glimpse of an ocean, a headland, a garden, a room, all of them tumbling through space, eventually falling apart and then redistributing themselves as atoms and waves that may or may not come together in some other form in some other time and place? My consciousness, then, is no more than a fragmentary world's brief memorandum to itself in passing, and its scribbled notes can never add up to a definitive statement.

But fragmented occurrences of matter and energy do quite evidently cohere and persist. Some persist in organic cellular structures with ergonomic work cycles. And some, over the course of time, persist successfully enough to become the sort of creature that I am myself, carrying on my back instead of a beetle's protective carapace a head filled with images of my own intentions.

This is what the subject is, the organism as a coherent object striving to persist, with its subjective experience as the focal point of its persistence. Subjective perception is part of the armoury of the organism that must manoeuvre in its world, negotiating the autonomy of this singular object among other objects. In putting the fragments of perception together into some useful order it is not merely leisurely occupied in creating the world's self-portrait. If, as it has turned out, through continuously augmented complexity in organisms over evolutionary time, the coherence of experience that is the foundation of self-interest in the human organism is better served by going beyond its original and limited cognitive sphere to represent the context in which it can more effectively function, the subjective mind, thus brought to power and eventually to the power of speech, cannot then turn round to this world cradle and say: 'By virtue of what you have made me I confer on all your realms my sense of reality to be preserved by you in perpetuity as your true and revealed nature.' I have no remit. I can only be grateful not be a mouse or a mollusc.

I am faced with two contrary facts of my existence, neither of which I can dispute. The immediate evidence of my own being in subjective experience is the given foundation of my understanding without which the world and life are nothing. In this respect the world itself is my dependant. Close my eyes, shut down my senses, become deprived of all power of thought, and the world is a blank. Yet this blank is the source of my being and it, not I, determines my subjectivity. I am the subject of my experience, and all that matters to me is that subjective representation of experience. It is this that I call my life. But the one that represents the world to himself did not will himself into existence as the subject but came into being readymade to be that thing. Something, something else, exists – before me, after me, with me, without me – and I am *its* dependant. My subjectivity can only be that something else persisting in and through me. I am first and always what I am not, before I am who I am.

When I refer to 'something else' do I just mean that I am finally an event that has its origins in organic evolution that in turn worked its way somehow out of the inorganic material of the universe that abides by its own universal 'laws' which themselves suddenly exploded out of the lawlessness of nothing at all? Whether I like the idea or not, since I am not the creation of my own will I cannot escape the idea of being willed elsewhere. My problem is not so much in finding the physical and then the biological causes of my having become myself, but in the persistence of the state of affairs that is the ground of there being physical and biological causes. The laws of existence do nothing to justify the existence of laws. I do not need to understand what this ground is. In fact, by claiming to understand what it is I would only add something more to the list of things I understand and never get any nearer to the principle upon which everything I understand is predicated. I need to accept something, something that can't be understood, something that is irreducibly something else, before I can proceed towards any sort of understanding that is always limited to the appearance of something represented by the understanding itself.

I can't simply call it 'nature' because it is nature that is the problem. I can't escape my nature. Nature is determined, so it is not nature that determines anything. I have to resurrect the *will* as that principle, the will that is nowhere to be found in science but only in metaphysics. It cannot of course be admitted in science, for the empirical begins with what is given and we cannot locate in what is given the principle for the necessity of its being what it is. That it could not be otherwise if it is to be at all, we might agree upon. But that it should be as it is can't be established within our knowledge of it, only as a fact preceding all knowledge, as the principles of reason can't be questioned by reason but must be accepted *a priori* as the ground of reasoning, and no one thinks that this is not a proper way to proceed. We should grant to the will once and for all the same irrevocable and unquestionable status as the ground upon which anything at all can proceed, including reason itself.

To invoke a principle of metaphysics as the ground of all empirical knowledge is to stand accused of sleight of hand in springing upon science a first cause and principle of creation from speculative philosophy's bag of magic tricks. But the will is not the cause, only the fact of their being causes, not in fact a principle but only a word sufficient to denote the insuperability of some questions relating to existence that are not to be answered by observing what is in the hope of discerning in its physical and behavioural nature its right to be what it is.

What cannot help its existence, because it has no will of its own to be or not to be, is the subject of the will. The will is what cannot be accounted for. The will is the condition of being you can do nothing about. It is the condition itself. The will is the persistence of the condition and not the locatable cause of it. But we need not insist on causes, it is only important to insist on recognising what cannot be averted.

Since Darwin we have been able to view the evolutionary biological processes of variation and selection as undirected adaptive survival strategies with neither a Schopenhauerian *will* nor a Bergsonian *élan vital* brought into the argument about how it all keeps going. If someone mentions the 'forces' of evolution, what is meant is no more than a figure of speech to describe the constraining principles of change and development. If there are other forces at work, then they are subject to the laws of physics, operating at microbiological levels of cohesion. If we admit the will into this closed shop, the conversation goes, we admit agency, and if we admit agency we admit God and all those tiresome arguments from design. But this is to misrepresent the necessity of the principle of the will simply as poor empirical science. It was never an empirical proposition. On the contrary, the concept of the will is necessary in order to assert the primacy of the *fact* of the universe as the field for our empirical investigations and knowledge of it, and under which the principles of physics, chemistry, quantum mechanics and evolution are subsumed. Something else came first, the primary condition of a universal state of affairs that allows chickens and eggs to come and go – not of their own free will but by some other primary will implicit but unlocatable in the state of affairs. Science may not like it, but until science creates its own constructionist hypothesis from its reductionist laws, the constructionist metaphor of the will in metaphysics, and in intuitive thinking, must stand as the ground of the 'must' awaiting a successor 'why'.

II

To live means to lack something at every moment... Paul Valery, *The Temptation of (Saint) Flaubert*

Technical language does not clarify what ordinary language cannot explain. Words are only approximations of a truth they can't define, the embodiment of the history of our misunderstandings. It is only by repeating ourselves that we are able to restore an idea to its pure rhythmic form free from language. The 'ego' and the 'id' did nothing but add obscurity to the common words 'I' and 'it' (*das Ich und das Es*) which are already layered with multiple meanings. 'I' can be anything 'I' choose, and 'it' anything else. I have to try to understand myself in some way that involves separating the 'I' in here from the 'it' out there. Freud, in calling up the ghosts of the unconscious to haunt our idea of the personality and its will, at least succeeded in restoring the 'it' to its 'I'. 'It' existed before 'I' did, and it resides in me as the progenitor of the 'I' that represents the subject.

Schopenhauer chose the word 'will' to define the founding concept of his philosophy, knowing that the will could represent a number of meanings in ordinary language and that he would himself be obliged to use the word in more than one sense. In one sense the will is used to describe a world existing *on its own account*, that is, underived from any other cause. It is the world's aseity, precedent and impervious to any theories of how it came to be. In another and simultaneous sense it describes its sustained persistence. This world that exists on its own account does not continually fall out of existence, appearing and disappearing as a random event. It sustains itself and perseveres in a continuum of changing forms and associations. It is always tempted to be, as though always lacking something, rushing to rebalance itself at every moment. Not only do insistent living organic forms survive, but fundamental matter and energy persist. The 'will' is an ordinary word to describe what is essentially the most ordinary thing in the world – the world in and to itself. The will does not belong to the fundamental physics of the universe, is not subject to empirical investigation. No empirical description of what the universe is and how it works touches the problem of the will: the will is the given condition on which its description is predicated.

We might ask: 'If all the particles of the universe possessed free will, would they choose to exist?' The answer to this question is, yes – because their will is not free, for their existence precedes and therefore precludes their will. They are already willed. But they are not willed by any agency that wills. The will stands on its own ground. This is the third sense of 'will', not the will manifest in the evidence of all that exists as the will of something else that wills, but the thing in itself that is the will.

What in Kant's mind was the noumenal world of 'thing in itself', in Schopenhauer's was the will itself. There is that which exists in itself and on its own account about which we can say nothing, and there is that which is represented in cognition and understanding as phenomenon. The worm's view and my own are similar, in that what we can know of the world is confined to the cognitive architecture that defines what may be known. What 'it' is always remains what it is in and to itself. The only world I know (and the different world the worm knows) is the one presented to my bodily senses and extrapolated in whatever neural chemistry I possess, and the worm likewise, and whatever I investigate (that the worm doesn't see the need to) does not touch the world itself but remains contained within that vast cathedral structure that is my consciousness. The ground upon which this edifice is raised is utterly lost to me.

The will is the fact of the world. It exists on its own account, it persists, and it is what it is in itself and is not and never can be what is represented to my understanding. The will in this complete sense exists prior to and outside of the forms of human cognition, and independently of everything I have ever thought or could think through their agency. Since the capacity to think at all is given by the very thing I am expending my thoughts on, obviously whatever I construct in my head about the origin and nature of the universe, every logical conclusion about cause and effect, any theory, rational or irrational, has a prior dependency on something I can know nothing of. *It* exists without me. But

I cannot exist without *it*, of my own volition, by some other 'will'. I do not command my being. I exist because something unceasing and inexhaustible has driven me here.

My mind is a very late flowering of evolution. Millions of years preceded it. There was light, and for the most part all of life grew towards it, the plants today still piercing through the darkness of the earth, the eye of the snake looking out from its inner darkness. In time there was not just light but illumination. Consider the degrees of apprehension inherited by all of existence. For the unfeeling and immobile garden cabbage, for the chrysanthemum, none at all, no more than a stone, yet they live for the light. Think of all the scrabbling towards the light from under the ground and over it. Every moving creature has some limited apprehension of the world in which it moves, even the blind slow worm and the mole and the bat, who do not count on the light, shape their habits to the actuality of their physical existence. And I, I cast around for some sort of comprehension and coherence, under the same unavoidable imperative, so as not to stumble, to fall, to fail.

If, out of this late flowering of evolutionary necessity, there is in me the temporary and tenuous power to create these abstract notions of reasons, causes, forms, and of my intentions, purpose, meaning, and to make them clear, as the light makes clear, this does not suppose that there is clarity, or reason, or meaning subsisting in the world. Such things subsist only in my disposition in the world. This accident of cerebral comprehension that differs, it seems, from the apparatus of the aster and the ant, does not legitimise the imposition of reason and partiality, retrospectively, on that unreasonable and impartial, blank and indifferent circumstantial will that imposed existence on me, and with it this much understanding. What I know is given by what I do not know. What my understanding encompasses, encompasses me. What I love is bequeathed to me by that which holds no love for me. My consent to my existence was never sought, my agreement is not required. I could not choose or refuse, and now that I understand the little that I do, it makes no difference – it makes no difference to the condition of my existence.

If I am allowed to make this much out clearly, it is on the understanding that some things will never be made clear. It will never be clear why this condition of being is the condition at all, why matter, energy, life are the condition. Wherever you fix the starting point for the origin of matter (fix it in nothing at all!) there is nothing in your theory that will explain why existence and not non-existence is the condition. How easy it is for things to fall apart, to break, to collapse, disintegrate, dissolve. How much a characteristic of everything's existence is its fragility, its impermanence, its return to dust. How soon we are exhausted. Yet it is not its dissolution that marks the condition of existence, but its persistence in spite of everything. If I understand the origins of life to have emerged from some primeval flux of 'soup and spark', I am offered no explanation of why, once formed, this unicell of life possessed the potential to go on living, to divide, divide and rule as though it were a rule that it should. Why must it exert effort? Why should it not fall out of existence immediately upon its creation, as though it had come into existence by mistake? Why should things be the most they can be and not the least? Everything, even the smallest particle, even the particle that is so small it can be held to exist only theoretically and in principle, is. Everything persists. It does not even just persist as a mute fact. It clings to its existence, insists on being and howls against non-being. Without an underlying a priori acceptance of persistence as intrinsic to life and matter the Darwinian theory of selection for survival could not make sense. It has to *assume* survival, and cannot explain survival. The mechanisms of survival, physical, chemical, organic, conform to our rational theories about them. But survival itself is completely unreasonable.

The intellect has no means at its disposal to go beyond what is as such. It cannot reach for what is not in order to find the source of what is. Every speculation begins and ends with the fact of existence, with what is as such.

My thoughts cannot escape me. And I cannot evade the fact of the world as the ground of my thoughts in the first place, since it is not 'I' who thinks but that which *is* that thinks through me.

All my thoughts take place within the condition that is given. That given condition includes the objects of my perception and the means of perception by which the idea of the subject is itself given. My intellect is trapped in this claustrophobic condition. It cannot proceed from the given condition to the giver, or to the cause of the condition's being given, without having to admit that its speculations and its reasoning are predicates of the given condition. It is therefore perfectly useless to suppose that the ephemeral images of my mentality, which are the temporary association of molecular material conditions already given, can by their to-ing and fro-ing *find* the giver in or among or behind the given condition. All that my introspection is capable of understanding is its own reflections.

Reason ascribes causes to effects. That's what reason is for. It is therefore bound to appear perfectly reasonable to mind, when stared at in the face by an existence thrust upon its attention like a ragged old man who accosts us in the street, to try to find the first cause that created the necessity of our being so violently interrupted in our eternal dream of nothingness. It is only a small step from admitting that the world exists in its own right with no further need of explanation or justification to asserting that what will satisfy my reason is that God shall be that which exists in this way, in His own right and not subject to any further elaboration on my part or anyone else's, sufficient in Himself and also very conveniently therefore the *cause* of the world about which I appear to be so exercised. By this way of reasoning I will in addition have discovered the added benefit of conferring on the blind will the hope of a revealed purpose, a certainty of direction, and even a benevolent intention towards its own creation. The will, by this method of reasoning, becomes *His* will, not blind will but omniscient will, His will as the agency of the giver, and not the given as the condition of the will. But, in reasoning with myself thus, I am only playing a game with the tokens and counters of reason, the gift of which is the one and only true origin of the game I am allowed to play.

All my propositions remain dependent on what are already given as the conditions and rules of thinking on which I ground all my ideas, concepts, causes and complaints. Thought itself cannot reinvent the condition of thinking simply because it wishes it otherwise, wishes that the sources of its thinking were as rationally grounded as reason itself, wishes reason to be absolute and not contingent on being born. God cannot be the prime cause. God can only be the secondary consideration of that insistence of mind that seeks causes, whose only true first cause is the given condition on which it depends.

The only thing I am able to say with any certainty about the true nature of things is that it is their nature to exist and to persist. Not to exist from any cause, not to persist for any purpose, but to exist on their own account and to persist willy-nilly. This is not in fact to say much at all, but it is the only legitimate starting point from which I can proceed to any understanding whatsoever, and it does at least avoid the error of thinking that from some further point of understanding I will be able turn back and retrace my steps so far and with such misplaced self-confidence to a point *beyond* where I started from, to an idea of a first cause or principle. For of course I can invent anything I like to be the first and final cause, principle, meaning, purpose, direction, historical inevitability or visionary eschatology, and assert such a thing to be implicit in the nature of things from the beginning. I can easily suppose such beginnings in the knowledge that they cannot be disproved except by asserting just such another supposition in its place. Paradoxically, to settle for a first cause implicit in the *fact* of existence, to insist that there *could* be meaning in the universe merely awaiting its unlocking, is to commit the gravest offence against its disinterested impartiality and its blank anonymity and against one's own rescuing consciousness. My consciousness and my reason are the only sources of illumination in the eternally dark vastness of the universe.

When that universe gave me my reason it did not know what it was doing. But I do, and I am in no mind to give back my freedoms and confer on *it*, on the blank and mindless *other*, those powers of intelligence that are *mine alone*, and to give them back for one reason and one reason only, out of mere timidity when confronted by my existential loneliness, when one cries out and no one answers. One should have more courage.

III

There is the dodo for instance. Says the moment one looks at it one sees at a glance that 'it looks like a dodo.' Mark Twain, *The Diary of Adam and Eve*

The scientific evidence tells me that the universe had a beginning and that it will eventually come to an end. Between these two imagined events the universe proceeds from a *point* towards ever increasing complexity. But in no sense can I infer from this fact that the will – that which I am satisfied to define as 'existing-and-persisting' – is in some way the agency of this growing complexity. 'It' persists but does not (as will, force, energy) thereby *propel* anything. The will is not the agency of the other, the will *is* the other. Complexity is the outward manifestation of existing-and-persisting, of the only manner in which the will can exist and persist. It is possible to imagine that this given condition of existing-and-persisting – of existing on its own account and persisting willy-nilly – could have manifested itself as a single, uniform and unchanging state. But in doing so it is possible to imagine it only as neither existing nor persisting, as the inverse of the actual condition that prevails, as not, as nothing. This is exactly why I have to accept my being and persisting as the starting point, as the given condition, simply because the alternative condition, of not being and not persisting, which I can so easily imagine ought to have been the case, is not in fact the case, is not given.

If the unavoidable nature of things is their existing and persisting, the unavoidable nature of existing and persisting is change. In the mountains only the wind, the stream, the pine trees, the clouds, the hare appear to be moving. But the mountains themselves persist in their outward stillness by virtue of their inner turmoil. Matter itself is bounded by movement. The shapes that movement casts up are only the forms of its constraint in time. In time they will be otherwise.

The mind is obsessed with causal connections and with settling permanent states on phenomena that could just as clearly be accepted as evanescent and indefinable. The species no sooner woke to consciousness than it began, like Eve, to distribute names and likenesses to things – and this for the good reason that, as a conscious human being, I am no longer simply that aggregate of material parts lost to myself, as the mountain is lost to itself, but I am aware of myself as one thing separated from other things of which I am also aware. Yet I may not take these tokens of separateness to be anything more than the way in which the phenomena of self and other manifest themselves, of their own accord and through no agency of mine. Everything in itself and by itself is simply *one* thing, which is the existing-in-itself and persisting-in-itself of the will. I can't see and can't understand the will itself, for since it is something self-contained that also contains me I am only aware of the forms of my understanding that the will has shaped for me. It is not one of those things that I have named with any success: it is itself the insistent namer of names that goes by no name of its own. If I offer up some understanding of it, my understanding is itself only the phenomenon to which it has given rise. I am allowed to be by being brought here, but I had no part in my starting out or arrival. I wake in the early hours while it is still dark, and hear the noise of engines arriving and departing, and wait for someone to inform me what the name of this station is.

Evolution can't explain more than the phenomenal manifestations of existing-and-persisting, the operant, prevailing circumstances of existing-and-persisting as life forms. It can't throw any light at all on why anything takes the trouble to be. I can discover the conditions and circumstances that allowed life to create itself from molecules of inorganic matter, but I am unable to discover what it is that 'allowed'. Change and variation are the evolutionary factors that permit the persistence and continuity of the forms of life, but I have no knowledge of what it is that 'permits'. I can see that complexity arises out of the necessary condition of persistence, that diversity must inevitably ensue from *one* thing insisting on existing and persisting on its own account, self-consuming and self-renewing, but I do not have the least idea what it is that dictates that it must be so.

If I am to think about anything at all I must believe three things to be true without question. That the fact of existence is the given condition of existence. That the given condition of existence is to persist in its existence. That existing and persisting must manifest themselves in perpetual change as the necessary condition of existing and persisting. On this basis I am free to speculate on any number of other things: on the origin and nature of matter; on whether matter is not in fact matter at all but now just an old fashioned conventional term for a quantum that is neither here nor there; how matter organises itself; how life emerged; how forms of life diversify and survive; how individuals and species evolve behaviour as well as physical forms; what the evolved faculty of consciousness is for and what degree of wilful autonomy consciousness confers on me. But I cannot examine the ground upon which these interests are raised.

I owe my being to the detritus of the years, to crimes and sins and broken crockery. As a product of evolution I am a product of waste, for that is what evolutionary history looks like. But it only looks like that if I assume it has some purpose or direction. Nothing is wasted, nothing is actually lost along the way, if the way is unknown. Nothing is certain, nothing is meant. I am certain only of *this* point. At any point in time life must always be the most it can be. The wastefulness of lived lives is never apparent unless I care to look down from this point to what is heaped at my feet. At this time I cannot say what was destined to be discarded, because nothing can be destined. Nature is not set on a determined path, it has no idea what it is doing (and we should not expect it to care since guilt comes only with knowledge). The path taken is defined by the paths not taken. Nothing is meant, and since nothing is meant nothing is wasted. But it seems wasteful to my ordered mind that fancies itself in control and obsessively looks for meaning and direction in its own ideas of order. For among the events of this wasteful persistence I can count the mind itself and its rational forms of understanding. The will in nature did in the end give rise to moral natures, and those moral natures do seek meaning and justification for being in nature. Whatever the unknowable nature of the objective condition of the will, though it holds no brief for me, it nevertheless undeniably has nurtured in me the subjectivity by means of which the objective is held to account. The will, as Schopenhauer says, is the strong blind man who carries on his shoulders the lame man who can see.

The whole of existence is beholden to my understanding. It exists as phenomena because my mind wills it so. Yet my subjective nature is also the manifestation of the will itself as one element of the complexity of its persistence. My mind does not stand apart from the will, but is given in it. Mind therefore is also will, the thing in itself. If the world exists as thing-in-itself, on its own account and self-sufficient, then mind as the manifestation of the will, as one complex item of the manifest will, exists in the same condition of thing-in-itself as mind-in-itself. But mind-in-itself is a rather different picnic. For it is not exactly describable as just one more object arising out of the will, which is always objective and indifferent. It is the subject, the subject of the will. As mind-in-itself it is subject-in-itself and holds its existence to its own account, is its own sufficiency. It elaborates a phenomenal world that obeys the laws of mind. In the attribution of mind to itself the will is filled with self-regard. What is *given* as will in the beginning, what in fact is still and must always be given for ever as will, is nonetheless given in mind as the subject of its own creation.

It is in the self-sufficiency of mind that I have my being as subject of the will. And what is so remarkable is that this situation has come about in true undirected evolutionary fashion from no other cause than the will's persistence manifesting itself in complexity. Mind is one of the complex creations of persistence. This organic unity that owns my name, that sits here and thinks and writes, came here as the result of the restless persistence of the will. I represent to myself the cognitive world of my experience because it serves my interests, which are in turn the interests of the will manifest in me. I came here at another's insistence, as the woolly mammoth and the cockroach, too, were bidden. If I represent the world of my interests in an intellectually connected way of which the cockroach is ignorant, then it is because it serves my interests more effectively and would benefit the cockroach not at all, which has no need of memories, ideals and dreams.

I did not will myself into this state of affairs. Nevertheless, here I am, with myself as the subject and the world as its object. I am the subject, and because I am the subject I write the rules by which the objective is governed. The will as thing-in-itself cannot be known, but the will as subject-in-itself is all that can be known. My mind is not mine but the will of something else that has burst in upon me. It is as deeply and darkly ominous to me as the blood that worms through my body. It is as much the flotsam of the floating world as the monkey's tail and the crab's claw and my true right hand produced by the same blind processes. And yet I alone am the light of the world. I am reason, I am knowledge, I am imagination, and because this is so despite all the possibilities of its not being so, I am the only source from which I may legitimately draw my justification for being. I illuminate a pathway through a dark and squandered world. Because my light is the only light I have, I must live by that light. I cannot cast light on the will itself. I can't expect to find meaning and justification for being in what is unknown to me, only in what is known and what can be known.

It is clear that meaning can't be found in the world because there is nothing in the world through which it can be externally given that is not already of my own making and naming. The will allows me to be, but it is not itself being. What it confers on me is nothing to it, but what I bestow on it is the knowledge of itself that it can never have except as subject-in-itself. The meaning of being is in being itself, in what I have become, and nowhere among the blind processes of my becoming can I point to anything to which I am obliged.

What It Means to Be Unreal

... that mindless, gross and contemptible idol which is called 'nature'... Thomas Mann, *Tristan*

When you know quite absolutely that everything is unreal, you then cannot see why you should take the trouble to prove it. E M Cioran, *The Trouble with Being Born*

You land, it seemed to him, on the shore of your own being in total innocence, like an explorer who was looking for something else, and it takes decades to penetrate inland and map the mountain passes and trace the rivers to their sources. Even then, there are large blanks, where monsters roam. John Updike, *Baby's First Step*

Just inside the edge of chaos seems the ideal place. Stuart Kauffman, *Investigations*

I

The spider has no particular idiom. Denis Diderot, *D'Alembert's Dream*

I write in an old house that was once a barn, with hidden corners, irregularities, cracks and gaps between and behind oak beams where other smaller creatures' lives are lived out unknown to me, as mine is lived out below unknown to them. In other words, I sit here at the end of time, where I always sit, neither in the world nor apart from it, accused by every moment that passes of being one of those poets despised by Robert Musil, speaking in obsolete idioms on great subjects as though just passing through on earth on my way to eternity.

I write these words in an old house with hidden corners and irregularities, cracks and gaps between and behind oak beams which, according to popular tradition here, were once ships' timbers that in the nineteenth century were hauled here to support a barn roof, timbers scarred by axes and two centuries of careless abandonment to wood beetles. But we are a long way from the sea, and much nearer to fanciful thoughts. The place is trimmer now it's a house and no longer open all day to the world and the weather. But the spiders, who were here before me, have made it their home also. Flies buzz in at the door and disappear into dark interstices in the roof beams. On the ground, spiders lurking in corners and behind bookcases seem to specialise in the dismemberment of woodlice, leaving small accumulations of rejected body armour in gritty dust heaps on the floor. Others, more ethereal, float on invisible threads, surprising me with their overnight industry when I come down the stairs each morning.

I could be more rigorous, I guess, in searching out their cobwebbed domains, but do what I will they return, and in any event I am inclined to give way to their claim to precedence.

Apart from the occasional disorientated scurrying some evenings across the floor, when they are at their most vulnerable, or the tentative descent of the more aerial species on threads from the roof beams, they generally stick to confined spaces defined by the angle of one object to another, and wait. Their domestic world is dark and angular, like a dislocated *film noir* scenario, their lives secretive, unobtrusive, hidden. Their activity consists in waiting and devouring and avoiding discovery. It is hard to imagine that a spider might have, or why it would need, a wider contextual perception of a world that is similar to my own, the director's cut, as it were, of reality. It is difficult to say what the spider would gain from the perceptual confusion of having to consider so much redundant and irrelevant information that did not concern it.

The spider's perceptual world is defined by what serves its interests, which are limited to its self-preservation and self-perpetuation, and the necessity of repetitive actions it can do nothing of its own will either to initiate or avoid. The spider that lives behind the toilet cistern in the bathroom can never, in an infinity of time, discover the shape or functionality or identity of a bathroom or why or how it came to be. In the context of all this gleaming porcelain, whose reality and true purposes are clear in my own mind, it finds nothing but the unconscious usefulness and efficacy of the angles and obscurities accidentally fashioned for it by causes forever beyond its knowledge. When your way of making a living depends entirely on unwavering obedience to the strictures of your nature, the introduction of a little knowledge is bound to be fatal. It is to the spider's benefit and essential to its successful longevity from generation to generation that it should know nothing, that it should be incapable of reflecting on the world as I do, that it should never know what it is or what this world is or what either of them are doing here. If the spider had a point of view, I imagine it would see the whole corpus of human knowledge, language, thought and belief as nothing more than the accumulated refuse of our animal bodily functions, a vast excrescence that may be of some indeterminate use to us but of no enviable interest to the spider.

Knowledge is added on. It does not appear to be fundamental to the working of anything that works. All of life's abundance and variety and swarming complexity contrives to exist and persist without the supportive armature of thought. Just because I am aware of that complexity and puzzled by it, it does not follow that the architecture of my thinking brain exists so that I may tax myself with questions about the nature of the reality it reveals to me. Thought is essentially functional, and with a limited functionality at that. Despite the illusion of illumination, I may be just as much trapped in my nature as the spider is in hers, both of us spinning out our not so different practices of deceit without either of us knowing why.

The thirty thousand or so distinct architectures of the spider's web are variations on a single theme of making a living by predation. We can assume that over the several millions of years before and after the carboniferous period, where early arachnid species first appear in the fossil record, spiders drifted, floated, walked and were carried to the niche environments they now inhabit, distributed over the whole world. Just as they themselves evolved, in unknowing conformance to sound Darwinian principles, their behaviour, and hence the patterns of their web construction, evolved as successful feeding strategies. Some of these web patterns are so impressive that we can't help but admire the skill and ingenuity of the spider from the perspective of our more deliberate and deliberated approach to the creation of complex artefacts, as though she proceeded from the starting point of an engineer or an artist, whose roles are interventionist, rather than blindly complying with the rules of self-organising behaviour that apply equally, in both physical and biological forms of order, to the formation of crystals and corals, blood cells and clouds, webs and booby traps.

It is now possible to use computer simulation models to produce parallel environmental constraints to those encountered in evolution, and to demonstrate how the geometry of the spider's web will adapt to environmental changes to the point of optimisation. A few fairly simple behaviour patterns interact to produce complex behavioural architectures. But it's not just the architectural aesthetics of the web that impress. The dinopid spider holds aloft a square net of threads spread between its outstretched legs and hauls in insect prey by gathering in its net like a fisherman. Yet the making, mending and trammelling of nets – something the spider can achieve in a half hour without an idea in its head – is not something we can do ourselves unless we have first been taught the skills, unless we have memories, unless we are social beings whose ways of making a living are dependent on the accumulation of a body of knowledge we are able to share with each other.

The diving bell spider, *Argyroneta aquatica*, constructs an underwater air bubble chamber, a submarine habitat for breeding and diving. Yet *homo sapiens* has no unconscious or incremental methodology available to it by which as a species it could invent a diving bell by accident – unless we consider thoughts themselves to be accidents, a different sort of evolved experimental instrumentality blinded by knowledge itself to the fact of mind as just another way to make things happen. For us, we have to work out the maths, the basic physics and the structural engineering – first in our heads and on paper before experimenting with the actual – and consciously address the main problem of how the bell we will produce in the iron foundry is to be supplied with its own pocket of air (the *pabulum vitae*, as Edmund Halley has it, who was the first to attach leather hoses to the foot of the bell) that the diving bell spider carries with her on her own person without effort or thought.

That the web-constructing spider got to be so smart simply by experimenting with its own excreta is something of an affront to the idea of intelligence. If everything can take care of itself by being left to its own devices, to 'nature', what is knowledge for, my knowledge of reality? If knowledge is merely something super-added, and even superfluous, what is the point of understanding beyond a certain practical usefulness? I suspect that there might be none. The fact of reality that is my everyday experience, that makes a bathroom a bathroom and not a place to hide, is perhaps no more than a mere epiphenomenon that results from the sort of contextual judgments we have to make to make all the things other animals construct without it. Who's interested in reality, in what and why, in *what else*? Not I, said the spider, not I, said the fly.

II

Truth repels, but delusion attracts, because truth presents us as limited, while delusion presents us as omnipotent. Leo Tolstoy, *Diaries, 3 February 1870*

The boundaries of the real are set by the near-sighted limits of the self-interests of the organism, the basic unit of self-centred existence. If this holds for the arachnid and its insect diet, it holds also, by indefinite analogical extension, for the human sphere of self-interest, and the human animal whose complex web of mental activity differs from the spider's web only in what it hauls in to serve its purposes. Its scope is wider than the spider's, but not as wide as all that. I only possess what I have been given and, like the spider, I cannot say that 'I' weave these patterns, only that in some way I am that pattern.

Reality is the net of perceptions I have woven in order to pursue my interests. My mind negotiates space, time and causality as deftly as the spider unconsciously designs the billowing rigging that is the centre of *her* universe. The spider's existence is a bounded, confined, formulaic and unreal place about which the spider has nothing to say. Were it possible for arachnids to comment on their lives, the conversation of spiders would be no more interesting than the conversation of people in general, preoccupied, despite their unique intelligence, with the immediate, the everyday, the banal, motivated, as Schopenhauer so aptly says, 'merely by want and illusion'. The pronouncements of spiders or insects do not count for much. In principle, nor do ours. Yet we believe that, out of the complex net of *our* thoughts and words, we not only construct the context from which we take the points of reference and direction that are essential for our survival and endurance, but we are also permitted to make definitive statements about the universe itself, stamped with authority and certainty. We even believe we have a duty to do so. If we are so clever, why are we so deluded? Perhaps for the simple reason that, as Tolstoy writes, 'truth repels because it is fragmented and incomprehensible, while delusion is coherent and logical'. The sense of an ordered relationship between things and the reason, meaning and purpose of everything is more important to us than the truth of things, if the truth of things is without reason.

There is no historical inevitability implicit in the complexity and diversity of life on earth, and no guiding principle behind it. Tolstoy's huge romance of Napoleon and Alexander has for its theme the grand delusion that great historical, epochal events have equally great and singular causes. A book of great length (a book that could never be long enough) was needed to encompass the many lives and incidents, the petty domestic as well as the romantic interests and occupations of the participants in these historical events and who were, in fact, the multiple and multi-faceted causes of them. History is not guided by a Napoleon,

Napoleon is simple the unifying theme of the imagination that requires coherence and logic. The sufficiency of an action in its time is not part of a larger purpose, and no final purpose can ever be exhausted by the enumeration of all the causes and effects we are able to observe and calculate. It is only the cumulative effect of infinitesimally small acts of free will constrained by larger necessities that allows us to invent, in the perspective of time and history, the laws of epochal movement and change.

III

We are a thing, an item of history, not an embodiment of general principles. Stephen Jay Gould, *Wonderful Life*

Whether in historical events or in the emergence or extinction of species, changes that appear large and sweeping happen at the micro-level of action and interaction, pressing against the limits of constraining circumstances and conditions, as much likely to fail as to succeed, to retreat and retrench as to advance, to collapse as to expand. Nothing given in the beginning determines anything in the end.

Of course, by establishing the fact of all conditions prior to the present condition, I can trace the causal connections by which the present condition came to be. No matter how lost in the dark wood I found myself, I could if I wished to take the trouble (bearing in mind the lesson of Hansel and Gretel and the treachery of nature) perfectly retrace my every step. But I could not thereby establish in any sense a direction given to those steps that was implicit in the first step. Once I have found myself in this *selva oscura* I realise, as Dante knew, that I am not here inevitably because I could not have done otherwise, but because I did what I did. I am no wiser about the laws ruling my condition than the soldier who sings, 'We're here because we're here because we're here.' I am always in *some* place and it is simply *that* fact that prohibits me from being in any other. We have maps only for the places we have already been. In the dark wood I stumble over obstacles and adjust my progress accordingly. The more my path is blocked, the more I must look for another way. If one direction is closed to me, I follow the one open to me, proceeding within limiting constraints, not following a determined route. All the causal constraints that I can identify and analyse in retrospect, all the incidents and accidents that hindered my freedom of action, add up to a coherent strategy of progress, and even a sense of inevitability. But none of them was given at the outset. I set out in fine weather. The present is not determined by the past, only traceable to the past.

This is an important distinction when thinking about evolutionary theory. Evolution as a process works, of course, from the past to the present – along the arrow of time that can't be reversed, time that is responsible equally for the dodo and the dinosaur, the broken teacup and the spilt milk that we must not cry over. But evolution as a theory works back from the present to the past. A 'law' can emerge only over time, the time it takes for the constrained micro-events of the past condition to be reconstructed as a sequence of events in retrospect. Those events themselves were nothing more than the miscellaneous and multiple firing off of infinitely small squibs doing simply whatever it was they were able to do in their time and place, with no eye for the future and what time would lead to.

Those minor negotiated advantages and concessions that make up the micro-diplomacy of sustainable coexistence at organisational level do not add up to a predictable outcome, let alone a partisan interest in any outcome in particular. This realisation is a blow not only to one's vanity but to the idea of rationalism itself. The only reasonable creature in the universe must concede that its powers of reason are owed to historical processes lacking in intelligence, and its very existence to nonrepeatable sequences of micro-events in the lives of pre-human organisms straining at the limits of their capabilities but with nothing to look forward to.

We are accustomed to think of evolution as the forward momentum of a series of successful adaptations through incremental changes that are preserved because they work or confer benefit or advantage on the organism. Evolution seems to be about success, about winning. But in every example of conflict and contention, say the confrontation of two stags locking antlers, it is the loser who determines the outcome. Until one of them gives way there is no winner. Winning is not an inherent quality of the winner but an event in time. The strong dominate only because the weak surrender.

In the evolutionary paradigm of incremental change and extension within constraints, what proves not to work, bit by bit fails and is expunged. What succeeds is the remainder of all that has not failed or, more correctly, has not yet failed. We say that the organism 'succeeds', as though 'it' had battled against the odds and come through. But in fact we cannot say what *will* come through, only what *has* come through, like those strangely shaped rocks in the desert left standing by the erosion of softer stone. They are not there 'because' they are made of stronger stuff. They are what is left standing when the weaker stone has been washed and weathered away and turned to windblown sand.

The classical Darwinian theory of natural selection is built securely on the principle of the regular and abundant occurrence of random and undirected variations in ontogeny that lead over time to the preservation of variant traits in biological populations, where the *fact* of their preservation provides the evidence that those traits have favoured advantage and survival. You don't get favoured variations so *that* the organism can survive. The mechanisms of inheritance were opaque to Darwin: 'The laws governing inheritance are quite unknown'. An understanding of the levels at which the replication of inheritable traits takes place, below the observable effects of breeding, was unavailable before Mendel, before Crick and Watson. Variation at the level of the cell, and at the level of the genetic sequence in the genome, provides the theory with its prehistory, with those elements of development for which there can be no fossil record, but only the record carried in the blood of the living organism. It would have pleased Darwin, no doubt, to have been able to imagine the 'propinquity of descent' at this fundamental level. But he would have been unlikely, once in possession of the knowledge of the building blocks of life, to have confused and conflated the means of construction with the causes that lead to it. It's not all in the genes. Replication is the remit of replicators, but they cannot themselves determine through their efficacy at replication how things will turn out. They are in no position to look out for themselves. There is no such thing as a wilful gene, only a working gene. How things turn out depends on what happens. The essential point about variation is that it is undirected. Variation is just the small limited thing that happens next. Its consequences are limited to three possibilities – either nothing will happen or something will, and if something does happen it will very slightly shift the odds against the organism, or very slightly improve its chances, and, in both instances, only eventually, over time. Evolution always looks like it works in the right direction because at any point in time what you see is what works (for the time being) atop the charnel house and dust heap of billions of life's superseded ancestors. The two Darwinian principles of variation and natural selection are the two voices in one endless discourse between incident and accident, where the incidents are the vicissitudes of organisational inheritance from which change, variation and diversity inexorably arise, and the accidents are the contingencies of a life being lived, whose success or failure will decide the fate of what it has unwittingly inherited from its past.

IV

It is not so easy to be an exception. But if we were destined to be exceptions, we must make our peace with the absurd order of chance, which reigns over our lives with the whim of a death squad... Imre Kertész, *Nobel Lecture*

Nothing can stand still. A universe in a continuous state of immobility can't exist, for it would be exactly equivalent to what it was before it came into existence, that is, nothing, outside time. Stasis is not living, not being, not existing, even at the microscopic, the atomic and sub-atomic levels of matter itself. Change is the order of existence. At this exact point in the history of the universe, at the arrow head of time, the fact that I am able to stand here as a metazoic organism and contemplate my own existence I owe to the contingency of change, and to the complexity that has arisen from contingent circumstances. Does anyone think there is a plan somewhere in all this? Is what I am now, and what the world has come to be, really the summation of all that has gone before? I think not. I think that what I see is the remainder of what preceded it – the residual forms of all the inconceivably numerous forms of life that no longer exist. I am hardly inevitable, and nor am I convinced that this is the best of all possible worlds. In fact, when I consider the immense diversity of life and how those lives are lived, they seem to me illogical, perverse, bizarre, heartless, bloody and wasteful. There is no real economy of means in evolution that has not been dependent, in the final analysis, on the most extravagant waste of resources. Not the way you would make things if you were the maker of things. The *fatefulness* of being is not in its order but in the arbitrary and contingent nature of that order. Its guiding hand is a fairytale Cinderella's, picking lentils out of ashes cast there by her cruel stepsisters. One will be chosen first and one last, but the first is of no more intrinsic worth than the last, or one more favoured than another.

It would be truer to speak, like Kertész, of *fatelessness*. The survivor suffers the guilt of survival, because survival is not the inevitable outcome of some seed that germinates with its fate already made in heaven. The survivor does not *deserve* to survive, hence the guilt that always attaches itself to every happy outcome in life.

Success is always precarious, provisional and, above all, dependent on the failure of others and what we have been able to build for ourselves over their remains, as we exemplify so often in the ruthless pursuit of power and wealth that, just the same, will not guarantee that the successful will not ultimately fall themselves. We know this in biology simply by the fact that precedent forms of stability have given way to new variants and have thereby gone into liquidation themselves. Change is always adverse, simply because, by definition, change is adverse to the present condition. Whether the variation in a particular trait is preserved or not, its advent destabilises the given condition of the organism in its world. Only the death of the organism, and the death of its progeny over generations, determines its emergence in a new form of organisational stability. Death determines it all, both what will fail and what will survive. Survival is not a sinecure. There is no incremental change that will confer a guaranteed benefit on the organism. A step is not a step forward, it is only a step, and that step is always unsteady, uncertain, conditional and intrinsically adverse to the present condition of negotiated stability, an outlier. The first step begins the longest, but also the shortest journey, and there is nothing given in the first step that will indemnify the organism against failure, or warrant that it will make the leap from uncertainty to a sure foothold on life. A successful complex stable structure is forever on the edge of expansion or collapse. Its complexity gives it a balanced stability, but no permanent security, like a man on a tightrope with a pole but no net.

V

The leaves are leaves again   no tree forgot Gregory Corso,
Reflections in a Green Arena

The tendency of the processes of evolution is towards ever greater complexity and diversity, and by implication towards an increase in indeterminacy and unpredictability. Nature does not create any ground for optimism. There is no case to be made for nature as a higher form of wisdom that, in this great sorting out, sorts things out for the best.

The order of nature lies, in fact, in deepest ignorance, in one remote and impenetrable act: that committed by the demon who gave the first push to a universe in waiting, the original cosmic fool who threw a stone into the water that no man since has been able to recover. Underlying all phenomena, from the beginning to the end of time, is this one simple *perpetration* that can have no name, and with which we can have nothing to do. This is the only singularity in the universe. All else is its diaspora of neutrons and neurons, atoms and molecules, waves and particles, grains of sand and mustard seeds, bacteria, lice, chickens, monkeys, men and monuments – the mish-mash of material existence that is the history of a singularity becoming many.

The tree gaudily jangling its multicoloured leaves in the autumn, a short time earlier was puffing out its green buds in May, breaking through the dead and mouldering kindling of its dry limbs with renewed insistence on its cyclical continuity. Although its ability to do this, encoded in the genetic sequence for protein synthesis, has an evolutionary history, it does not, in putting forth a new shoot, recapitulate any of its previous experience to inform how it will proceed. We need acknowledge surprisingly little history in order to thrive. We need very little of the past in order to make a living in the present. The humus of unimaginable numbers of leaves shed over millions of years has nurtured nothing in the tree beyond the present moment. It unfolds as it does not as the summation of all that has preceded it, but because it is a fixed and bounded entity locked into its present, and cannot do otherwise. Its lineage, the story of how it came to be thus and not otherwise, can be traced back via tiresomely repeated processes. But none of this is really history, just the present repeating itself. What nature *is*, is defined by the limits of what it does and the constraints on what it is able to do.

Everything in nature lives in the present. Animals, for Schopenhauer, represent the sufficiency of the present moment, satisfied simply with the fact of existence and the integrity of experience. And in the *Eighth Elegy*, Rilke says on the same subject:

> With all its eyes the natural world looks out
> into the Open. Only *our* eyes are turned
> backward…

Only we, who are creatures of natural history too, have inherited the illusion of space and time and seek the satisfaction of our needs and wants, desires and ambitions beyond the immediate present in the farther reaches of hope. The mind creates the illusion of freedom from the constraint of the present moment, calling on the experience of the past and the possibilities of the future to extend the available space in which a man might forage. My imagination would appear to be unlimited, able to step out of the confines of the here and now into mental spaces that intrude into a future that has no reality and a past that is already finished. I can set out utopian plans for people not yet born, and recreate the past in my head peopled with the shadows of my mental construction. I appear to have limitless creative freedom, roaming just as freely in impossible realms as in the known world. But when I examine my freedom more closely I discover that I am just as confined and constrained in the options open to me in my wider mental landscape as the dung beetle is in its narrower, more earthly one.

All my mental discoveries have a prior dependency on all that has gone before. In physiological terms I have the cranial capacity and an evolved brain structure that permits language and communication. While that capacity is innate, language itself is not, any more than mathematics. The capacity for reasoned thinking needs the materials of thought, the abstract representation of the concrete by which I can articulate and communicate concepts, and I must learn these. Unless we learn, even the capacity for learning, left without external stimulus, shrivels away. All that I can learn, in the beginning, is what is already known. My language is not a new language. These words are secondhand and joined together in a permitted syntactical manner. They are not my words, these are not even my sentences. I have plucked them from history, from out of the past. I cannot write originally, I am bound to echo what I have already heard, what I have read, what has been said before. I imitate, in spite of myself. Writing, I break a rule only to mend it again. I cannot transgress too far the limits set for me – set not just in some book of rules, but set by myself in order to understand myself. To fail in this is to become incoherent. It is the order, the sequence, the juxtaposition, the proximity, adjacency of individual letters, words, sentences that determine sense. Though the sense of a sentence is a greater entity than the sum total of the words I use, there are limited ways by which the sense may emerge and, however large the meaning, those ways are small. Without prior agreement to these ways between writer and reader, speaker and listener, no communication can take place, nothing can be understood. This means I can say nothing original, because the truly original is incomprehensible. I can only communicate variations on a known theme, expressing my thoughts in familiar terms, reshaping the familiar into something new but unable entirely to suppress what has already been said and therefore already implicitly meant.

The artist, as much as the philosopher and the scientist, no matter how original, can only build on the past and, however revolutionary, must work within the convention and can push only at the boundaries of what is already given. Art – whether painting, poetry or novel writing – is technically limited and socially constrained. Art forms do not exist in the abstract, and they are not simply the formalisation of the individual psyche. They are limited, in fact rather narrow social activities that can neither be practised nor appreciated without a large number of learned rules. Art cannot even offend unless someone takes it upon himself to accept a set of limitations to sensibility before his sensibility can be affronted. To take offence is to see one's own rules of decency broken, to recognise a disjunction between what you expect and what you get, a deliberate misfit in the agreed upon language of art, like an arbitrary obscenity introduced into the middle of an address to the Women's Institute. The motive for writing a novel may be pure inspiration (though unlikely) but no novel gets into circulation except within the constraints of what is saleable, what is readable, what a number of people in organisations of economic self-interest decide to do in relation to a commodity that may have had its origins in a world of the spirit but has its end as an object of some temporary interest to the few who will accept it as such. A book may have the power to expand the mind's horizons, but in essence it is a slight cultural artefact, governed by social and economic rules and permissions, an object among other objects in a world of objects.

Thought does not transcend nature. It is wedded to it. The idea of the limitless freedom of thought is an illusion since it is always dependent on the limits of its vocabulary. The past hems me in, weighs on me, contains me, even as I exercise what I call my freedom, just as a fish swimming around under the weight of the ocean is both free and suffocated by the medium of its freedom, or a tree pushing out leaves must eventually reach the limits of what it is allowed to be.

But doesn't my imagination transcend nature? Have I not the intellectual power to deny my material nature, to transform myself by thought alone into pure spirit and an immortal soul outside space and time, and therefore am not bound to this body nor constrained by the instrument of my thinking? But no one has ever discovered the soul outside the idea of the soul. And no one has yet recovered the limits of the self from the limitless emptiness of its absence.

I can't think without the instrument of thought, in the absence of the electrical and chemical activity of my material brain. My thoughts are not random productions but have developed along complex intersecting tramlines laid down by repetitive thinking, so I *secure* some thoughts just as I secure the continuity of my personality from minute to minute and day to day. Wherever I look outside the constraints of my thoughts to some principle superior to my thoughts that will give them their validity as the interpreter of what is given, I do not find their creator, I only find what they have created. To turn to God is to turn in the first instance towards an inherited convention, a corpus of historical thoughts. How can God be an unencumbered thought, an original insight? God comes fully formed in words, and with initial capitals that not even the denier of God fails to acknowledge as His due.

From the beginning I perceived nothing for myself, I chose nothing for myself. I was force-fed words and what words were to stand for. I was bullied into modes of good behaviour. When I was bad I was bad only in relation to what was held to be good, and the good I borrowed from those who would lend it to me. Books opened my mind, but only in so far as my mind enabled me to open a book. My mind swims in its medium, unable to escape from it. Its freedom is limited, though it may seem infinite, just as the sea is to a fish or the air to a bird. What hems me in is the perpetual presence of the past in the formality of the present – my body, my brain, my thoughts, my language and the poverty of my vocabulary, the limits of the beliefs that I inherit like verbal clichés, the deep psychological sources of my emotions and my decisions and, in the final analysis, the inescapable condition of being something in particular and not something else, the condition of being born.

VI

...but I would certainly love to know...whether it is simply by some irony of nature that the particular instance arises from the happening of nothing in particular, and that the ultimate meaning turns out to be something arrived at by taking the average of what is basically meaningless. Robert Musil, *The Man Without Qualities*

To get down to cases, what a turtle does, day in, day out, is the most that a turtle can do. A pigeon does the same. ('No other thing in the world,' writes James Thurber, 'falls so far short of being able to do what it cannot do as a pigeon does.') You can't fault anything in nature for being less than itself, nor can you ever, except in human fable, point to the folly of its over-ambition. It stays within its limits, and we applaud it for doing so. That's what the nature of nature is, and what we mean to praise when we admire nature for its imperturbable depths and primal silence. No living thing except the human is discontent. There is no creature in nature equivalent to a Madame Bovary.

However grand the designs of nature appear to be, they have emerged out of the accumulation of small tangential relationships between one thing and the next, just as the pattern in a piece of lace or the figure in a carpet depends at any selected point in time during its making solely on the next loop or the next knot. Nothing holds together except by loops and knots and attracting and repelling forces that are the basic building blocks of material cohesion entangled in time. It is our own especial fate to be able to abstract from all this becoming the indelible shape of its past.

The ability of birds to fly is an evolutionary adaptation, or technically, perhaps, what Stephen Jay Gould denoted an 'exaptation' to distinguish between a physiological adaptation to the environment, like growing more fur to keep warm, and something developed for one use that turned out unpredictably useful for something else. Flight probably falls into this latter category, as an adaptation developed gradually over time, as the formality of a body cooling system evolved into the rudiments of wings that would eventually separate the feathered bird from its scaly reptilian ancestor.

Given our backward looking perspective, we might be tempted to think that all the time this was going on the *potential* for flight was somehow present but suppressed in the primitive avian species, like a spring that would eventually set that possibility in motion, that its 'nature' in fact was to work towards some form of perfection and that that perfectibility was already in the creature as a sort of eminence in waiting. That is to say, that we might believe that everything by its nature is *less* than it could be, since history shows that everything does, in fact, change and develop, and earlier forms are replaced by later forms, so that nothing might be said to have achieved the perfect fulfilment of its nature at any particular point in time – the evidence of history is against it, and the form of an organism can't be said to be its fixed and final form. When we look back over time, at the evidence of millions of years of existence and the forms of life superseded by more suitably adapted creatures, we see nothing but waste, the skeletal deposits of failed lives piled up, one imperfection heaped on another. These are, Darwin wrote in a letter to J D Hooker, the 'clumsy, wasteful, blundering, low and horridly cruel works of nature' by which we came to be. We owe our existence to multiple, unpredictable contingencies, to accident not necessity, to chance not inevitability.

Lacking any purpose, life does not and cannot fail its purpose. Nothing is wasted, only consumed by time. At any moment each life is all that it can be. Everything that is must be something. The turtle that swims in the sea is no less the perfection of itself because some other creature lifts itself skyward. Nature has no aspirations. If anything changes, and change it must, then what *will* change is determined by what *can* change. Nature on the grand scale might be described as the great inter-relational regulator of all that is, but what actually happens does so not on the scale of a sweeping epic but at several small, distinct and non-negotiable points of interface, just as the sudden wheel and turn of a flock of starlings in flight is not the result of individuals acting in unison as one body, but only the effect of each one turning at a single point relative to its neighbour.

Nature can be describe mechanically, and its boundaries defined by the limits of the possible.

It is easier, in fact, to understand the nature of nature by cataloguing what is unnatural or against nature: the miraculous and the magical, prayer and the successful petitioning of a will outside nature, water running up hill, tears flowing from stones, voices in your head and the sudden reappearance of the long since dead. If these things were true, then it would also be true that the nature of the universe is such that anything might happen at any time without semblance of sense or order. But, just as nothing can be created out of nothing, *anything* can't be made out of something. Otherwise, as Lucretius says,

Men could arise from the sea
and scaly fish from the earth,
birds hatch out of the sky...
and any tree bear every fruit.

Or, again, as Musil reflects, without order arising spontaneously out of large numbers, 'we might have a year with nothing at all happening, followed by one in which you could count on nothing for certain, famine alternating with oversupply, no births followed by too many, and we would all be fluttering to and fro between our heavenly and hellish possibilities like little birds when someone suddenly comes up to their cage'.

For 'nature' read 'order'. Nature has infinite material to work with, but finite ways of making things. The reordering of bits of the universe in line with our wishes, hopes, desires and fears would rightly be called supernatural events. But there are no supernatural events. There are only natural events and nature, defined, is order within limits.

VII

Therefore the mind ought to be more astonished at the hypothetical duration of chaos than at the actual birth of the universe. Denis Diderot, *Pensées Philosophiques*

Given enough time, all random processes become orderly. Wandering particles, blown sand, spider's silk, cloud vapour and strangers on a train all sooner or later come into contact, collide, rebound, cohere, confer in some tentative relationship to create a semblance of order – a 'slumping together', in James Clerk Maxwell's phrase, of multitudes of events lacking uniform causes into observable uniformities of pattern or behaviour. Order is a less mysterious state than chaos, for we would have to explain how a permanently chaotic universe would contrive to remain in perfect equilibrium and never find itself in conjunction with itself. A clockwork universe without randomness must by default be ordered and unchanging in its essence, which is clearly not the case, and a random universe must by reason of its randomness eventually become ordered.

Isolated random events lead over time inevitably to some form of connective order, not because order is implicit in events from the beginning, but only because it can't be helped. At some point the whole connective process speeds up until order rather than randomness becomes the rule, as order begets more order. The direction is from chaos and randomness to order and complexity. Time, once admitted into the universe, can't be reversed. As events unfold, suddenly the original universal phase of timeless incoherence comes to an end, and some sort of tangled order prevails.

Absolute chaos, unmitigated randomness, simply does not exist in the universe. The rule for being, for existing, is that the matter of the universe must exist in some way. That all is chance, that one configuration of the universe could exist as easily as another may be true, but that *any* configuration could exist as easily as this one is refuted by chance itself.

There is less chance that every fundamental particle that makes up the fabric of the universe could go on forever following a random independent existence and an isolated trajectory than that, given the large numbers of particles involved over time, it would enter into some sort of relationship with other particles wandering on similar journeys. Though the universe has been going for a long time, it is a not so long compared with infinity and it has already settled into what it has become, at home with itself, long before it has had time to exhaust what it might have been, whose possibilities are now excluded from it by its own probability.

The fact of the matter is that the universe is not made up of innumerable separate 'things' bound together by the 'laws' of physics, but of 'events' that may be, at quantum level, one thing or another or neither or both. That in the end they are something is a matter of probability rather than inevitability, and what they have thereby become is not a predetermined necessity but merely a necessary fact.

That there might have been billions of other possible universes in other configurations is not in doubt, but the miracle that it turned out to be this one, and with us in it, and not another one is not after all so surprising – for where else among the billions of possibilities can we stand to make such statements but here in this one, whether we believe there are multiple universes or an infinite number that have already been and gone? The most curious thing about the universe is that out of all its possible states it has produced only a single point of view.

All observable large events or entities must at bottom be the result of a concatenation of small occurrences or intimate relationships. Impressive effects, like rainbows, peacocks and butterflies, arise out of lesser, more immediate and confused circumstances at tediously obscure levels beneath our perception and attention. Large events and entities as diverse as weather and animal species and defeats in battle appear to us as isolated and disconnected things only as a result of their distance from earlier causal epicentres, as the mountain is from its original geological turbulence and the chicken from the precursor dinosaur. We can observe everything only at a point in time, in the expanded, diversified form of the universe and everything in it, but yet nothing exists except by virtue of its connectedness. The connectedness of small contiguous events limits and constrains how things proceed or change, and what ultimately emerges as order and, to our perception, separate and independent orders of events and things, is connected to and dependent on unretractable actions that in themselves were not making anything, but only proceeding step by step into the possible. And what is possible, of course, constrains all our freely chosen actions.

Nest building proceeds contiguously, one act at a time, with no pattern in mind. Unconscious behaviour hormonally released, unselfconscious comings and goings and head shaking bring forth a construction whose final design involves no preconception. Human house building proceeds from a pattern whose end is envisioned from the beginning. That is the difference. Yet it is not all unconstrained creativity. Building proceeds brick by brick and from the ground up in a progression ruled by the inescapable material constraints of the physical world, in the same way the bird plants its feet firmly before building into the spaces it can reach. And our creativity is confined within the limits and habits of thought, restrained by cultural and social inheritances and acceptances. When Dorothea Brooke was designing ideal cottages for the tenants of the estates of Middlemarch, her highest conception remained a cottage, and the proposed improved lines were along familiar ones involving staircases and fireplaces. No wigwams, no longhouses, no glittering palaces either. There are no really radical revolutions, because we can only ever proceed within the limits of the possible, and the possible is not a step towards an imagined future but the next available possibility of reordering the present.

The nature of everything is defined by the constraints within which it persists. This principle applies to the material and the immaterial alike, to the water molecule and the water rat, to atoms, mice, men and ideas. The principle is twofold, but at bottom the two constraining realities are one and the same. The first might properly be called the ontological constraint of a thing's being something in particular, the existential space it occupies that separates a water molecule from a carbon atom and a frog from a prince. The transformational possibilities of one thing becoming *anything* else are severely constrained by its persistence in what it is. A soldier may become a general through a sequence of events that translate him from one status to another, but not every soldier may become a general because the self-organising constraints of an army ensure it persists as an entity of some generals and a lot of soldiers. Most soldiers will persist in their roles and the organisation as a functioning whole will persist in its identity while accommodating relational shifts in some of its component parts. The second is the behavioural constraint of the limited number of actions or options available to anything in any given circumstance. The transformational possibilities of a molecule or a cell are limited to the very few things it can do next in relation to where it has come from and the few places where it can go now. People persist in their poverty or their ignorance because the possibilities of transformation lie beyond their immediate grasp or comprehension. We can work only with the things that are to hand, and those things serve only to confirm the boundaries of what we are and what we may become. The soldier becomes a general not in the way a frog becomes a prince in a fairy tale, but by writing letters, passing exams, filling in forms, being in the right place at the right time, by doing whatever it is he needs to do next, constrained by what he is permitted to do in his particular circumstances. That these two constraining principles, what a thing is and what it is permitted to do, can be separately defined is merely down to history – the length of time that has elapsed to fill the world with widely segregated entities such as frogs and princes, soldiers and generals, and the shortness of any history we need to have information about in order to persist in our enclaves, in the way that leaves grow on trees and ice crystals form on their branches in winter without reference to the entire sequence of preceding events that have brought them to this point. But they are the same. What anything will do next is dependent on what the next possible thing is it can do.

Every event is a unique event, but each event conforms to a pattern that repeats itself over and over again. This is as much so for the growth of crystals and the limited number of possible permutations in the ways open to us to put on a shirt or a pair of shoes. There are only so many ways in which events unfold and only a limited number of ways in which they *can* unfold. The formation of a snowflake is a unique event, both in temporal terms and in the unpredictability of the individual snowflake pattern. Yet what is predictable is that snowflakes will form in given climatic and environmental conditions and that snowflakes will look like snowflakes. The way water molecules line up in ice dictates the regularity of their hexagonal crystalline forms. But where and when the ice growth will branch out depends on random fluctuations during growth and the inevitable breaking of symmetry at critical points in that growth. The underlying architecture of physical processes and the capacity of matter for constrained self-organisation and growth means we have to take seriously the idea that self-organised structures underpin the forms and formal behaviour of organic matter, and that the conventional theory of evolution is a secondary mechanism of development and diversification that cannot be invoked to explain the fundamental organisation of life.

Evolution is a retrospective review of how life has diversified into a complex and interactive biosphere from what, in the beginning, was a relatively simple configuration of self-organising molecular structures. Nothing compels organisms to evolve. It is probably wise to view the nature of the universe as intrinsically conservative, struggling at its heart to be, in essence, nothing, as though regretting the loss of equilibrium and the breaking of the symmetry of existence and non-existence. But the price of conservatism, of stability, is a permanent state of criticality, always on the edge of being other. Paradoxically, to remain the same everything will edge out into the next available state of equilibrium, change in order not to change. Treading water might seem like a good analogy for standing still, but the trouble is you can't keep it up. It's not a stable state, it's a state that will run down to a new and disastrous state of equilibrium as energy is expended. A small, random misjudgment might lead you to flail out with an arm, which could get you to learn to swim, and you might save yourself. Your state is always critical, your options limited, tentative, provisional. The survival of the fittest is not a law. It is a narrative of history. We look for causes in history, who won and who lost the battle of Austerlitz, what could have been directed otherwise, but in the thick of it men are moving to act in the only ways open to them. There is no grand strategy in the mist in the morning with a gun in your hand. There is no contextual strategy for evolution. There is only contiguity. This happens, and that happens, and order emerges out of what does happen and what can happen. The robustness of a self-organised universe is so great, so hard fired in the actuality of incalculable and inconceivable numbers of repeated acts, that the introduction of knowledge into this regimen must be seen as nothing more than error, hubris, the superficial vanity on the part of mind (which does not know itself or understand what it is). If molecules can line up in ice to make a snowflake and cells can organise themselves in bodies to combat a viral invasion, then spiders can construct webs, bees honeycombs, birds nests, the angler fish can catch its prey, the lion hunt the antelope, the chimp groom its mate, without the necessity of understanding anything, without context or perspective, without history, without purpose, without consciousness, without memory, without emotion, without knowledge. Contiguous self-organising behaviour can account for everything that happens – up to the point where mind intrudes to weave its own web of appearances that the mind itself must answer for.

VIII

What does what it should do needs nothing more.
The body moves, though slowly, toward desire.
We come to something without knowing why. Theodore Roethke,
The Manifestation

So what is knowledge, and what is knowledge for? Why, if everything in the universe lines up in accordance with proven rules for order and stability, can't we leave 'nature' to take its course, cease our conscious efforts and striving after understanding, and go with the flow of a self-regulating universe? For if contingent and contiguous self-organisation within self-defining limits works, then it works because it has produced what must be, at least for the present (and the present is all we have), if not the best of all possible worlds, the best of all probable worlds. Why *can't* we follow our own nature? Our problem is we do not know what our nature is. We know what a fox's fox-nature is, which is defined by the limits of all that a fox can do. If the fox were free to choose its own behaviour and determine the moral nature of its actions it would not know what to choose, for it is the absence of choice that determines its nature. Our own ability to choose our actions excludes us from that self-determined order of nature decided for us by the absence of choice. As self-conscious beings we have many freedoms, but among them is not the freedom to return to a nature that does not include those freedoms. The fox that carries off my chickens is following its own nature. But is the thief who breaks in and carries them off also following his nature? Nothing in nature guarantees the sublime will arise of its own accord from the dictates of necessity.

The emergence of complex behaviour – in molluscs, worms, crustaceans, insects, animals – does not require the presumption of either knowledge or intention on the part of the organism itself. Patterns of behaviour, in this respect, are formally of the same order as the distribution of physical attributes in the body plan, or the pattern of colouration in the evolution of defence mechanisms. The fox no more 'decides' to bury some of its food against a future shortage than the leaf insect 'decides' to hide itself where it will least likely be discovered. There is no plan in the tiny skull of the swallow when it begins to build its nest, or when it turns its head and sets off south for the winter. There is no aesthetic satisfaction to be enjoyed by the bower bird once it has completed its arrangement of miscellaneous objects of attraction. The social organisation of ants and bees requires no social conscience any more than they themselves need an architect's drawing to get on with the construction of their socially organised colonies. Complex social interaction might appear to require some level of conscious awareness, but one can just as easily extrapolate from the blind interactive behaviour of lower insect and animal species the likelihood that primate social organisation and familial interactions can function without it.

Before we can say what knowledge is, we are obliged to recognise how much is accomplished without it. How small and superfluous a thing knowledge is. What a minor aberration the mind is, a sort of pig's snout for speculative foraging, none of which is needed but all of which determines the inescapable context of my being. I would be mistaken to believe that the world that appears before me purely in my consciousness in some way partakes of my knowledge of it, is complicit with the mind in making itself known, that my knowledge of the world is in fact the world's declaration of itself in comprehensible terms and not something relating solely to my own interests in it that I impose upon it. What I know about the world and what happens in it are separate facts that never meet.

The more thoroughly we are able to describe an organism the more certain we will become of the limits of the nature it can't transcend. By filling in every aspect of its biochemical and genetic structure and its behavioural life cycle we just confirm the ways in which it cannot be otherwise. Nothing is more or less than itself. Nothing is more or less than the limits its self-organised behaviour will permit. And all this takes place, age after age, without the backdrop, the painted scenery of representational 'reality'. The unconscious creature is neither content nor discontent, neither happy nor unhappy with its lot, unable to distinguish being from nothingness. There is no context for its actions, decisions or judgments, only the availability of the immediate next possible action, decision or judgment constrained by necessity, all that it can possibly be or do contained in all that it has already become. There is no requirement in theory or fact for a strategic judgmental context, for a perceived reality in which informed choices or judgments take place on the basis of assessed options, only perhaps for some functional abstract structure to sensory data sufficient to mediate behavioural relationships between the organism and its environment. Mistakes are clear cut – they just don't work. Errors of judgment are not misunderstandings (what is there to understand?) but mistaken directions that ultimately correct themselves through the rigorous and unforgiving evolutionary suppression of failure. Everything in nature is blind to its own being, disengaged from reality. Neither being nor reality is part of life or part of nature, but only a feature of consciousness, a dimension added to something contained within nature and not the dimension in which nature sits.

No living organism knows or needs to know how the system works in order for the system to work. All it needs to 'know' in its unconscious way is how to persist by searching out the limits of what works and arrive at a state of equilibrium in which it *will* persist, to find its niche by exploring which niche works for it. Given a basic autonomous work cycle that *does* work for it, what happens next in this complex biosphere is governed by the accidents and incidents of evolutionary opportunities and constraints. Since it can't by its own self-willed effort stray far from its state of equilibrium, has no need to, no incentive to, no ability to, those accidents and incidents are minor events in a stable and stabilising environment. The system works for the organism without the need for any other form of knowledge that approaches what we mean by knowledge. The organism does not need an awareness of its wider environment, any picture of the overall complexity of the environmental context, the knowledge of what a thing is or what it is for or what the world is like in any way at all for it to have a perfectly defined place in it and an ability to function in it just as though, to all appearances, it knew exactly what it was doing and why. In so far as the organism embodies 'purpose', it does so only as a function of the performance of its work, the work of persisting, of persisting within the limits of what it can do. Nature knows nothing, and does not need to know anything. It only needs the habit of doing things in limited ways, and does not need to know what it does or why or in what wider ordered universe all this takes place, for what immediate purpose or to what end.

It is easy enough to illustrate the case, if only we do not intrude into this empty space our anthropomorphic habit of thinking, do not lend to mindless nature the stuff in our heads that is part of our nature and has nothing to do with anything else. Bird nest building, for example, is a complex constructive behaviour that can be explained without believing that something is going on in the bird's head simply because something is going on in ours. In the first place, there is no necessity for a context in time and space for this activity. When nesting will happen – the temporal range of the bird's behaviour – and where it happens – the spatial relationship of the bird to its nest construction – are not *a priori* cognitive necessities for the bird, only for us in the act of observation and analysis. It can just as easily (and in actual fact much more easily) take place in a flat continuum of non-contextualised actions as it could in the typically 'narrated' contextual world of consciousness.

The construction of nests by African species of village weaver birds is well-documented. The behaviour is stereotypical and seems to be hormonally initiated. The weaver bird has evolved a preference for the green or yellow-green materials that have proven to be the most flexible materials in practice. The male bird gathers nesting material and appears to respond to a stimulus at the point of satiation to return to the nesting site and begin consolidating the strips of leaves it has gathered into the nest structure. It does this often in an experimental or exploratory manner, with some false starts and failures, working with the end of a strip in its beak, doubling it back, poking it into spaces that will take it with a vibratory movement of its head, producing knotted or woven textures that would arise in any circumstances from a regulated pattern of pushing and pulling the ends of adjacent material. The basic ring structure that is the foundation of the overall nest arises from the bird's tendency to weave in all adjacent directions above its head in relation to its fixed position on the nest substrate. That fixed position and consequent orientation determines the plane along which the nesting chambers are formed. Each stage creates its own stimulus for behaviour to begin, and for that stage of the process to be completed – the 'ceiling', for example, comes to an end when the weave finally shuts out the light, and if, experimentally, you shut out the light before the structure is complete, weaving will stop.

Complex structures will arise out of a combination of constrained physical limitations and hormonal signals to stop and start an action that in themselves are the biologically organised extensions of the same physical constraints.

Suppose we were to introduce the idea of intention and choice into this scenario. In what ways would the described behaviour change to improve the bird's nest-building effectiveness, having come this far? It is impossible to conceive of any benefit. If all these constrained actions, added together into a whole, create a consistent pattern of behaviour that permits the weaver bird to persist in its individual and social existence as an adapted organism, what would be the effect of placing all this in a contextual world of understanding? Only disaster could follow, by adding alternatives and choices to a course already long since and successfully determined without knowledge. Knowledge will not increase the probability of success, only the likelihood of error. Behavioural variations can only prove themselves over time in exactly the same way that all successful variations are settled over evolutionary time. It is the blindness of this behaviour that ensures success and continuity. The surest way for any creature to undo millions of years of evolutionary success is to try to understand what it does. The dangers of contextual judgment are obvious from our own experience of misunderstandings, mistaken choices, wrong pathways, fatal errors. Yet, clearly, in evolutionary terms we have been more successful over time by using our power of contextual judgment than in going on living without it, by taking matters into our own hands than by simply relying completely on the natural processes of constrained contiguous necessity to build societies and civilisations in the way that termites and chimpanzees have created their particular social structures.

Yet in trying to understand the nature and limits of consciousness we have to concede that a much larger bulk of our behaviour than we might like to confess to is anchored in that same substratum of autonomous contiguity that we share with termites, sticklebacks and bees, and a genetic make-up that overlaps with the DNA of worms, flies and pumpkins. The stickleback 'selects' a home and a breeding ground for itself without recourse to conscious judgment. It knows how to protect its territory and its young. It can be aggressive when it needs to be without knowing just what leads it to make that judgment, and it will retreat when retreat serves its best interests without knowing where its interests actually lie. The bee knows where to find a patch of clover and knows how to communicate its whereabouts to the rest of the hive, and yet it has no ideas about any of this. Crowds of creatures – ants, bees, crows, gulls, fishes, frogs, cattle, primates – have social or group systems where territorial and spatial relationships, competitive advantage and co-operative benefits have worked themselves out in self-organising ways through the pursuit of self-interest.

External stimuli and internal responses, recognition and reaction and appetitive drives towards some goal are bound up in these patterns of behaviour. It is only in anthropomorphic moments of weakness that we allow ourselves to think that this interaction of inner and outer worlds must involve a representation of reality and that these internal responses must be a sort of thinking. To us, our consciousness of the world *is* the world. We have no means of separating the two things without losing the knowledge of the one by the elimination of the other. For us, consciousness is all in all. But in evolutionary terms it is something super-added late on in time, and we would be wise to assume that just as our bodily forms are 98% chimpanzee, our behavioural norms might be sculpted on an armature bequeathed to us in much the same proportion.

However, that is not to suggest that there must therefore be a direct connection by inheritance from one illustration of behaviour to another, from one functional body plan to an analogous one – though doubtless many links can be found between them. I only want to assert that there are sufficient numbers of analogies to establish the fact that functional behaviour and complex social interactions are able to subsist successfully below the level of conscious awareness and deliberated choice. To complain, for example, that there can be no homologous model for primate and early hominid ritualised food sharing because one was vegetarian and the other carnivorous is to miss the point of the principle by trying to establish a causal connection. The principle is the ubiquity of self-organising behaviour that serves a particular end without any particular need, on the part of the animal, to know what that end is.

The essential part of our life is lived, as it were, without us. If we can suspend belief, for a time, in that illusion of the self within the self, of the homunculus, the ego, that seems to sit, like a spider at the centre of her web, holding the threads of coherence together – if we can momentarily cancel out the unlocatable abstraction of the self itself, we can catch glimpses of ourselves not as selves inside our own bodies looking out, but as figures mechanically propelled along in a world crowded with other objects but carrying within us a unique sensory appendage that allows us to know we are in the world and to knit what we habitually think of as the reality of the world out of nothing more than the fragile firing of neural networks in our cranium. The mechanical constructions of the spider that Keats called 'airy citadels' are as nothing compared with the net of connections we make in our brains that fabricates the whole universe in which we move, attuned as ethereally to conceptual understanding as the spider is to the vibrations of the air. The equipment of understanding is a late elaboration of evolutionary neurobiology on a substructure that was already working – and naturally still is – not only as a self-organised auto-catalytic cell structure, but as a set of interactive behavioural imperatives and established habits that go on happening underneath whatever it is we like to think of as our human social, cognitive, cultural and self-motivated individual lives. For the inescapable fact is that the larger part of our motivation – literally, what moves us – has nothing to do with 'us' at all.

The hedgehog that has bled to death in the road, its self-organised integrity spilt out of its open belly, is no longer a blindly pulsing living entity, but blindness itself, a blank, linked to life only as the host environment for maggots, as a discovered source of nourishment for flies and magpies. Nothing that might be described as the animal's inner self or being escapes the failure of the animal itself. There is no separating the act of living from that which lives. And I myself, the self that is in pain, that suffers, that cries out, that fears for 'its' life, under anaesthetic subsides to no one and nothing while the body 'I' inhabit struggles, heals, recovers itself until 'it' awakens and reinstates its awareness of itself as 'I' and the illusion of the separateness of life and the one who lives it.

This body and the mind that grows within it are the given

ground of being. Immediately upon my involuntary manifestation and coming into existence as an organism, I am at once not only given this one possible ground of being, but deprived of any other possible ground of being. Those later daydreams in which I spend the most part of my waking life, of deciding courses of action, of speculating on what might be, what might have been, what I might become or what is to become of me are, in spite of the mind's free rein and the imagination's limitless bounds, of small compass. I am stuck on these two thin legs with a beating heart and heaving lungs whose failure (at their discretion alone) might at any moment cut off my life. Blood and fluids circulate in my body. I am compelled to stuff bread and cheese and potatoes into my throat as obsessively as the blackbird outside the window gorges on worms and equally, but discreetly, evacuate the stinking products of this self-indulgence just like any other creature. Cells divide and grow, organs go on performing their determined functions, to be interrupted only by some environmental dislocation, cancerous growth or accumulated decrepitude. No matter that I wake each day with the self-awareness and the self-assurance to believe I can decide how I will live my life, the 'it' that allows me the comfort of this illusion provides all the ground rules of my existence. I can cry out in protest from my narrow prison cell, but I have no more hope of not being what I am than the butterfly that cannot escape the confines of its wings. If this is my fate, the real horror of it is to realise that the mind, in which the landscape of reality is laid out as a painted representation of myself and the world, is the production of the same blind forces that created the bat's unerring talent to sense a mosquito in the dusk, not for the purpose of capturing reality in the manner of a photographic plate but as an instrument for the effective pursuit of uncompromising self-interest in perpetuating organic existence. I sit here with reality all around me, both inside me and outside me, but my knowledge is only a means to an end, a map of the logical connections of the world to my interests and my next available opportunity.

IX

...the remote vegetable-reptile-saurian background of the human soul. John Cowper Powys, *In Defence of Sensuality*

I must now assert, in a miscellaneous way, the facts I can longer evade.

I did not, could not, will myself into being.

I am forever in the orbit of the other, whatever that other is and whether it is at all, if being is only the sense of what is when nothing in fact is.

Whatever freedom of action, thought and imagination I possess, it has been conferred on me through evolutionary adaptation in the same way the snake got its poisonous tongue, the monkey its tail and the hominid its descended larynx. I say so. Man spits out words the way other creatures spit venom.

The body and its brain are one functioning organism, and whatever they create together in my mind remains a pulsation of the blood – heart and mind being one in our language.

The fabrications of the brain are additional functional adaptations of an otherwise perfectly adequate vertebrate neuro-anatomy. The thing runs itself – bones, lungs, legs, liver, blood, veins, heart, kidneys, kneecaps, eyes, fingers, breath, brain and its five million sweat glands.

Why should anything coming out of the brain activity of this animal object deserve the name of 'truth'?

Nothing needs to know anything in order to proceed in its course.

The body makes all its own decisions.

Even snowflakes make unerring choices.

Since everything can decide to be as it is just by making least-effort decisions, why should our representation of the world have more truth in it than it needs? The least of our truths suffices us.

No living creature knows or needs to know exactly where its interests actually lie. It finds them not through positive crawling towards, grasping and seizing opportunities, but in a negative way, through failure and sacrifice, carving out being from non-being, becoming something in the absence of everything else that might have been, becoming possible through the collapse of everything impossible.

Inorganic matter coheres, refuses to go away. Once life got going, though it defies the imagination to think why it should keep going, it held on to *form* with the same sort of tenacity that keeps the planets in orbit.

Why introduce consciousness, that aberration? Just as everything ceased to falter in its nature, we were given a choice of errors – that is why we are so passionate about truth. Our lives depend on it, and others must die for it.

Judgments are right not when they have identified the

truth but when any other judgment is not available.

Millions of creatures have learned not to ask questions. They have been brought up the hard way, dying for their mistakes and leaving posterity to thrive by their deaths. Step out of line, question your nature, and the entire cycle begins again. Choice only opens up more possibilities for error. So many have died in our stead that talk of freedom seems like a betrayal. The least said the better.

There they go. The jackdaws poke about for a while in the chimney pots. The bees buzz in and out. They are looking for something, they can't say what. They fly off. Pigeons take their place. Wasps find a nesting place through a hole in the chimney mortar. Now they are busy. Do they know if they are happy? Why would knowing make any difference?

Evolution has not excised our reptilian brain stem, only built a superior architecture on top of it. It still grumbles away at an ichthyosaurian level, submerged, hidden from conscious view.

All our thinking amounts to this: to have become the world's supreme trickster.

To possess knowledge is to possess the faculty for extreme cunning. It's a joke played on us to be allowed to contemplate the puzzle of experience in order to solve it, to understand it, to find meaning in it. We are so cunning we excel at deceiving ourselves.

It is evident that species can go to war, and even totally defeat and wipe out their enemies, without a plan of campaign, silently and without trumpets – witness the chimpanzee wars of

Gombe and the reports of infants torn limb from limb.

Animals will sacrifice themselves to protect their families, with nothing more to go on than the chemically-based bodily signals of consanguinity to substitute for love and affection, the benefit of which is evident only long after the event itself in the formulaic increase in the probability of the forms of survival.

The slightest inefficiency, the least disruption to established and consistent behaviour, the breakdown of regulation, are disastrous for most species. Individuality, freedom of choice, discretion, preference, all threaten the stability earned by generations of the dead.

Adventure is always, in fact, misadventure.

We ornament but cannot quite disguise the beast inside. We flush away disgust in chrome and porcelain chambers, clothe our nakedness, dress for sexual attraction, undress for sex but cloak it in a narrative of lovemaking, elaborate our eating and drinking into decorous social rituals, glamorise our armies with brass buttons and medals. But the beast is not fooled.

We haven't used our knowledge to overcome disgust. Our aversions are fundamental – filth, rotting flesh, stink, other people's shit. We are not godlike creatures of mentally controlled equanimity. We even make God partial, for He shares our aversion to snakes and scorpions, and tells us we must abhor the osprey and the osifrage, the nightjar, pelican and the qaath of uncertain etymology.

All our roles, codes, manners, morals are conscious elaborations of patterns of behaviour already given in evolution and the evolution of social and group relationships for mutual benefit, self-interest, self-regulation and co-existence, all of which run mechanically in non-human groups. These extend to altruism, defence, all forms of herd behaviour, scavenging, food sharing, sex, breeding, home building, power orders, leadership, envy, mimicry, conflict, migration, invasion, ecological dominance, ritual, communication and apparently rational actions, all without the need to know anything, without understanding, without a single thought entering any head.

Everything that appears to spring from thinking, to proceed outward from inward reasoning, actually emerges from below and implants itself in thinking, makes itself heard in our thoughts and words.

Knowledge is not the fact of the world. Thinking is not its metier. Thought is part of the biology of a living organism, an extrusion that oozes from the brain like a cloud of cuttlefish ink, confounding our enemies, confusing ourselves.

What we know of the world is read from a palimpsest written over what has already been written and never quite erased.

Five experiences of not being: How do I know that I could wander through the world, play a part in it, make a living in it, without knowledge of it? Firstly, because I already do, since my body conducts itself in the world of its own will and not mine, and I constantly turn to it for confirmation of myself. Secondly, because the pattern of my behaviour is built from precursor forms that have required no knowledge of the forms of the self or the shape of the world. Thirdly, because there exists among phenomena the phenomenon of blind-sight or mind-blindness, where subjects can see but do not know they can see, act in response to visual information without that information ever translating itself into knowledge. Fourthly, because my earliest memory, which I can date from the age of two years, of falling twice from an open door down stone steps, has imprinted in my mind the possibility that there can be a cry with no person yet known to himself who cries, and a disorientation that can struggle autonomously to right itself without a prior agreement in principle of the separateness of self and other. Fifthly, because I can conceive of experience as being no more than the flow of inconsequential encounters and buffetings that do not accumulate to anything that might in all reason be called a life lived in the world.

To say that we will know what it's like to be a bat when we have all the information that the bat possesses is to misunderstand the verb to be. The bat manages without knowledge. It has no inner life. If by information is meant the flow of sense data and the bat's evolved strategies for acting in relation to it, then we have no need to develop a theory of subjectivity with information accumulating like alluvial deposits into 'something' which we then call knowledge or mind or experience or being, a body of 'something' burdening a body to whom information is like the wind blowing through grass. To know what the bat knows would be to sacrifice all knowledge for no knowledge, to abandon being for emptiness not empathy.

It appears that strategic judgment takes place in the prefrontal cortex area of the brain where we plan complex tasks. But judgment reverts to an autonomic process in the periaqueductal grey region of the brain for decisions related to immediate danger. One can assume that the contextual landscape differs also, the immediacy of judgment not extending to what or why a thing is, as I duck to avoid a buzzing insect without evaluating its danger or at a bird flying at the car windscreen even though rationally I know there is a barrier between myself and imminent danger. Our knowledge of the facts is contrary to the visceral experience, but the body rules because it always has.

Even dust deep in space can form itself into spirals resembling the double helix of DNA. Can we not believe, then, that the whole of reality is the self-invention of dust?

The universe has brought everything into being through the gradual accumulation of connections between one material element and another. So the agencies of sand, wind and the elements have ultimately been able to fabricate both microprocessors and morality.

Do I, unknowingly, act always in my own interests, even when I am good, helpful, self-sacrificing, for some advantage that unconsciously accrues? Are all gestures towards others in some way signals to myself, self-assurances and self-aggrandisements? Do I wait in the wings for what I have enacted to unfold, so that I might step out centre stage as the main character, diminishing the rest to supporting cast as though they, but not I, are mere mortals?

Love. What is that? Love, lust, adultery, promiscuity, desire, jealousy, that murderous borderland where a wrong turn in sexual advantage delivers a stiletto to the heart or where, as in the mating practices of the mantis and some species of spider, decapitation and death are the ritual order of life? What leads my life to what it has become – that ankle, that smooth skin, her red high-heeled shoes passing on the pavement? Or a red spot on a yellow beak, a pigeon-coloured breast and the sudden gleam of feathers seen through trees at dusk?

X

So rather than labelling an object by what point it is passing through, you need to label its motion by this matrix of degrees of freedom.
Brian Greene

Action requires no more ground of truth than the necessity to act.

All actions proceed from judgment, but not all judgments require knowledge as the *a priori* ground of judgment.

There are three grounds of judgment, all of which are circumstantial variations on the one single ground of the necessity of judgment. Unless we posit a state of affairs where nothing ever happens, a universe in equilibrium, a steady state where absolute emptiness prevails merely waiting for something to come into existence, then the world that does in fact exist continues in its state as a process of change and continual reconfiguration at points of connection between one thing and another, at the level of fundamental particles and at all levels of being and becoming from ice crystals to social organisation, at all degrees of organised activity from catching prey to planning space programmes.

There is a point at which a thing is what it is, suspended in its state of being like a humming bird hovering before an open flower, and a point at which it ceases to be exactly that same thing, becoming other, making a transition from one wing beat to another and to a state of ceasing to be altogether, each connected contiguously from state to state, constrained in what it will become by what it was a moment before. Just as we know that underlying the mystery of the coherence of music the continuous form of what we hear must be made up from moments of sound already lost to the past, to the observer the point of transition from one state into another, from one phase of stability to the next, has the appearance of a continuity that must in fact be the appearance of multiple micro-states re-establishing temporal coherence. These critical points of transition are points of decision and judgment that are limited in degree by the range of potential actions available at that point, and by the limited number of possibilities that are open for one form of order to move into the next phase condition. These constraining principles apply in all circumstances and for all forms of order, regardless of how much self-determination we might like to ascribe to them. The three grounds of judgment are therefore (1) judgments of inescapable and non-negotiable necessity, the rules that govern the existence of phenomenal matter throughout the universe, (2) judgments made by living organisms, by autonomous agents processing information encoded in autonomic systems, and (3) judgments made on the basis of a superficial layer of representational information manipulated in the neo-cortex of one of the higher primate species. This third ground of judgment enfolds the other, primary grounds of judgment, and the fact of their being subsumed under and integrated into the higher brain functions that manage phenomenal representation thereby ensures no one can ever prove definitively that a judgment taken freely in consciousness is not in fact a judgment taken autonomically or by necessity that is merely presenting itself for notice in the mind.

Now it may seem illegitimate to describe the physical processes at work in the universe and at the heart of matter as 'judgments' when we usually reserve the word 'judgment' to mean the freedom to make decisions based on the evaluation of information, to weigh up one thing against another, to discriminate between alternative possible modes of action. But in all instances the point at which one thing changes is a point of decision or judgment in relation to an immediately available possible state of order, for nothing is free to embrace the impossible. If we preclude judgment from these events, we are perforce required to imagine in their place merely arbitrary and random occurrences that only accidentally and occasionally find themselves in a temporary state of order that might instantly become any other sort of order. The forms of order that we do in fact observe would not arise. Since what we do have is precisely this order and no other order, then it is legitimate to describe as judgments the point of transition at which the act of closing down on one state of order and not another is more likely than not. The ground of the judgment of necessity is true to the principle that governs all the grounds of judgment – that what *is* has been left standing, as it were, in the absence of all other possible states of being that proved improbable, and what is left standing is evidence of the efficacy of error in determining what shall be, not in any ordained or positive or deliberate way, but simply by abandoning and discarding everything else.

In art we are taught to draw by outlining what is not there, to create the object by cutting away the surrounding space, and in sculpture to reveal the finished form by removing the outer husk that does not belong to it. The invisible makes the visible possible. Necessity is less the force of will that determines what shall be, than the falling away into oblivion of all that cannot be, so that what remains is the revelation of the invisible, the gift of the impossible.

The blind fact of the ground of judgment of necessity, that perpetuates the visibility of matter ordering and reordering itself in forms of being, does not give way to a more refined or subjectively considered mode of judgment once matter has ordered itself into the forms of organised autonomous living agents. What is life? It has to be some formal extension of the order of inorganic matter, defined as the propagation of thermodynamic work cycles in self-organising systems. That hardly constitutes an entirely new order of being in the world, with its own original ground of judgment removed from the prevailing ground of judgment of necessity that drives the continual shaping and reshaping of all the other material forms in the universe. Physics still rules. If life is a more complex self-organising unit than a snowflake, none the less it abides by the principle of the judgment of necessity, which is that, in part and in whole, viewed analytically or synthetically, it can only act within the constraints of what it can do to propagate its form of order, can only move into the next space available to it, buffeted by its neighbouring relationships, compelled by the impossibility of being other, in a series of continuous and contiguously connected acts of necessity. While all this may add up to a scuttling crab or a scurrying mouse, the appearance of a creature at home in the universe deciding at each turn what it shall do or where it shall go is as illusory as the idea that it may decide at any moment what it shall be or what it shall become.

What determines a creature's being-in-the-world and its subsequent behaviour, despite life's unlimited potential for variety and diversity, is its nature defined by the limits of the possible. Everything repeats itself, with only the smallest scope for error or differentiation, all of which in any event remains contiguous in its contingency, explicable by local effects that might, in the case of errors of replication, flower into some bizarre reordering of parts that can only tentatively subsist in a world not made for it. Although the world is filled with exotic creatures, it is not hospitable to strange efflorescences of the usual, whether these are small unsustainable genetic shifts in cell replication, or albinos in African tribal hierarchies, or schizophrenics in an ordered society. Evolution is the description of the ways in which life manages not to fall out of existence, of the restoration of equilibrium through the consolidation of successful variations into encoded forms of replication, of the success of the least possible divergence from proven norms. If life works by the perpetual expunging of varietal forms that do not work, and the encoded reinforcement and replication of what does work, then living creatures can no more permit themselves unconstrained freedom of judgment than any other observable form of material order.

Information received is information processed, by an organism already prepared to act upon it by virtue of the necessity of the same acts in previous lifetimes, now encoded in the replication of itself as what it is. Like the flower hidden in the bud or foetal horses galloping in the womb, life unfolds in the world inescapably ruled by necessary relationships with it, and not as some new unexpected form of mindful curiosity that stands apart from it. Which is to say, the possibility of subjectivity forms no part of the necessity of being, and where subjectivity has arisen, later in evolutionary time, it can be seen as an extension of the information processing that takes place entirely objectively and unconsciously in every living organism, systemic in humans as much as in every other form of being.

Keats's 'airy citadel' is a wonderful description of the spider's web that conveys both the phantasmagorical, eerie and unearthly quality of this sublime structure, and the workmanlike construction of a practical stronghold where the spider rules the lives of lesser creatures who stray into its web of deceit, making a living and a larder out of silk and body segments. It is at once a centre of being, where the spider holds the thread that links it to the rest of the world, and a phenomenon of nature for which the spider can take no credit. It is an admirable analogy for the human mind, that centre of human subjectivity from which we hold the world together in a net of concepts, but whose existence depends on the complex architecture of the brain for which we, as a construct within it, can take no responsibility. Both the web and the brain are ordered constructions whose order has evolved on the principle of the necessity of judgment applicable to all forms of material order, and the principle of natural selection that has resulted in the distribution of viable forms of order.

So, the presence of the self in the world and the flowering of subjectivity, and the phenomenon of the objective existence of the world as an observable fact, have both arisen through the natural history of the brain and its judgmental architecture, to provide the human species, that most manipulative of animals, with a third *phenomenal* ground of judgment, that of mind, which, while by no means free of the ground of judgment of necessity or of autonomous, instinctive decision-making, is no longer entirely dependent on the blind contiguity of judgment that ensures the survival of species unaware of any other ground of judgment. The human species has inherited some freedom of judgment by building its airy citadel not from silk but out of the fabric of space, time and causality.

If all this seems too much to swallow, it is only because, as creatures with minds, we find it impossible to conceive of mind as something objectively given and not as the one thing to which all objective phenomena are subordinated. Nor are we able easily to place ourselves in the mindlessness of other organisms to the point at which we can recognise that it is entirely feasible to be in the world and of the world without any awareness of being so. The concept of 'being' requires a sense of reality that lies beyond the scope of the sensory apparatus of creatures with brains but no minds. That the whole world can get along without the introduction of mind into it is evident from all we know of the history of the universe up to the emergence of socialised mankind. That this one creature alone has an idea in its head about the world creates no dependency in the world on the truth of that idea. It's just another phenomenon. Ideas have less presence in the world than leaves blown in the wind. They are insubstantial and irrelevant to the integrity of the world and life. They are the mind's means to its own end. That end is to be able to make judgments for action in the context of phenomenal representation, but our representation of things does not touch things themselves. They are what they are in their own blank, blind, unknowable nature. Nothing in the world is required to have any reality in order to be, only in order to assume their place as fictions in the mind.

XI

...that imaginative episode we call reality. Fernando Pessoa, *The Book of Disquiet*

Migrating birds find their way around the world, flying great distances with unerring accuracy. For the human mind to emulate this performance we need a headful of concepts about time and space and objects in space, including ourselves, notions about the relationship of one thing to another, and ideas of causality and the potential consequences of our actions. This is what constitutes contextual as opposed to contiguous judgment tied inexorably to what is permitted by the proximity of the next available possible state. What happens in the bird's brain is not dependent on any sort of conceptual or contextual judgment, on memory, perception, observation, on an internal map of the world and the bird-like self within it. What, in a mechanical way, may be happening is that the earth's magnetic field affects the stability of light sensitive protein molecules, and it is this relationship that can signal the bird's orientation, with the whole mechanism built into autonomous behaviour that is surprising and baffling to our understanding but requires no understanding whatsoever on the part of the bird. The bird's judgment is free from error because its judgment is shaped by molecular constraints imposed by only marginally alterable encoded genetic sequences that are non-divergent. To imagine overlaying those judgments with another level of 'knowledge' would be to introduce uncertainty and deviation – in a word, error – into its undeviating course. The very nature of stability in an organism lies in the evolutionary suppression of originality. It follows that the opposite is true for contextual judgment, where the scope for error is unlimited. But in exactly the same way that error is expunged through contingent evolution, and right judgment sustained through constrained contiguous acts, errors of judgment in human evolution have been just as bloody and wasteful, just as red in tooth and claw in achieving a level of dominant stability for the species in weighing our successes higher than our failures, despite the terrible and scarcely bearable cost.

What we have arrived at, through the selective processes of evolution, is a state of organic and organised existence engineered through a cranial capacity for symbolic representation where we and the world and the objects of the world exist together, phenomenally and contextually, in a sort of impenetrable palimpsest written over the unseen, inconceivable, unknowable actuality of the universe – an understanding made clear for the first time and for all time by Kant. The world of consciousness is the represented, phenomenal world behind which lies the 'thing-in-itself', the never to be disclosed 'noumenon' to which we are forever blind. Unarmed with the idea of biological evolution or with concepts of self-organised autonomy, Kant could not begin to speculate how an organism's sensory and behavioural apparatus, that allows it to function perfectly adequately in its own domain with no representational understanding of the world whatsoever, could translate its orderly relationship with its environment into a representational mental framework anchored in space, time and causality and inherit the *a priori* ability to make judgments about quantity, quality and the relations between one thing and another. And no one has attempted to do this, to establish the evolutionary ground of *a priori* mental judgments in autonomous organic behaviour, since only science can make the attempt and science will not begin with philosophy, will not compromise its empirical credentials with what it sees as some superseded historical Kantian mumbo jumbo that questions the very notion of the reality that is science's bread and butter. But none the less such a translation and inheritance has taken place. Purely contiguous and contingent modes of judgment, that are the mechanics of life and matter, have by themselves permitted the emergence of contextual modes of judgment which have freed the human species from solely mechanical acts of judgment, those of necessity and instinct, and endowed the human being with the capacity to remember the past, imagine the future and plot the causes and consequences of his own actions.

The world and the self are real to us. But that is to say no more than the seamless integrity of the way in which the brain represents the self and the world is called 'reality'. Reality is an essential illusion. The world would be of no use to us if we did not represent it in terms of our own potential actions and interests, if its shape were constantly just colourless, amorphous, formless distributed matter, if it entirely disappeared from consciousness each time we blinked, if it was lost to us every time the mist descended, was forever a mystery and a puzzle to our understanding. And we would be of no use to ourselves if we did not discover ourselves as something more solid than the insubstantial self-imaginings of the brain, wraiths, dreamers, amnesiacs. Only when some part of that underpinning cerebral foundation cracks, some genetic malformation of the neural pathways makes dysfunctional links, or we suffer organic damage to the brain, or catch ourselves deluded by some misapprehension

– only then are we made aware of the evanescence, the instability and fragility of the personality and its perceptions of reality. Does that mean I am not permitted to assert that the world is real? Far from it. Of course the world is real! If the mole can find its way in the world in the dark with its useless furred over eyes and fossilised genes for seeing, how could our minds not have evolved to be the prefect fit to the same world, with all its mental imagery and knowledge modelled to the shape of our interests in it? We can't afford, in evolutionary terms, to have doubts about reality. We are as wedded to it as the turtle is to the ocean and the bird to the air, to its north and south, to the high purchase of its viewpoint. Reality is the ground of the finality of judgment.

We make decisions in the context of our perception of reality. Even though the wellspring of many of our judgments lies below consciousness, we have our being in consciousness and reality and that is where we act out our lives and endure the consequences of our actions and our judgments. That we are so exercised by the rightness of our judgments, by what is real and what is illusory, what is true or false, what must be so and what cannot possibly be so, testifies to the vital necessity of minimising error in judgment. If we accept that evolution is driven by the elimination of error, the cumulative effect of erroneous judgments and their consequential actions will decide our demise. Whether any of our ideas are true in themselves is a sophism. What matters is that the adoption and consolidation of ideas should secure some sort of stability or power base in the same way that territoriality does. Hence, in the human landscape, ideas, and ideas of truth, are disputed territory and the conflict of ideas as much a part of the evolution of populations as war, disease, famine, migration and the economic bases of power. William James and F C S Schiller were right to define truth, for all practical purposes, as that which works. What is true is what we all agree, at least tribally, to be true. Intrinsic truth is nowhere to be found. No 'truth' adheres to particles of matter. The 'reality' of the world is of no use to the flatworm, the fly, the lion, the lamb. No context is needed, no sense of the passage of time or the dimensions of space for the bird to weave its nest in the spring, or the spider to spin her web. Only in the mind – that abstract airy citadel constructed by the brain – does reality count, and it counts only because the value of contextual judgment lies in the elimination of error to reveal the truth of our final judgments – the only truth there is.

There is no 'is'-ness in the world, only a presence in the mind, only a confabulation of pictures of the world that enables us to make a living driven by the same blind impulses that drive the ant, and what the ant achieves by chemical signals and pheromones, we excel at by the cunning association of our interests in the world with the world itself.

If the notion of reality is mere surface perception, are we not entitled to ask if there is not another reality, a 'real' reality behind this one, that we should be able to make Kant's noumenon reveal itself? Kant gave the name 'noumenon' to what cannot be understood except when translated into 'phenomenon', to offer a word to say what the world is in itself when it is not what we say it is. The noumenon, therefore, by definition, is *impossible* to know. Since then, of course, every thinker unable to *let go* of philosophy has taken this up as a challenge, determined to find some contradictory or mystical way in which the unknowable can be known, not content that Kant once and for all put an end to the matter. The answer will always be that there is only one reality, that of phenomenal representation. The unknown presents itself to us in the only way possible, as the known, as the phenomenal representation of the mind. Mind *is* that representation, the sole formal presence of the reality of the self and the world. The alternative is not the revelation of another, deeper truth, a more real reality, but to know nothing, to be nothing. We have the experience we have, or we have nothing at all.

The evolution of consciousness is the evolution of the ground of judgment. Contextual judgment arises as a development of higher brain functions whose foundations lie in the integral grounds of the judgment of necessity and the judgment of contiguous encoded processes. Conscious judgments, just because they are conscious, are not released to float free in a separate moral universe unhitched from the neurobiology of the conscious agent. They remain as integral to organisational behaviour as the appetites and self-preservation strategies of the stickleback. From this perspective we need not tax ourselves with the perennially recurring question of the 'freedom of the will'. And biology should not get involved with what is essentially an outmoded theological debate just because occasionally it is possible to prove that what we believed to be a free act of choice was in fact determined by pre-emptive instinctive cognitive reactions, or by subliminal psychological influences. There is no separation of the 'will' in the context of judgment from the holistic biological unit that wills or is willed. Freedom of judgment is not an *absolute* freedom in any metaphysical sense, only an elaboration of other forms of judgment that now makes use of contextual information and conscious experience to increase the effectiveness of its judgment. Freedom of choice is not about freedom, but about choice and the efficacy of judgment. To pivot 'freedom' against 'determinism' as an either/or is to find ourselves back in an unproductive debate of no consequence. Not even the wiggle of a worm is determined, let alone man's destiny, only constrained by the limits of the possible, and freedom of the will is similarly constrained, neither free nor determined.

The whole of existence, life and light, the earth, the

cosmos, is predicated on no thought or word. Thoughts and words grew out of it. If the word was in the beginning, then it was our word, the word with which we began. The world was something before words were, and remains in essence what it was before the mind was. It continues blind to itself and its own being. Only, here and there, like candles being lit and blown out in dark windows, the forms of reality flicker in the cranial recesses of our post-reptilian heads, which are like so many Lascaux caves, representing a dream world of things that are our desires and hopes. Existence itself is the dark night outside. The light of the world is an electromagnetic wave and the eye that sees it a receptor that translates it into a network of signals that activate the nervous systems of creatures who live above the surface of the earth. But nothing thereby is illuminated. The interaction of light and life creates movement and action. But out of that witch's brew of the elements, out of ceaseless action and becoming, nothing becomes, nothing comes of it. Neither knowledge nor purpose, sense nor meaning, certainty nor finality is distilled from it. The deep meaning of the world is its own unreality. And that I cannot find, and nor can I speak of it. Only this island of consciousness is real. To that fact alone can I look for the justification for being.

On the Other Side of Silence

For he had discovered that there were a great number of hours to get through every day, even when one put in the maximum of sleep. Georges Simenon, *The Man Who Watched the Trains Go By*

I defy anyone to explain anything without the body. Denis Diderot

You have yourself confused with somebody else. Raymond Carver, *Intimacy*

I

There, through the broken branches, go
The ravens of unresting thought... W B Yeats, *The Two Trees*

To be is to be conscious of the possibility of not being, to know in the midst of life that there is such a thing as absence. Life is suspended between two events, birth and death, about neither of which do I have any direct experience. Life is all on this side of the divide that separates me from the void, from the void of non-being before birth and that same void of non-existence that resumes after death. Both events are facts of which I have knowledge as facts. But being born and dying are, as experiences, acts of living, and I have arrived too late to have any knowledge of the one, and I leave too soon to grasp the experience of the other. Yet without the knowledge of these two great facts I could not know the difference between being and nothingness, since a continuum of being without knowledge of either a beginning or an end is an undifferentiated form of experience with no distinction between what is and what is not. To exist without the knowledge of the possibility of not existing is, it is true, to be *something*, but that experience of being something is not anything that can be distinguished from being nothing.

The troublesome nature of being is that we are on the one hand nothing become something, and on the other something that can never know what it is to be nothing. They are the two contrary forms of a sort of immortality that nonetheless never quite reconcile us to the idea of absence. The contingent relationship of being to non-being does not alter throughout all eternity and we are forever one with the world's emptiness. But because all our knowledge of being is contained within being and we have no knowledge of, and no possibility of knowing, the emptiness that preceded and will follow our being, so we are also immortal in the sense that we know only living and can never know death or directly know emptiness, so that our living neither begins nor ends but is all in all.

The possibility of happiness or unhappiness with this state of affairs depends on how we deal with this knowledge, the knowledge of those two dismal facts of the involuntary act of coming into existence and the equally hapless inevitability of falling out of it.

The obscure unconscious recognition of a state of being in life without knowledge and without self-awareness, a state of innocent obedience to laws given and accepted without question, before wilfulness, discrimination and freedom – and with them the freedom to act according to one's own will and therefore, implicitly, to err – this recognition of a state before such aberrations crept in lies dreaming in the two figurative trees of knowledge and life by which guilt came into the world. Twinned with the ghostly memory of lost innocence is a dimly understood causality, that it is knowledge itself that has introduced the idea of death and exiled us from that place where we might have remained subordinate to a will not our own with all the possibilities of immortality to be plucked from the Tree of Life, had we not taken it upon ourselves to choose freedom and death by first being tempted to eat of the fruit of the Tree of Knowledge. Once knowledge is introduced there is no escape from death, but neither is there any freedom from knowledge itself, from the perpetual burden of consciousness, from cruel and devouring thought.

The *inconvenience* of being born is in being forced to come face to face with the unrelieved perpetual *presence* of the world in consciousness as a sort of tinnitus of all the senses. To be born, says Cioran, is to inherit a 'special type of sleeplessness'. To understand simply the *effrontery* of consciousness in translating mere *existence* (as trees, clouds, grass, frogs exist) into the uninterruptible bedlam of *being* one would need to enter into the lives of insects, worms and animals to locate the primal state of living-without-knowing-we-live in which they partake of the world's essential emptiness. *We* of course can only look into this with our minds, and on each occasion where we allow the mind to intrude into mindlessness in order to imagine the animal's own representation of its universe, we succeed only in introducing some parasitic form of ourselves, so that what looks out from the eye of the lizard or the wasp is only a modified version of the self and not the other, the ever alien other that neither knows nor can be known.

To the revealing mind that roams around in this new world of knowledge and self-awareness, there appears to be a semblance of intelligent reciprocation that inheres in all phenomena. We inhabit a world of objects and events that attach themselves to us, wrap themselves around the centripetal ego with assurances of their inextricable relationship to us. It will always naturally appear so to us since the mind is the great interpreter and intermediary between the body and the world in which it flourishes. Hence several things at once have been allowed to intrude as causal connections between the deep unknowable and indifferent universe of non-being and that knowledge of being in a world that seems to exist solely in its relation to us. The mind, in the course of the evolution of its self-interest, has managed to connect the phenomenal world of appearances to some purposive activating devices that exist for no other reason than to torment and taunt us in our state of undress. They go by various names: God, destiny, fate, heaven, the stars. They can be appeased by spells and prayers, flowers and sacrifices, magical names and rituals and homeopathy. The mind, proposed Goethe, is like the silvered back of a mirror under the universe in which man, the 'true Narcissus', delights in seeing his own image everywhere. Even those who think themselves free of illusion and superstition, in everyday life believe in the reciprocated affection of their pet dogs to which they are tied by a leash. Those who know nothing else, nonetheless are sure of their dog's intelligence and the regard and esteem in which they are held by the evidence of its liquid-eyed gaze.

Our significance lies neither in our being nor in our doing, not in any self-sufficiency in existence itself nor in any deed that passes unnoticed and unacknowledged. No, always our significance is derived from a fundamental need for our awareness of the world to be reciprocated in some way – by God, Nature or Providence, by our fellow men, our children or, failing these, by a dumb animal we keep for this sole purpose. Even the great Schopenhauer allowed himself to be deceived in this way, finding in his dog the companionship, constancy and appreciation lacking in his contemporaries and in the human species at large. And indeed the dog in its nature is wiser than man, who never learns the limits of his own nature, for the dog always obeys its true master – which is the guiding constraint of evolutionary necessity that has moulded the dog's behaviour to its own interests. The domesticated canine has advanced its self-interest in food, warmth and shelter by learning to respond to human social signals. Assisted by our own selective breeding of the species, we have succeeded in attaching to ourselves an alter ego that we drag around with us wherever we go, or one that we can leave behind to greet us on our return so that we can know that in some manner we have arrived home, when in fact, as the dog already knows, nature is indifferent to us and what is reflected back from the dog's looking-glass eyes is a reciprocated emptiness. If we could first surrender all that is human and uniquely representational and constructive about our minds we might begin to see dimly what the dog sees – not our multi-dimensional world of experience and meaning, of love and self-regard, but only an outward looking hunting down of sensory impressions, linked to a cycle of behavioural patterns with which it is genetically and habitually endowed, unable to recreate by any means the self-centred notions of ourselves to which it appears to be so devoted.

II

If we had a keen vision and feeling of all ordinary human life, it would be like hearing the grass grow and the squirrel's heart beat, and we should die of that roar which lies on the other side of silence. George Eliot, *Middlemarch*

There is an unbridgeable divide between silence and knowledge. It has only once been bridged, in the course of the mind's origin and development. But now there is no going back. We are on one side or the other of the divide and the great silence we have left behind knows nothing that we know, and we in turn cannot return to it and know anything of it, any more than we can know the experience of what it is like not to have been born.

All organisms function unconsciously in a self-organised way in pursuit of their self-interests. All the physiological and behavioural characteristics of an organism have evolved around making a living in a particular niche environment, co-evolving along with that environment in competition with the rest of the biosphere in which every creature, every cell and every molecule is going about its business. What is superfluous to its needs for the most part drops away, atrophies, like the brain of the sea squirt or the eyes of the mole, all the tricksy behaviour we observe in, say, the trapdoor spider or the angler fish being just those diverse and bizarre propensities that serve its interests. There is no context for this behaviour, no known world wider than its interests that would require every creature to process large quantities of irrelevant information before concluding just exactly what part of the whole meets its needs. Evolution has limited the dimensions of the world in which an organism persists and thereby increased its energy efficiency by never having found it necessary to widen its horizons beyond its needs. Contextual awareness, that is, some form of consciousness, is of no evolutionary advantage. It is a waste of resources. It is more expedient, in the long run, just to do and see what happens than to work out what might happen in advance and get it wrong. Mistakes correct themselves so long as we don't have the freedom to go on making them.

Consciousness is a sensory mechanism for exploring the outer limits of interestedness. The caterpillar will never, throughout all eternity, recognise a need to read the *New York Times*. Yet such a thing, such a creature that does exactly that, has come into being. We ourselves operate within a large context of the oversupply of information. Few people read all of the *NYT*. Some read sections here and there. Most people in the world do not read it at all. The majority of the world's population will in fact not know that there is any such thing as the *NYT*, though they will know there are such things as newspapers in general. In consciousness, the limits of our interestedness are no longer predefined by the restrictions imposed on an organism's meanderings by not knowing anything at all. But consciousness still serves our self-interests – it is just that we need constantly to edit where we place the limits on information. Because no mind works exactly within the same limits, no two minds are alike, no single conscious experience in one head is replicated inside another and, though the *a priori* framework of cognition is given and held in common, as the segmented locomotion of the caterpillar is common to caterpillars, what is *known* in consciousness has no uniformity (no one can know *exactly* what

I know).

Since consciousness is the only basis for making definitive statements about the world, it follows that the postulate of a single reality is merely a categorical convenience of language and society and entirely irrelevant to the primary functionality of consciousness, which is to serve the organism's self-interests by identifying what things are and modelling the possibilities of what they might be and of acting in the light of that understanding. Far from being the one and only arbiter of the real, the mind simply aids the organism manoeuvre towards satisfying its needs and interests. It taps into a huge amount of miscellaneous and largely useless information, but actually utilises very little of it. Even so, the immediate data of consciousness is severely limited, in accordance with the economic principle of self-organised evolution for self-interest. Despite what we think we know, we don't really know much at all.

Like any other organism I am immediately aware only of the environmental data within the range of my senses, and there are sights and sounds that remain outside the range of my experience. I do not hear whispers in the next room or the perpetual turning of worms under the lawn or the rustling in the grass that the blackbird hears. I do not see what is out of sight or see what anyone else sees. I do not, cannot share another's pain but pursue the object of my attention without regard for the cries that do not reach me or for the death of a stranger behind a closed door. We are each focused on a limited world of experience not much larger in itself than the sparrow's. The greater, seemingly almost infinite accumulation of inferential data that is the mind's knowledge of the world is not therefore the same as the experiential world of consciousness. Just as the individual human being operates within a spatially and temporally defined sphere of direct experience, the mind, while it ranges beyond the present moment to the past and the future, to theories of the origins of matter and the outer limits of the universe, only cocoons us, as it were, in a kind of life support air bubble of thoughts and concepts and representations, like an astronaut's space suit that acts as a protective membrane between the adventurous representative of the universe and the infinite nothingness of the universe itself. That membrane that keeps us safe can, of course, be punctured. It tends, for our own good, to self-repair so that, like a lizard that re-grows its tail, we can readjust the mind's lost equilibrium by editing out the intrusion of the abyss and the monsters that live in its deeps, or by retelling the stories that make up the idea of the self, or by reshaping our memories into the narrative of a life that never need hear what is never to be heard or to see the hidden face that never must be looked upon. In the north African setting of Paul Bowles's novel, we see the self temporarily sequestered under the sheltering sky, and forever isolated from the lives of others. We cannot know directly what it is like to be another person. But we know that their sense of self has its own orbit and, while we circle each other elliptically and pass by and pass on, there is no greater danger to the integrity of the self than to become captive in the orbit of another's sphere of consciousness. The word 'Africa' itself can be made to stand for a world of chaotic swarming that is deep, dark and impenetrable, resisting any attempt at simplification and the possibility of attaching it to one's own self-contained idea of the world. Each time we pronounce on the shape of reality from inside this singular skull that knows only a fragment of the world, we should also utter the word 'Africa' to remind ourselves of the world's and our own essential incomprehensibility, to acknowledge, as Pessoa says in *The Book of Disquiet*, 'the existence of people, of climates and changes in the weather; the terrifying objectivity of the world…'.

This, then, is the threefold condition of being that is imposed on me by being born. Firstly, I am forever cut off from the deep, silent and uncomprehending anonymity of life itself, from the emptiness of the life that has been left behind that has no argument to pick with an equally empty universe. Secondly, I have inherited the inescapable and burdensome presence of the world and the cacophony of experiences that assaults one's senses along with the awareness of the isolated consciousness that must bear it, neither of which can be put off until the return to infinite silence in death. Thirdly, I must face the disappointment that the reality of the world and the self has its substance in the sensory order of the mind, and whatever truths and values I derive from my experiences are the fictions of my own invention that can never stand on their own ground, objectively given, as the justification for being. No matter how much we elaborate the forms of reason and order that the mind alone brings to the world, it makes no difference to the underlying and undermining condition of being, which remains undisturbed. All our thoughts are arabesques performed on a high wire strung across the abyss. So be it, since it is so. Any philosophy or attempt at understanding that does not acknowledge these three conditions of being is doomed to repeat itself endlessly through all time and never discover the sources of its delusions.

The only trustworthy response to life is perpetual astonishment. To remain unsurprised by this unexpected and unjustified sudden descent from *nowhere* into a state of conscious being in which nothingness has shrivelled to something that can only be imagined contained within it – to be without astonishment at this turn of events is to be plunged in the ocean of consciousness as though it were the infinite *everything* of the universe and not just *something* in a small corner of it where the mind sits like a sea anemone sifting saltwater ripples in a rock pool. But when one is suddenly caught by this surprise, when one literally becomes an astonished man, it is impossible simply to plunge into life, to swim in it unselfconsciously like a flounder, as though there were no other possible medium in which life can be conducted, no possibility of coming up for air. This is the position the poet and poet/philosopher finds himself in, not quite born a slave to consciousness, unable completely to let go of his formlessness and take up the mask of someone in particular from whom there is no escape. Pessoa, in his *Páginas Íntimas*, wrote mysteriously: 'For poetry is astonishment, admiration, as of a being fallen from the skies taking full consciousness of his fall, astonished about things. As of one who knew things in their souls, striving to remember this knowledge, remembering that it was not thus he knew them, not under these forms and these conditions, but remembering nothing more.' There is a special sort of joy and a special kind of anguish that are neither plainly happiness nor simply pain that cling to this state of mind of one who is always seemingly on the point of taking leave. It is a half-lit life not to be envied, but it illuminates the world it leaves behind.

Consciousness never leaves the world. It contains it all. The world is the whole of all that it knows. Because of the fact of consciousness the great nothingness to which it and the world belong can never enter the mind. Always there is something. We have to go out of our way to make an imaginary sketch of nothingness, but it is never less than something simply *called* nothingness subsisting by permission of somethingness. Always there is world. In his *Eighth Elegy* Rilke writes:

> Never, not for a single day, do we have
> before us that pure space into which flowers
> endlessly open. Always there is world
> and never nowhere...

'Mere creatures,' says Saul Bellow somewhere, 'look

with their original eyes.' The animal constantly looks out into openness. It is not, like us, turned towards the world of things and objects, to the invariable presence of the world, tied to reflections, memories, absences – and to the idea of death and the suffering self, of which it knows nothing. It lives always in the timeless succession of the present moment. We ourselves cannot grasp this 'pure space' into which the animal gazes and the flower opens. For us there is always world, conscious awareness, our eyes, as it were, turned, twisted around towards the world of objects, and 'never outward'. For, although we naturally think of the world of objects and things as something outward, they are, like our whole sense of being, knowing, thinking, dreaming, remembering, imagining, an inward transformation of that outer world. We never fully gaze outward. Our gaze is turned around and we look upon the world as a reflection, like the romantic tourists in a grand landscape used to view the scene in a mirror so that it could be contained as a framed pictorial representation, an object in particular. To be able to grasp this outwardness would be to answer the Zen koan-like question: when a flower opens, what does it open into? For we are locked into the somethingness of objects in time and space and can never turn our gaze completely outward without sacrificing all knowledge of being inward.

If consciousness is a 'special type of sleeplessness' our only conceivable escape from what Bellow has so aptly called the 'claustrophobia of consciousness' is some form of somnambulistic existence, sleepwalking through life without either sadness or joy, free from pain and grief but also without gladness. But the experience of consciousness, that is to say the experience of knowing we exist, is inseparable from the experience of pain and suffering. Under the heading of suffering I include anxiety, disappointment, guilt, regret, envy, loss, apprehension, the frustration of ambition and the fear of death – those phantoms that belong to the mind only, that supplement the suffering of the body and extend pain beyond injuries sustained by the nervous system to the anguish of the mind that reflects on its own misfortunes and its destiny. We can acknowledge that the animal organism feels pain from its injuries, but we cannot go so far as to say it dwells in an existential realm of suffering, that condition of knowing we live, knowing we suffer and knowing we die. The spectacular bloodiness of life, its violence and aggression, its destroying and devouring, are unconscious acts indifferent to the individual forms of life. Life devours itself and spews itself out again, endlessly and enormously, as a continuous process in which no single organism accumulates to itself the singular knowledge of its being or demonstrates any empathy with the separate existences of other organisms. It is indifferent. It is indifferent because it has no reason to stand apart from the processes that created it and no means by which it may do so. Its separateness is an accident of form. Life fights instinctively for its preservation without being able to value what it is that it has thereby created as the form of its extension.

But we, who know ourselves, suffer our lives. Suffering is the gift of consciousness and self-awareness. We ask, fruitlessly, why we should suffer, but there can never be an answer within the condition of being, only in non-being. An alternative to pain and suffering in this life would not turn out to be the thing we wish for, happiness and bliss, but a life of somnambulistic indifference, the deep secret truth of nature incubating in every soul like the reborn creatures in the 1956 film *Invasion of the Body Snatchers*, who no longer feel pain or loss but at the price of never knowing joy or happiness. They represent life in its nakedness as pure will. If we are not to suffer the death of a child, if we are to be like sheep grazing next to a dead lamb, then neither can we love her, or get pleasure from her company. The living organism has no particular need of consciousness. Life has a self-sufficient and self-organising trajectory to which self-consciousness adds nothing. Living itself is mere indifference to life. But *being* is not the same as living. Being is knowing, a perpetual wakefulness to conscious experience in which there is no sleep, no rest or respite or retreat to moral indifference and a blissful state of unknowing.

III

Knowledge is the plague of life, and consciousness an open wound in its heart. E M Cioran, *On the Heights of Despair*

Now, in speaking of consciousness, one must make a distinction between a general state or condition of consciousness which is everyone's inheritance, taken for granted and to which I need pay little attention since, as far as I am concerned, consciousness is just the everyday medium in which my life floats, like a fish swimming under water unaware of the weight it bears, and that state of acute conscious awareness in which I *suffer* my existence and am never free of the painful knowledge of death that prevents me from surrendering completely, forgetfully to life.

To possess a high degree of consciousness, to be always aware of yourself in relation to the world, to live in the permanent tension of knowledge, means to be lost for life. *Knowledge is the plague of life, and consciousness an open wound in its heart.*

To be happy (to use that ridiculous word) is to avoid thinking. The happy man is he who wakes each morning to pick up the momentum of an energy focused on the outer, on tasks and activities, who is forever moving forward, knocking things apart, nailing things together and 'passing the time' in between until it is time to sleep again. Only some illness or failing suddenly alerts him to the fateful condition he had all along inherited but paid no attention to: that it has been his destiny all the time to carry death in his heart, like the accustomed ticking of a clock you no longer hear. One might consider this happy state a *suspension* of consciousness – though technically and actually conscious, for all practical purposes he might just as well have remained in an animal state of outward-facing integrity, of self-organised sufficiency, that simply goes on living until its heart stops. This is why pain, illness and tragedy are important in human life, for unless that plain sailing, habituated, innocuous pacing through life is disrupted he never shall know what it is to have lived. For always living is dying. It is having lived, not living, not life itself that counts, for only the presence of death in life removes life from the uninterruptible present tense and permits one to live in eternity. At one level of consciousness I am somnambulatory man, an automaton whose conscious awareness merely permits the representation of my obstacle-ridden life course through which I am unconsciously propelled and which donates to my struggle an enhanced capacity for solving problems. At another level I am transfigured man *afflicted* by consciousness, burdened with the perpetual presence of the world, engaged in a struggle to redeem myself from the abyss of nothingness of which I have suddenly become acutely aware, as of an open wound. We cannot be conscious without suffering because of it, we cannot know without the pain of knowledge, we cannot be without the anxiety of what it is to be.

Yet, as Schopenhauer says, there is no pain in knowledge itself but only in the habit of reflecting on our condition of knowing, of having all that we would wish our condition to be thwarted by the knowledge of what it actually is. We would be capable of no such knowledge, we would live as imperturbably in the present moment as sheep or wolves, oblivious to the dimensions of reality, were our experiences not events in time but events of the here and now only. In a static universe that was merely a massy *point* without movement or change we would be unable to form the idea of any sort of awareness or experience. But because the universe is constantly expanding, moving and changing, and life has evolved also, not as a fixed commodity but caught up in the careering, pell-mell course of whirling matter and we must go along with it, the brain's modality of time-perception is the root cause of the emergence of consciousness and the duration of experience. 'Time,' says Schopenhauer among his *Parerga and Paralipomena*, 'is a contrivance in our brain for giving the *utterly futile existence* of things and ourselves a semblance of reality by means of continuance and duration.'

For Schopenhauer the animal is the embodiment of the present, calmly enjoying the present moment in ways largely lost to the human, for whom the present moment is a transitory bridge between the hopes, plans and anticipations of the future and the shrivelled up memories of their final resting place in the past. Yet the present moment, too, must have its duration, or else we find ourselves caught up in a Zeno-like paradox in which, no matter how finely we cut the moment, we are left with no substance to the present that will allow the accumulation of experiences that makes up the past. The perception of the flow of sensory experience is the great illusory construction not only of consciousness but of primitive organic nervous systems in other forms of life, designed to accompany the flow of movement and change that constitutes the nature of both matter and life and at the same time allow the organism to cut out of this flow the critical static moment at which it must act in relation to its experience. Henri Bergson writes in *Matter and Memory*:

> The fundamental illusion consists in transferring to duration itself, in its continuous flow, the form of the instantaneous sections which we make in it.... You define the present in an arbitrary manner as *that which is*, whereas the present is simply

what is being made.... Practically we perceive only the past....

However, the perception of the past does not occur *in* the past but in the flow of the present, along an overgrown path. Memory is the road more travelled. It is not so much that the past is *recovered* along that road as reinvented, for, while the path may be conceptually the same path, in practice it is changed. We tread down a blade of grass and the path is changed, yet we refer to the same path. We revisit something called the past that conceptually remains the same unchanging and fixed set of recollections, yet each time we walk all over it and it shifts like gravel under our feet. Not only can you not step into the same river twice, as Heraclitus says, but you can't, says Cratylus, step into a 'river' even once, since the river is only a mental construction that has already flowed away. Clearly the mind must 'make up' not only the continuity of the present but the coherence of the past, or our perceptions would be only of the fragmentary present instantly replaced by another fragment, lacking continuity and duration, sensed but not making sense. We need think only of Funes in Borges's famous story to get the idea of how everything, and language in particular, breaks down if we don't allow one relatively unchanging thing to stand for something that is not in fact one thing at all.

> It irritated him that the 'dog' of three-fourteen in the afternoon, seen in profile, should be indicated by the same noun as the dog of three-fifteen, seen frontally.

One cannot live in a world of particulars only, unless one is a dog. 'To think,' continues Borges, 'is to ignore (or forget) differences, to generalise, to abstract.'

All memories are new memories. We only remember what we have just remembered. Recent research in neuroscience seems to bear this out. This is Joseph LeDoux, author of *The Synaptic Self*, reflecting in *Edge* magazine on the lab work of Karim Nader: '...each time a memory is used, it has to be restored as a new memory in order to be accessible later. The old memory is either not there or is inaccessible. In short, your memory about something is only as good as your last memory about it. This is why people who witness crimes testify about what they read in the paper rather than what they witnessed.'

While we are habituated to think of memory as a great permanent storehouse, it is hard to sustain that view of how memory works, if only because it is impossible to conclude just *what* it can be that is stored in it. Certainly it can't be the raw data of consciousness, since these would not resemble the substance of memory but the entire unedited version of all sensory input, most of which can't be stored anywhere: for example, we are unable to recollect the relative positions, size, shape of every leaf on a tree at one moment and then a minute later – for each and every moment of what undoubtedly we did see at those precise moments. We don't remember the true size of things. When we revisit a childhood place, a house we lived in – it is always smaller than we remember, and invariably we have got some detail wrong that in our mind we were quite certain about. We know from experience how often we disagree with other people's recollections of a shared past, how indisputable facts expose and contradict cherished certainties, how old newspapers disabuse us of firsthand truths, how diaries stare back at us and seem point blank to *lie* to us. And we now know also that drugs can affect the reconsolidation of early memories to the extent that a remembered 'experience' is irrevocably changed, evoking the possibility of removing painful recollections, editing, as it were, the idea of the self that our memories help create, that figure from the past, desperately held on to, remodelled without its faults and its guilt.

Personally, I have difficulty recollecting anything in

sequence. Hence my writing is like a patchwork of associated pieces that just look as though they belong and want to stay together. If memories really are the product of uncountable numbers of crossed wires, a tangle of neurons and synapses and synapse-strengthening proteins, then the notion of time, and one's life lived in it, as a *line* might seem a practical but ultimately unsatisfying way of thinking about time – as something thin and attenuated and lacking the depth of experience itself and the multiple simultaneous recollections of experience that are associated together, but not associated in any sequence. I prefer, with Ford Madox Ford, 'impressions' to 'memories' – it's good enough that the past seems to be what it was, and preferable to being something else that has nothing to do with me. I find myself constantly forcing a linear narrative of events, to connect intersecting lines as though obeying a formal convention, a grammar of remembering, when in fact what is 'past' is 'present', in tangles and layers, like a forest floor where last year's leaves are mixed with this autumn's fall, over which there are large areas of dark shadows and occasional unexpected patches of light.

Time is the necessary modality of experience, without which we cannot be said to have consciousness or knowledge or experience. But time is the enemy of stillness, of the deep contentment of the present, of motionless, impractical, uncivilised absorption in the accumulated moment. The moment escapes us, like a melody blown away on the wind, and we spend our lives forever locked in the vast library of the past, turning over the pages of our thoughts.

The consensus in the literature seems to be that the present moment – a moment of 'perception' in consciousness – has a duration of about 100 milliseconds. That is, that's the time taken by neuronal activity to make up a perception, cut out a slice of experience before moving on to the next slice which, when run consecutively, like the rapidly moving frames of a film, recreate the movement we observe. It may be that the numerous modalities or dimensions of the actual experience are processed at different speeds and in different parts of the brain – shape, depth, colour, cry (the beauty of a thing, the desirability of anything, the fear of it – how different these are from the mere geometry of it) – to be recomposed into a whole. But of course what the mind thus composes is not the thing itself but the perception of it, made up not of its natural elements, of which we know nothing, but of its aspects and modes of interest. It is our personal representation of the world we are engaged with at a particular moment, the selective processing of a limited amount of information from which we make up experience through a continuous process of recollection from moment to moment.

The flow of conscious experience may seem to us a mirror image of the world itself, yet, looking at it from a purely functional perspective, the concreteness of an experience is an evolved instrument for practical living, shaped to the contours of the external world, wrapped around the movement it encounters, primed to abstract from the immediate data of consciousness the dimensions of the mind's interests acting on behalf of the whole bodily organism.

It is unlikely that the mind should have emerged out of the organisation of the nervous system simply in order to be the observer of phenomena, just to bear witness, or we should contend that the frog's tongue evolved to savour the evening air and the rat's eye to appreciate the sunset from down in the ditch under the barn. Rather, it is to know the time and conditions for action, and to differentiate the object of interest from the miscellany of data that makes up the sensory world, sufficiently to act upon it or in relation to it.

Life is essentially lyrical, a continuous flow outward into the 'open', an expansion and dissipation of 'being' into 'becoming'. It is a lyricism constantly interrupted by moments of attention that stop the flow as the organism unconsciously seizes the moment to act and then leaves the moment behind as it moves further into the open, unaware of the past, forming no relationship with events, holding on to nothing. In consciousness, though everything flows away into the past, everything remains. The world, by rights, should be empty, but it is always full. The river remains. Consciousness is wedded to what it has made, and the river flows into fullness and not into its essential emptiness. 'Always there is world'. The ungraspable lyrical flow of change and becoming is translated by the mind into things that are, objects with attributes and aspects that do indeed move and change but remain in their conjunctions real and actual. A tree is always a tree despite the impossibility of such a thing's actually being in the world, of its ever being anything other than the mind's notation of it. The mind's notation for 'tree' sets limits to its extension in space, ignores the perpetual movement that prohibits its fixed extension, consolidates the diverse phenomena of leaves, fruits, seeds, twigs that are themselves notations for something else, discounts the tree at midday in the sun and the tree at midnight under the moon, discards from the idea of a tree the leaves dispersed by the wind and the leaf-mould lodged between its roots, overlooks the variegation of each leaf in favour of some notion of green and yellow, and passes over what it does not know about the synthesis of cellulose or the metabolism of exogenous nutrients. The mind decides, over and over again, how much knowledge goes to make a tree and what will become of the blurred and uncertain sensation of anything in the process of its creation and notation in ideas and language and memory.

Ask a blind man how the retinal input of light can make

a tree, or a deaf man how the sound of rain on the leaves comforts the mind on the edge of sleep, to get some idea of consciousness as artifice. Take a moment to look with the eyes of the woodpecker to understand the usefulness of a tree in the absence of the idea of it, and to ask what is a wood without the capacity to consolidate into one collective noun its subsidiary contributory singularities that are themselves only abstract mental notations. The answer is in the sound of the woodpecker pecking, whether you can hear it or not.

Newton wondered how light 'produceth in our minds the phantasms of colours', and since then no one doubts that colour is not present in the external world as an attribute of things themselves, but is a quality of perception produced by the interaction of the eye and the brain. Yet despite the strength of this analogy we go on believing that green trees, blue skies, black clouds, red sunsets, terracotta roofs are exactly the same as the words and ideas we use to describe them and not, in fact, something else altogether that the mind represents as objects of its own composition, in the way that a child transforms an alien assembly of fur, fluff and glass beads into a bear and an object of familiarity to which it is attached. The world and all its objects, with all the qualities that characterise those objects, do not present themselves ready-made to be reflected back in the mind as though minds were mirrors and cannot help but represent the reality of the world in all its colours and dimensions. To the adult suddenly recovered from infant blindness, the unfamiliar and unlearned world of light is a dazzling, disorientating and painful experience, a mental confusion. Objects suddenly made visible do not equate to anything previously known and objectified by means of touch only. Their visual representation, scale, perspective, dimensions, functions, shadow and substance are alien distortions and redistributions of previously familiar experiences, perversions and contradictions that do not enhance and complement the reality of the perceived object but detract from it, as though one had suddenly discovered flaws in a perfectly shaped crystal that only the light can reveal. An object known by touch alone is sufficient in itself, and in its very solidity seems in possession of its own truthfulness. But the sudden intrusion of visual elements produces an alien array of new impressions, not least of which is the ungainliness, asymmetry and ugliness of objects once known perfectly, that have become monstrous.

The mind is made for the light. It allows the blind to see. The blind and deaf Helen Keller was able to use the metaphorical language of sight and colour because she understood that the mind itself is metaphorical, that there are 'correspondences' between the outer and inner world mediated by the senses, but one's conception of the world is a self-willed act of the imagination. Consciousness cannot be without the potential for hearing and seeing even to the deaf and blind, or without the capacity for language and vision, since the brain evolved in a seeing and hearing animal. Without the development of those faculties the mind would be denied the metaphorical, it would be denied knowledge and understanding, and denied futurity. For the other three senses of touch, taste and smell detain the mind in the present. An object to the touch is that object in its fixed presence, visited over and over again only as itself with nothing to offer beyond its immediacy. Taste and smell are also sensations of the immediacy of things. If we try to imagine a future state using the faculties of taste and smell alone, all we can find is the past, the madeleines and cinnamon shops of memory. We can never close our eyes to the world, even if we are blind to it, for it is in us. Always there is world. We no longer have the unconscious ability to navigate through it, like a blind bat flying unhindered through the dusk, but we carry the weight of it with us from birth to death, from the past to the future, as a burden.

This, then, is our life, washed up on the shores of light

from the impenetrable deep ocean of unconsciousness. I cannot escape the world by going to any length – meditating on infinity beyond God, journeying to the future to escape the present – for, as Pessoa says, everything, 'sky, earth, world is never anything but myself.' My life is lived in a perpetual state of insomnia that sleep itself cannot bring to an end. Sleep is only a temporary and confused respite from one sort of existence merely for the moment replaced by another, equally real or unreal, one sort of dreaming rising up to take the place of another, like shadows coming and going whose paths cross and connect and which then just as mysteriously disappear. What one can never escape is one's being. I am pinned here as the birds are to the sky, who lift their wings to fly away but can't free themselves from the act of flying.

IV

There is always the sun when the sun shines and night when the night falls…. There is always what there is and never what there should be… Ferdinand Pessoa, *The Book of Disquiet*

We wake to consciousness only to discover that there is something not quite right about this state of affairs. A crack soon appears in the surface of things and goes on widening until there is a an unbridgeable divide between hope and experience. Not only does the world remain the same, day after day, but we discover that we ourselves are also the same, not reborn from one day to the next, but condemned to repeat ourselves indefinitely until it is all over. We spend so much of our lives trying to leave ourselves. Our hope is always of being someone or something other, a childish dressing-up. But all we are allowed is the tedium of always being ourselves and never becoming other. If just once we were to experience what it is like to be other and newly created, it would be at the sacrifice of duration. It would be the experience of being discontinuous – not, in fact, to be born anew but to be finished.

It turns out, after all that effort, that life is mundane and banal. We go about the business of living just as any other creature does, but we are interminably aware of our own presence in space and time, of the repetitive return of work and days. At the essential, unreflective level of life (and what need have we to be reflective or philosophical?), engaged simply in the act of living and in labouring to sustain life, boredom is found to be man's true existential condition. Once having risen to conscious awareness and left behind that purely unconscious state of living that knows nothing of tomorrow, what is revealed to us at once is both the indefinite number of days that must be filled and the pointless futility of all our activity that takes us no farther than the necessity of occupying time and space. Schopenhauer writes:

> This is a consequence of the fact that life has no *genuine intrinsic worth*, but is kept in *motion* merely by want and illusion. But as soon as things come to a standstill, the utter barrenness and emptiness of existence becomes apparent.

We play games of patience, but 'the cards have no value in themselves'. We are like characters in a Chekhov story, filling the time by playing cards, paying visits, going for drives, all the time realising we should be working for the betterment of mankind – but to what end? In Chekhov's stories so often do good works, dreams of love and a better world come to nothing, to disillusionment, the waning of energy, boredom – with the question always immanent: What is all this for, what is it that we should know that no one is telling us?

For the most part we live partially eclipsed lives of light and shadow, living among clouds and mist, dreaming or half-asleep in an indeterminate state between being and non-being, remembering and forgetting, just sufficiently between consciousness and unconsciousness to know enough of pain to wish to unburden oneself of the weight of existence, yet awake enough to recognise that the pain of existence is all there is on this side of silence. Even for one saved from death who, as in Chekhov's story *Typhus*, sees life rise once more like a new dawn, in the end 'joy gives way to the boredom of everyday life'.

In order to live one must more or less forget the mystery and mockery of being and go along blindly. Or at least translate the absence of usefulness, purpose and meaning into a formulaic prop of some sort so that everything that conspires to deny any intrinsic value to life is thereby incorporated into it – as a moral, religious or utilitarian code or mantra to live by – and its terrible aspect neutralised with *words* and *thoughts*. The very condition that absolutely denies life any meaning is thus set up as its actual justification. But the shadow of disillusionment is never far from us, and darkens our moments like a cloud across the sun.

If life were a passing parade, and we merely the spectators of it, we might watch it pass with a wry smile ('a spectacle worth seeing, altogether significant, and at least entertaining,' as Schopenhauer says) and acknowledge its rowdy cacophony, its gaudy display, its strutting insistence on being seen and heard, before it, and we ourselves, fall back into eternal silence. Like a day out at the seaside, we might be grateful for a momentary distraction from the grey uniformity of all our days and the days of silence which are beyond counting. But life is for living, and there is nothing we can do about it. We can rise above it only for a few insightful moments before we are forced to go back to the mundane routine of living with which we are tasked. Life is a chore and a burden. I am not like other creatures that are destined to scurry along the ocean floor or dig themselves tunnels under the earth, mindlessly, thoughtlessly, unconsciously driven they know not where or by what and not caring to know. For the effrontery of consciousness lies in more than an enforced state of insomnia. Not only am I perpetually awake to the world, I am obliged, endlessly, wearily, to do business with it. I cannot forever sit dreamily in an armchair and let it float by. I cannot hide from it or evade it. I am called upon to act, to fill the hours, to work (as Adam was condemned from the very beginning as the price of knowledge), to strive, to accomplish.

Yet as soon as one stops for breath, there it is again, hovering over us, the spectre of the uselessness of all our endeavours. We are back at the seaside building sandcastles that the next tide will wash away. Because we are conscious beings we now know what we previously did not know. We know the world of our experience as an interrelation of subject and object, knower and known, of things that exist in space and endure in time, possessing qualities and attributes and subject to the laws of cause and effect. These are such things unknown to other forms of life that none the less still live. We *know* – but what is all this knowledge for? It is only sufficient to empower us to continue our existence in time and space by manipulating the counters of experience for that purpose. A purpose beyond the perpetuation of the *same* condition is never made known to us. If we choose to introduce into this game something that is outside our experience – let us say some sort of eternal reward for having lived and strived and borne all the insults of life – on analysis it turns out to be only a compensatory wild card to console us in *this* life and, indeed, when we look closely at it, if it were to come up would serve only to perpetuate the same life in a slightly ameliorated form (one that would in fact be certain to confirm one's first view that the true existential condition of life is boredom). The real trial and test of life is to endure it without purpose.

The purposes and strivings of human beings serve the ends and aims of life only in the sense that work is done (as beetles roll balls of dung to some end, and the burrowing owl stores dung to attract the beetles that collect it), work cycles are completed, energy is dissipated, tasks are accomplished and, in that hackneyed phrase that serves to underline the utter pointlessness of everything each time we utter it, *life goes on.* Life has no ultimate or even secondary purpose outside life itself, no internal significance beyond the act of living and reproducing and perpetuating itself, which it can do just as well blindly as it does in possession of the knowledge of its own being. It only *appears* to have the possibility of sense and purpose over and above the preservation of organic integrity *because* it now presents itself in the mind in all its mental relationships of subject and object, action and reaction, being and nothingness. Once there was a single continuum of undifferentiated existence. But the instrumentality of mind lies in this: to break up the continuum of existence and construct from its parts an ordered universe in which the self, the subject, has dominion over the other, the object. And while this powerfully serves the ends and aims of life through the preservation and perpetuation of the interests of the subject, it has also laid bare the terms on which the self must do business with the world, and revealed the limits of perpetuity. There would be no cruelty or tragicomedy in this state of affairs had not the idea of the self emerged into consciousness. There is nothing tragic in the sense of life itself, only in the assumption of the self as its proprietor who will one day be evicted as not the rightful owner.

We live simultaneously in the future and the past, and never in the present. If the present were sufficient for us our existence would not be difficult to bear. It would perhaps pass by, minute by minute, as an ever-changing scene to which we had cheerfully become accustomed. Many people do manage to pass their lives in a state of enviable and noble idiocy, like Platon in *War and Peace*. In Platon Tolstoy created a character who embodied that rare being who is capable of being completely human, humane, wise with inventions and proverbs that appear on each occasion to be newly discovered, who has no idea of himself other than as the agent of his own experiences, who consumes his life minute by minute, 'looking out', as a dog does, and does not remember what he has just said, cannot repeat his own idea, cannot recite the same line twice, where everything seems invented for the purpose from moment to moment. There are many instances of such *good* people in life, here epitomised in fiction. They seem to sacrifice their lives as they go along, whereas the rest of us dwell in ourselves among our anxieties because we find that the self is always bound to time.

We are torn between anxieties about the future and regrets about the past. We have, we may think to ourselves, got off on the wrong foot. We are not who we would wish to be. Mistakes have been made. We have taken a wrong turning. We have made a bad marriage. We have worked for nothing. We have invested unwisely. We have less than we might have had. We are less than we might have become. We could have been contenders. Worst of all, we discover the most unpalatable fact about ourselves: that the more we strive to be what we are not, the more we confirm ourselves in what we are, as though we had stepped into quicksand and the more we struggle the more fast we become.

The truth of our lives evaporates into the air. There is no substance to hold on to. Nothing from the past accumulates to a defining moment. We are not our own biographies.

But the future must be planned for, worked towards. It presses upon us whether or not we choose to think about it. Our days are numbered. We eat into the promise of the future and find in our mouths the taste of the past. We rush helplessly towards the end, towards the diminishing light, until for one brief moment all we know is the past and nothing more can serve our futurity.

To be a fish in the sea or a worm underground is to be something inseparable from the weight of the ocean pressing in on all sides or the immovable earth above, to be confined by the immediacy of things to the perpetually recurring moment. Creatures able to raise their heads above the surface of the earth know the privilege of horizons, but only the mind knows anything within them or beyond them. To *be*, purely and simply, is to *know*, to be divorced from the integrity of a life lived without knowing to which the concept of 'being' as such does not apply. Being is all on the other side of silence, and only from this side, from this point of vantage, can we cast a glance backward to the deep unknowable form of existence from which the mind has emerged. In *that* world the spider spins its trap for the unwary fly, but knows nothing of what it does, the how and the why of it. The fly does not know what it should be wary of, and struggles to escape only because the thread's resistance triggers its efforts. The spider is not triumphant, the fly is not sorrowful, there is no guilt in the heart of one or regret for a wasted life in the other. It is life, just life, one thing not many, the organism and its world one and the same. When once that integrity has been broken apart, it is lost for ever. No longer is a life one thing, but two – that which knows and that which is known, the living being and the world in which it lives, that which contends with the condition of being and the universal condition of non-being that defeats it.

I need to make a distinction once more between the loose way in which we use the word 'knowledge' to describe the inner world of the unconscious organism and what is meant by knowledge in consciousness. We cannot enter the inner world of other creatures, for to do so would require us to abandon the forms of representation and understanding, which are the tools of our enquiry, in exchange for a blankness upon which nothing else is imprinted other than the sensory responses of the organism as a whole. We may perhaps make the case that animals, birds, insects possess knowledge in the sense of 'knowing how' while admitting the probable absence of 'knowing what'. But this is also too much of an unnecessary assumption. It is no more than a figure of speech to say the bird knows how to build its nest, the bee knows how to return to a patch of clover, the ant knows the best site for colonisation. Complex patterns of behaviour regulated by sensory and chemical releasing signals and instinctive actions that can be mathematically modelled do not in themselves constitute 'knowledge'. They indicate, on the contrary, the evolved efficacy of survival behaviour that can achieve sophisticated levels of organisation in the absence of all knowledge, as cells clearly organise themselves in the body without access to some other accumulation of knowledge separately or discretely held apart from what cells actually do procedurally.

Knowledge in the formal sense of knowledge in consciousness is knowledge of form and order. We too 'know how' to walk and find our way home through familiar streets without much more information in consciousness than the dog has in mindlessness, and probably with less information in terms of sensory data and instinctual competence. But to 'know' – to apprehend the form of things in the context of space, time and relation – is not simply to process data for optimal organisation and regulation, which can be done unconsciously by machines. To know is to introduce to the brain the form and order of the world of experience – a second order representation of it that can be manipulated intentionally by the mind in the way the hand holds and uses an object. Explaining what it is 'like' to 'know' in consciousness is, of course, completely impossible. Whatever information we accumulate 'about' consciousness and its mechanisms, it will always amount to something less than and other than the experience of consciousness, since all such analysis and data and verbiage themselves remain within and dependent on consciousness. Describing consciousness as something else does not get us any nearer what it is. And, paradoxically, it is only the imperative for the representation of form and order that *is* consciousness that prompts the search for the terms of its understanding outside itself.

The truth of knowledge as the knowledge *only* of form and order becomes evident if we attempt to see directly into things in their formlessness. The moment we entertain the idea of the formlessness of things-in-themselves we immediately fall short of that possibility by perceiving only its form, as something knowable. To know is to know the form of things and their relation in time and space. The immediate data of experience remain incomprehensible except in the forms and the order of their relations. Understanding is the correct imposition on the immediate data of experience of the forms of order that in themselves define the understanding. Put rather obscurely, knowledge is knowledge of what knowledge is, not what experience is. At a certain point, any further attempt to be clearer becomes self-defeating. One can only describe what is beyond comprehension metaphorically, peripherally, like walking on the stepping stones of reality unable to step into the flowing stream of things as they are in themselves, only pass over it.

We inhabit the deep unreality of being but apprehend only its reality. The latter is built upon the foundations of the former and is indebted to its permissions. And one may only speak about the mysterious presence of reality in words and thoughts that must not outstrip themselves.

V

Order is the mind finding itself again in things. Henri Bergson, *Creative Evolution*

Since the beginning of time our formal thinking about the reality of the world has been a quest for its formal nature. In a world where the very concept of time ensures that constant change is its underlying condition, we define reality as that which is unchanging. It is a quest that is implicitly futile from the beginning. It has, perhaps, its origins in Thales and the Milesians and the search for the essential *substance* of the world. It continues with Plato and in all subsequent expressions of idealism as the search for the persistent *form* of things. And it endures in modern science as the global co-operative endeavour to create a final explanatory theoretical framework from which nothing will escape. In all this we do not see the reality of the world made any more or less real – what we see, in fact, is the mind itself at work, not in the act of discovering the true nature of the world, but in shaping the world to the mind's forms of understanding. Such forms of understanding serve the bodily organism in the exercise of power over its environment and support its way of making a living. Only secondarily does this reflective mode of perception present itself as an abstract, contemplative process dissociated from the act of living itself: that is to say, mere philosophy.

Substance is the materiality of the world with which the mind must do business – the serious business of survival and continuity founded on tooth and claw transactions with a world whose underlying evanescence as thing-in-itself is quite literally immaterial. Form, in the generally understood teleology of form, form for some purpose, use or intention, is equally a serious business matter regarding the shape of our actions and intentions on the same intractable materiality of the world. It should not be surprising that at some point in the evolution of the brain of a hominid standing upright, looking at the horizon and with the freedom to grasp the world with its *hands*, that the matter to hand should eventually present itself to its perception as a multiplicity of things manageable in their permanent substance, in the forms of their appearance as the forms of its intentions towards them and its relation to them. And during all this time the formlessness and mindlessness of the world continues beyond, below, the mind's knowledge of it, untouched by it. Reality is the shape of the mind's representation of the world of experience that serves the bodily organism by positioning it adversarially in the context of substance, form and order that it might successfully contend with the world and not be defeated by it.

Have we sufficiently recognised the degree to which the hand has determined the emergence of mind? Without the necessity to grasp an object with intentionality, the object as something separate and something in particular need never have become manifest. In the absence of objects, the subject itself could never have arisen. But, more than that, the opposable thumb that allowed these things to come to pass is no doubt responsible for the subsequent development of abstract thinking. If I imagine going through life without the capabilities that the thumb lends me, living in a society of people without thumbs, it becomes difficult to conceive how we would have overcome our clumsiness to a point where we would be able to make subtle differentiations between abstract concepts. Were we not able already to refine the gross physicality of objects themselves into things more precise, how could precision of thinking have evolved? It is much easier to imagine that the mind, lacking the dexterity of the hand as its model, would have evolved a rougher and more approximate way of dealing with the world. Perhaps we would have remained animistic believers and it would have been impossible for philosophy to have found a hold anywhere – because it had no thumbs. It is the hand, as Anaxagoras says, that makes man wise.

The forms of order that the mind imposes on the world are the forms of a functionality that best serves its own interests. The mind is equipped with a grammar of order that, like language itself that reflects the same order as parts of speech, distinguishes the otherwise undifferentiated data of consciousness. There is a logical hierarchy to this grammar, a history of co-ordinated parts from which order is derived, that language is patterned upon. Its primary component is the verb. Movement, action, change are perceived even when we have no information about what it is that moves or changes. Substance, that which we subsequently associate with movement, is, sequentially, a later concretion of movement. Animals, ourselves included, react instinctively to sudden movement, whether we are aware or not that the movement represents concretely any personal danger to us from the material object that we say 'moves'. And organisms are adapted to diurnal and seasonal changes that are changes in general and not changes to any *thing* in particular. Substance is the noun, that may take the role of subject or object, the initiator of action or that which is acted upon. We ascribe to substance adjectival and adverbial qualities we say it possesses, as though these were separate things that accrue to it or limit its substance or its movement. In this way the world is laid out *formally* for our convenience, interests, needs and potential actions in a narrative coherence not only as subject, verb, object but in its teleological forms of purpose – that is, what we mean and what we mean to understand when we ask what things *are*. *That* things are, and that they cohere in some approximate purposive form of order, is the essence of conscious knowledge and understanding. But this defining and descriptive necessity of mind is a matter for the mind only. The mind is not a window on the universe, only a derivative of it. What we are in possession of is a translation of a text whose original has been lost. We refer to it, and defer to it, constantly, for it is all we have, and all we have of what we cannot possess, and all we know of what is lost to our knowledge.

Reality is a phenomenon of mind. The world's second order representation in consciousness is all the reality there is. The very 'isness' of things is the mind's formulation of its perceptions, beyond which the idea that anything is something is just that speculative idea in the mind. We may believe (why wouldn't we, in our own interests?) that the world is formally set out exactly as we see it (inordinately convenient, given that nothing but consciousness is interested in it), as though we had thrown a light switch on in a room where armchairs, wallpaper, carpets and mantelpieces all at once spring into being, when in fact it is the act of illumination we are seeing and not things in themselves. As in any other form of environmental adaptation, like the eye itself that evolved from simple light receptors for orientation, we have acquired reality, as we have acquired more complex vision, but what is real is not inherent in things, only convenient and contingent, no more than colour and perspective are to be found in things but only in the brain facilitated by the eye. Reality is the figment of the mind and the mind's need to know what it is dealing with, but its solidity is fragile, sustained only by our intense seriousness towards it.

We call some scenarios real and others dreams. Animals also dream, rehearsing in sleep the next engagement with the world of their attention. How do we know that one is a dream and the other real? Why should the scenes of our dreaming mindscape be less real than our waking images? Perhaps all that separates them are degrees of seriousness. Asleep, we are waiting to awake, and wakefulness is not truthfulness, only attention. Reality is not a scenic representation of things incoherently connected, as dreams are, but the world presented to the mind in the forms of our constant preparedness to act in relation to it, requiring the continuous maintenance of order and coherence between the self and the world in its substance, form and relation, so that it does not slip from our grasp and out of the reach of comprehension to become fragmented, unrelated, random, arbitrary and dreamlike. On those occasions when reality does fall apart, we know it for what it is – the fabric that our brain cells have woven becoming unravelled, the cinematic illusion of directorial control winding down to flickering celluloid.

The reality of the world and the self in experience is a mental construction mediated by the *a priori* modalities of the mind for representing phenomena in space, time and relation – the nature of that relation being the representation of form, order and causality in which the mind recognises itself in things. As such the reality of phenomena in perception is teleological – that is, everything bears some relation to ourselves and our interests, immediately or potentially. Hence all our perceptions are accompanied by some sort of feeling, attitude or mental preparedness derived from that relation. The quiescent potentiality of everything to be something is the subliminal background of everyday reality in which things appear to present themselves to us ready-made *merely* as objective phenomena passively existing alongside us in their own right. But on examination there is nothing we perceive that is not imbued with the potentiality of our relation to it. The ocean, we might say, is the ocean whether we know it or not and exists as an ocean outside our relation to it. In so far as it exists purely as *something* in itself, outside our conceptual acknowledgment of it, it does not have any relation to us. For the mollusc and the fish who live in it, the spider drifting in the current on a matted raft of vegetation, their relation to it is not phenomenal in the sense that there is a separation of one thing that *is* the sea from another that is *in* the sea. That relation – between subject and object – is a mental construction, without which everything remains at one with itself. In the absence of that mental construction there can be no intentionality of action, for intentionality is dependent on the relation of subject and object. We might in principle gaze at the sea for a thousand years, as the early hominid quite possibly did, without forming any more notion about it or intention towards it than the walrus. But to trap fish with nets, build boats from trees and carve paddles, we must first discover intentionality, since instinct alone can't make a canoe, and intentionality can only arise once we have moved from the state of instinctive integration with the world of our perceptions to the representation of phenomena shaped to our potential actions.

For every organism whose actions are instinctive and whose relationship to its environmental niche can be explained in evolutionary terms of trial and error, the question of the reality of the world need not arise. The world is not for looking *at* but for acting *in*. Only consciousness makes the world appear real, *phenomenally* real. Conscious awareness is awareness of *something*, and that something always presents itself phenomenally in the teleological forms of its relation to us. Such a relation in perception may appear a purely passive one, asking nothing more of us than the acceptance of the reality of the rolling sea which has nothing to do with us, yet how can the sea be allowed to surge unless the mind intervenes to let it be so? The mind hungers after its own interests, formalising them in the shape and movement and order of phenomena abstracted from the deep ocean of unreality from which the mind is absent.

Consciousness introduced into experience the representation of a struggle that had hitherto been conducted blindly. That struggle is the struggle between subject and object, between the active interests of the organism and the resistant material of the world to which it must accommodate itself. It is an interaction that has never ceased since the beginning of life in the first amoebae to the higher animals – but always entirely and successfully conducted without the intervention of mind, with no division between subject and object in experience, between the knower and the known in this exchange. The subjective nature of experience is, in evolution, a later conventional fiction, one of the operant features of a mind that translates the flow of information, action and reaction in instinct into information about the world in intuition. It is fruitless to conjecture *what* an animal experiences if the 'what' of experience is a convention of mind that the animal does not possess. Its experience must be some other kind of experience, one that consists of the organism's stance towards the information that reaches it and its potential actions and behaviour in relation to it, without the necessary presence of any secondary representation of it as something else.

Consciousness creates a world apart, shaped by our intentions towards it. We are never without an attitude towards it, without a readiness to pronounce on it. Our knowledge of the world is the material of our being. Absent it, and we ourselves no longer are. In the absence of mind, the animal organism's attitude towards experience is an appetite to act in relation to the flow of experiential data. It is a process that expends itself in the act of living. You can't look inside to see what it is 'like' to have that experience. Since the bat does not think, it cannot be in possession of a grammar of thinking – there is no 'I' that thinks and therefore no 'bat' to know what it is like to be a bat. Inside there is nothing to see, for the subject and its object are not 'set up'. It's just an integrated process that flows away along the trajectory of the arrow of time, the river we can't step into.

But consciousness is precisely the experience of what does not flow away. We are locked into a sense of reality whose permanence seems to us indisputable and self-evident. It is, after all, we believe, vouched for by experience itself. The experience of reality is a sort of locked room puzzle. We do not know how it got in there, but once it is inside it cannot be doubted or denied for as long as we are unable to escape from it or conceive of anything else that might be called reality outside of it that isn't just what we know of the inside projected out into a world that we shall never experience. We define reality as something concrete and certain to distinguish it from illusion, dream, madness and imagination – something externally valid as opposed to the mind's own creation. Yet that very solidity is evidence of the mind's insistence on the reasonable nature of the material it has to deal with, a mental landscape of coherence imposed on an outer realm that gives no account of itself.

The reasonable nature of reality is not given in the immediate data of experience. Its reasonableness – that is, its substance, duration and its connectedness with the self as the subject that perceives it – is mediated by the mind whose function is to create the spatial, temporal and causal connections that define reason itself. Reality is a dependency of mind whose actual presence as fact is never in dispute (though what constitutes that fact always is), whose connectedness is inevitably fragile since that connectedness depends on the mind's powers to sustain a coherent narrative within, and not outside, the realms of reason. Were we not perpetually engaged, consciously or unconsciously, in creating a continuous narrative experience of reality, all the incidents of our experience would be episodic. They would flow away, irrecoverably, passing away in the flow of time without memorial. All experience would be discontinuous and therefore incoherent, since coherence is not an attribute of what it is we experience but a construction of mind and memory.

My experience of the reality about me is impossible to sustain simply on the basis of the continuous flow of data emanating from the external world from moment to moment, on the basis of a pre-constructed formality of parts that reach the eye as sense objects faster than the brain can process them. How can the constituent parts present themselves *exactly* in their correct relationships *before* I have had time to see what they are? Walking down the street, my eyes looking first in one direction and then another, paying attention then letting my attention wander, my mind alert or my mind elsewhere – I am able to unscramble raw signals and navigate with ease through a world I seem to know yet have not until this moment encountered. What is this place I have come to and why, as I walk ahead, does its immediate presence not evaporate behind me and follow the moment into the past where, surely, it has just fled? I can't, after all, stem the flow of time, yet neither one of us, the world or myself, flows away. But from a purely organic perspective, we both do. The flow of data is facilitated by the organism's senses, brain and nervous system. The organism acts or does not act in relation to the flow of data. It requires no prior assumption that the world is necessarily and permanently real, and no representation of the self as a substantial entity inseparable from the organism, for the organism as it is in itself to function in the world as it is in itself. But the mind does demand both these things, both the substantiality of the world of experience and that which experiences it. The mind itself is not the facilitator of the flow of sensory data, but the creator of a sense of order (surely the true sixth sense) for the organism's instrumental purposes. The data must conform to ideas of order if it is to be comprehended. Order cannot arise directly and ready-made from the data of experience (which are arbitrary and unpredictable) but must be imposed by that which experiences. That order must conform to the categories of the understanding that determine its coherence, just as fingers obey the molecular ontological rules of order for the hand. The mind is another component of the body plan.

The mind harbours the continuous presence of the past in order to sustain the perpetual narration of the present. The sun is the same sun, the street diverges left and right, it's three in the afternoon again and the shadow of myself walking is not a mystery to me. Yet once I could not have known these things. I only possessed the potential to know them. Were they waiting to be discovered, unarguably real (what is real about three in the afternoon?) or did I make them up, once I became confident in the sufficiency of my own judgments?

I possess more doubts than certainties. But the certainty least subject to doubt is my conviction that the external world exists and that I am the author of my own perceptions. To deny this is, logically, to require the fact to be true in the first instance. This sort of certainty is necessary, but it has a fragile dependency on the regulation of perception that permits both the idea of the self and the integrity of reality to sustain themselves. That regulation has a parallel in the body itself. We churn out bodies, as a species, as resolutely confident in their final design, construction and efficacy as production line programmers in an automated car plant. We expect everything to go to plan because it usually does. Just exactly how the totality of that plan process works in every detail, and above all its guiding principle, remains mysterious. How noses and toes become themselves in the absence of a body plan in advance of their organisation is the intriguing puzzle of a self-organising system. Nothing appears more complex than the structure of the brain. That such a complex interweaving of billions of neuronal connections in the brain should arise of itself without a prior imperative or design demands that we recognise the fact that the more complex a function the less amenable it is to forward planning and the more dependent, therefore, on the consolidation of trial and error, accident and incident, change and mutation over time.

Things don't always go to plan. Genetic mutation and

the breakdown of order in foetal development will trigger abnormal growth – the fusing of bones, the eruption of breasts on the thigh, conjoined twins, gigantism and cyclopia. Such dysmorphism extends also to brain development, to genetic conditions that will affect behaviour, learning, social interaction and, by implication, limit in one way or another the concept of the self and its relationship to the external world. What it is to be 'normal' is fluid. What the self is, and what the self's order of reality is, are equally uncertain.

The norm, what it is to be human, is the consensus given by the collective presence of other humans. What defines being human is not one thing in particular, but the sameness of everything, and that sameness, that conceptual continuity, is dependent on a self-organising biological system. How that nearly but not quite perfect individual biped (for we all carry an inheritance of deleterious genetic mutations) then copes from birth to final demise depends in turn on the consistency of its interpretation of sense data which, as something that relies on brain function, lies within the same category of biological and neurobiological processes as the body. Being human in terms of possessing hands and feet in the right number and disposition, and being human in terms of the ability to recognise the consistency of oneself as agent and the world as the formal material content of one's existence, are ontologically one and the same. They are the contingent forms of sufficient order, evolved in one continuum. My sense of order is just that – the human organism's sensory order. Such a perceived order is no more the revelation of the absolute nature of things than the body itself is the realisation of a pre-existing idea of the human.

Fundamental physics and biochemistry can describe the essential nature of the upright bipedal primate *homo sapiens*. We know approximately how *homo* came to be, but understand less how *sapientia* got into him – largely owing to the persistence of dualism in our intuitive thinking, rather than just the intractability of the problem itself. The organic integrity of the body extends naturally to its mental capacities. Because mental images and concepts are immaterial, vague, abstract, unlocatable, it does not follow that they are something other, free, unlimited and unrelated to the rest of existence. Both sound and light are accounted for as physical quantities, yet we think music is something unbounded, free, and independent of the sound quantities that make it, and a vision of heaven is absolved of any debt to light itself. But they are not. They have quite specifically limited constraints, and are irremediably tied to physical quantities – not least to the body itself, which has determined not only the physiology of *homo*, but the scope and nature of his wisdom. There is no music outside the physiognomy of sound, no vision without light, no poetry without the heartbeat, no axioms of philosophy until, as Keats says, they are proved upon our pulses. 'Our most sublime thoughts,' says Stanley Kunitz in *The Wisdom of the Body*, 'have their feet planted in clay; our best songs are body-songs.'

The fact of death seals this fact: the wisdom of the body precedes the wisdom of the mind, which is a natural extension of it and does not and cannot have a separate existence. The mind has evolved as the instrument of the organism on the same pattern of self-organised development as its body. It, too, functions within constraints imposed by the needs of the whole living organism to further its own welfare. The mind is constrained, in the first instance, within the cranium as a complex brain function. Its capacity for rational understanding (*sapientia*) operates in a systematic fashion, not randomly, arbitrarily or inconsistently. Without such systemisation the mind could not sustain either a sense of reality or an understanding of connectedness. This connectedness, the creation of the self and its relationships, is given at the outset only *in potentia* (mediated by the *a priori* categories of the understanding), as language is given, to be developed entirely by the buffeting of experience and close encounters with the cultural limitations of the world outside the womb that will shape the narrative of the self and the ordering of reality. What is given at the beginning, in nature, is only the imperative that things should not fall apart, not that they should be indisputably anything in particular.

We owe the '*sapiens*' in *homo sapiens* to Linnaeus and his taxonomies. When, after much deliberation, he chose '*sapiens*' to distinguish us by, he did not have in mind man's 'wisdom' but his self-awareness, his knowledge of a separateness beyond the cognitive reach of all other creatures, the knowledge of his own mortality, of the self's relation to the world and, ultimately, to the mystery and meaning of being in an infinite sea of non-being. '*Sed homo noscit se ipsum*' – 'But man knows himself'. We are of the same line as other animals, but man knows himself. The whole history of philosophy and religion and the search for meaning and moral order is suspended by that single 'but'.

VI

Nothing is more unlike him than himself. Denis Diderot, *Le Neveu de Rameau*

The illusion of the self seems immovable from its position as the householder in possession of his property, who gives all the appearance of being master in his own house. The self – 'myself' – was, for Descartes, the 'first principle' of philosophy: I can doubt everything, but I cannot doubt that which thinks and that which, in the course of thinking, may doubt everything else. I am not my body, because the essence of my self 'would not cease to be what it is, even if there were no body'. The illusion of thinking is that there is 'someone' doing the thinking and, although we are only able to discover ourselves through thinking, the fact that this 'someone' must itself be the product of thinking is hidden from us. Yet, from the position of my adopted Cartesian first principle, I can observe that the rest of the animal kingdom gets by without *my* first principle, and on the basis of that evidence I may therefore doubt the necessity of being in possession of this first principle in order to exist. From an evolutionary perspective, we must treat of bodies, not souls. I may surmise, as a social animal within the primate species, that the self is an expediency of the body, an expediency which relies to a great extent on having the same degree of certainty of its existence as the body would have if it could know itself. If the body could know itself, what would it know? The self is a late arrival on the scene: not a first principle, but a secondary principle. The self, in the perspective of evolutionary history, is a newcomer, a product, not the producer, not so much therefore the master as the tenant, unable to discover by any means the name of his landlord.

We are blind to our own indeterminacy. As Descartes discovered, if we wish to start from a point of absolute certainty in order to make intelligent noises about the world, that starting point must be the apparent absolute of the self. Knowledge of the self, of the 'I am I', the one who knows, can be separated from the 'that is that' knowledge of the self's experience of the world. Yet the subject, the 'I' that perceives and thinks, and the object, the other that is perceived and thought about, cannot be separate entities. They lie along the same plane of representational phenomena. Their separateness is a matter of functional relationship rather than the certainty of one given absolutely as the mediator of the doubtfulness of the other. If we were able to perceive our knowledge of the self and our knowledge of the other from a point outside either, they would appear from this distant extraterrestrial perspective equally and indifferently weighted phenomena of consciousness, both being mental constructions of the brain in the body. One could not guess, from that distant viewpoint, the vanity with which these singular creatures carried around with them, like proud antlers, the delusion of the self and its self-created qualities. The 'I am I' and 'that is that' of conscious awareness are the evolved conventions by which the organic unity of a life expresses the primacy of the self (the subject) that will act as its agent and create the rules by which it will govern its own experience (the object). *Cogito ergo sum* is merely a reflection, not an absolute judgment, a restatement of the condition that the phenomenon of the self is unable to escape: I am only in so far as I think I am.

The individual human organism, the bipedal animal with its extraordinary brain, is the only true protagonist in this story. The self that thinks, decides and acts, and the self to whom experience happens, is the organism's representative fiction. In essence the self is a purely metaphysical quantity. As far as the interests of this primate species and its group relationships are concerned, self-interest alone is sufficient to drive its behaviour – self-interest without the 'self', for what else is the self but the conscious expression of the unconscious range of self-interests that precedes it? First there is self-interest, then there is the self, the self as something, as someone, to whom those interests relate. Not at all something that exists, but a phenomenon of consciousness, of mind – the whole point of mind being to establish a formal perceptual relationship between the organism and its environment for its benefit, and to set up the self as the inviolable subject of its experiences. Hence the inevitability that I may doubt the truth of my judgments, those judgments being about the various shapes and qualities and causes of what I experience, but not doubt the reality of that which judges, since it is my interests that are at the heart of my judgments. External phenomena are variable and at the periphery of my attention, but I myself am never in doubt. If I experience self-doubt, it is not a fundamental sort of existential self-doubt, only an uncertainty about my powers to sustain my own fictions. The self is a pragmatic, not an absolute truth. The fact of self-consciousness as a phenomenon should not be mistaken for the self as a fact in possession of consciousness.

I am no mere conduit of my experiences. I am not here to act as observer and recorder – to what end? There is nothing objective about my experiences. They exist as matters of fact only as 'my' experiences not as untainted phenomena that exist somewhere else as something else unrelated to me. Whatever is out there in the limitless universe reaches me only as limited bits of information filtered through a few organs of perception that evolved for that purpose, and along incredibly complex but still finite neuronal circuitry whose architecture has already determined what I will be able to make of it all. Every living organism is the same in this respect – what it can 'know' and what it can do in consequence is governed by the architecture of its physical and neurological frame and how that has developed and adapted to its need to make a living in its environmental niche, whether that particular niche is a hole in the ground, a rock pool or a city. The hole in the ground is not a window on the whole world, the ripples in the pool do not connect to a knowledge of the oceans, the farthest reaches of man's imagination do not extend beyond the outer limits of experience. Experiences, not things, are the forms of order. The forms of order I observe are not presented to me as the unequivocal nature of the things that I observe, as true for a mollusc or a mole as they are for me, but as the forms of my understanding of them. The primitive animal inhabits its own non-conceptually ordered world, created by repetitive cycles of behaviour, of action and reaction, of outer stimuli and inner drives, that produce regular patterns of interrelationships between the organism and its world, with nowhere for understanding as such to sit. The mind, the conceptualising extension of the brain in the body, has a functional architecture to determine form and order in consciousness, to subordinate randomness and intrinsically meaningless arrays of data to the exigencies of purpose and intention, to formalise phenomena into the shapes of its interests, and those interests into the form of the self that shall govern them.

In the normal person, the person not betrayed by a pathology of the personality or the nervous system, one's everyday experience is a fundamentally rational relationship between the figment of the self and the phenomena presented to it – the 'I' that understands and the 'other' that is the material of the understanding. It is the essential ground of being that the self, as phenomenon, should persist and endure in time and space in perfect unison with the forms of its experiences as things that are in themselves rational, ordered, substantial, possessing duration in time and space and having some relation to the subject that experiences by virtue of being the objects of that experience. I am not surprised when I rise each morning to find the sky above my head and the ground once more beneath my feet, to discover that a day has passed and yet be able to recollect myself from the vanished past to be the continuation of the person I was yesterday. Yet these are all very mysterious things. If the sky is substantial, it is more substantial as a word, as an idea, as a persistent perceptual notion, than anything that constitutes its actual physical presence in the world. Why shouldn't the sky fall in, as Chicken Licken feared in her limited perception of the universe? Isn't the sky completely untrustworthy as anything but a convention? It does fall apart, clouds and mist obscuring the vision of the world beyond it, granulated elements of rain and sleet descending on our heads, the blue, ethereal, safely distant arc becoming black, oppressive. What keeps the sky a thing that is blue and high above us, what makes it other than merely the air we breathe, what sanctions it to be the canopy of the world and the not the insubstantial, thin emanation of the earth that opens on to infinite reaches of an emptiness that is not sky at all? A word, a notion, a convention to certify and substantiate its dizzying indefiniteness. It is above me, as the ground is below me, because I need a place to stand. It is pure relation. When it is not relation it is nothing, nothing I know, nothing I can understand. And who am 'I' who stands here, looking up at the sky? I am a living organism seeking orientation, that is all. My notation of 'sky' and 'up' and 'earth' and 'down' are one with the notions of 'I' and 'my'. I am no more substantial than they are, and all I possess of them is my relation to them, a relation essential to the rational order of the mind that preserves the continuity of the self from day to day, and the integrity of the self and its experience despite the fragmentary nature of both. Chicken Licken had a perfectly rational order of mind. Not only did she base her belief on the evidence of her eyes when the acorns began to fall from the sky, but she took upon herself the burden of moral responsibility to act on behalf of the interests of the rest of the populace to warn of imminent catastrophe and to seek a higher authority and a greater power to act to avert it, all in the name of reason.

Reason does not establish the truth of reason, it establishes the foundation for judgment and the justification for action. Reason is relation, the interests of the self represented by the order of experience. My experiences 'make sense' not because they are 'true', in some inherent qualitative fashion, but because they are apprehended as a set of relationships, of which 'I' am one, and not as episodic singularities. In the non-mental animal world those relationships are not presented in perception but locked into evolved patterns of behaviour. That behaviour is a continuum of responses and patterns of activity that in its own way confers order on what otherwise would be, and in themselves actually are, merely episodic encounters. So, in a primitive way, the animal 'makes sense' of its world by remaining trapped within a framework of instinct. We, in quite similar if more sophisticated ways, with our capacity for conscious representation, make sense of the world through the basic building blocks of reason that require everything to be something, with duration in time and extension in space, to which we attach quantity and quality and relation. To be sane, to be rational, is not to be wise or be in possession of the truth, but only to have the ability to sustain the continuous sense of connectedness between the world of experience and the idea of the self.

One can be both sane and stupid. For the individual's everyday experience to remain coherent and understandable, one does not need to know very much, and the little one does know need not stand up to scrutiny. The essential physical extension of the world never needs validating – it is given in common to the mind *a priori* and corroborated through continuous experience and learning. The connectedness of the self to its experiences is also given in the form of the unassailable fact of subjectivity. But the question of 'who' the self is and 'what' it experiences and understands has no single answer. It has no answer in philosophy, and we are no nearer an answer in science. It is answerable only by identifying the continuous narratives of order by which the mind relates the world to its interests, and those narratives are as numerous as the minds to which they belong, or at least as numerous as the shared interests of groups of minds.

The interests of the organism, which we must equate with the interests of the self that is its subjective conscious representative, though numerous, are limited. They are in the first instance limited, like those of all living creatures, by immediate necessity, the necessity of survival, making a living, reproduction. The wearisome, repetitive activity of millions of creatures scratching, scraping, foraging, snapping, biting, bleating, humming, forms the incessant background turmoil of the world of nature living and dying. This is the world of work that humans must also occupy, our days consumed in self-preserving, self-promoting, self-assuring thoughts and deeds. Our mental capacity for representation allows us to extend our interests from the immediate and episodic to future needs – planning, scheming, working out imaginary scenarios of cause and effect, discovering potential future interests and forms of security, deciding and anticipating courses of action beyond any immediate need to act. None of this can be achieved without the artifice of the self. Unless, in the mind's representation of the phenomenal world, it is also able to represent the entity whose interests it serves, no phenomenal relationship can exist between the object of interest and the subjective form of that interest. They remain one and the same: the organism acting in an instinctive and integrated manner in pursuit of interests of which it has no idea or can make any evaluative judgment. Not having a mind, and therefore not having a self, doesn't, of course, stop judgment happening. It just doesn't happen in any representational context.

The self that is the subject and, as subject, contains both 'my' mind and 'my' body cannot in fact be more than the sub-construct of the body and its brain (the organism) acting in its own interests. 'I', contrary to my intuitively held belief, must be something *less* than the totality of my body and my mind. I am not who I appear to be to myself, because I appear to contain that which, in reality, contains me. Although the body is the entire living organism, it appears only as a figurative element in the fiction of the self it has created. When I reflect on what I know of my body, I soon discover I know very little. Even were

I to exhaustively study medicine and anatomy and biochemistry and genetics, I would never achieve a higher level of self-consciousness that would include my whole body. I would merely add to a corpus of knowledge about the external world, an externality that includes my own body. I am, or at least I appear to be, more real to myself than the body of which, ontologically, I am the dependant. In this model of the constructed self, my body is both familiar and alien. I walk about in it all day long and sleep in it at night, but it, not I, is awake or asleep and it, not I, determines the fact of myself and my being and, ultimately, my mortality. I am not, in this representation of myself, simply the body's self-consciousness. I feel its aches and pains and injuries as I feel the mind's anxieties, but those feelings are intrusions on the equanimity of the self that suffers them. The body is a burden and a constraint upon the self that bears it. I suffer, therefore I am.

Just as the self is less than the body, the self is not as wide as the mind. I am not what I think, nor everything I think. The mind knows many more things than the self will make use of. What the mind may know is almost indefinitely extensible, but the self operates in a much smaller sphere of interest than all that it might be interested in. Given choices that must be made and decisions that must be taken in pursuit of self-interest, the self chooses not to take up the sceptical position that there are several sides to every question, that all the facts are not yet known, that expert opinion needs to be considered, that assumptions need to be tested, that authority must be questioned – that, in fact, one can never act because there will never be a point when the basis for action will be known with absolute certainty or the consequences of an action unequivocally predicted. The nature of the self and its reason for being is to act, to act on behalf of the whole organism and its immediate, or at least fairly proximate interests. And those interests are essentially selfish. So the self makes up 'its' mind selectively from information available to it, and does not withhold judgment in consideration of all the other information that might be available or may forever be unavailable to it. Life has never been a slave to epistemology, and thinking is mostly superfluous.

The self is the social history of an idea. Self-sufficiency has its limits. Even in the most isolated and solitary circumstances I am unable to construct an idea of the self that does not acknowledge some sort of social or linguistic history to which the self belongs. I need society first before I can survive without it. Even so, shipwrecked on my island, I am always a social animal, never something of my own construction. Alone, the names for things flower in the desert. I reason with myself when there is nothing remaining to me of which I need to be convinced.

One can hardly see the point of the self as the locus of consciousness were the self to be no more than *entertained* by the spectacle of what it knows. The self as the locus of consciousness is the necessary consequence of having become the locus of power for the individual living in groups. Attached to a rock beneath the sea, I would have no cause to care who I was, because who I am does not make any difference to what I shall become. Only in the context of a social group do 'I' need to be someone, able to assert myself in relation to the others with whom I contend. What a fall from grace this is, to discover that the self is not the given first principle of being through which the truth of the world is revealed, but an evolutionary instrumental configuration of consciousness, a social appendage to the social animal competing for power and finding a place among other self-interested individuals where it may exercise its will.

The justifications of the self are, at bottom, about power.

The limits of the self are determined by the limits of its power to secure a space for itself within its immediate social context, within its peer group or sphere of influence, between itself and its rivals or enemies, its friends and relations. In this respect it is only a raising of the game played out hour by hour across the entire biosphere. The spider's game of power is conducted in a corner of the window frame, securing the fly four times its body mass on the end of a single thread from its abdomen. It has no larger authority, and hides from the sources of power in the wider, darker, unknown, indefinable world of obscure conflicts in which it takes no part. The dominant male hamadryas baboon rules his own group, subdues recalcitrant females, leads the violent rout and displacement of rival troupes, creates his own necessary sort of order within the larger social order of the tribe. But these are the limits of its power. Its actions are governed by context and self-interest. It does not have a more reasonable view of the wider world, or another set of internal references that would lead it to act in a contrary way. All this is conducted unconsciously. Were the male baboon to become conscious of his own self, marked already by nature with a red badge of courage, he might just have sufficient self-consciousness to award himself medals.

The self is a small, local thing that stays close to its origins. Even the well-travelled soul remains, in essence, provincial.

In common with other primates, the human sphere of power is a social, tribal one. The individual has, from the beginning, a need to command the attention of the family, tribe or society into which it is born, for the sake of its own welfare. The fact of coming into being is a novelty among numerous other pre-existing facts that, as in all instances of self-organising and self-sustaining forms of order, limit the scope of that novelty to its least disruptive quantity. The self that is born into the light of consciousness is also born under the shadow of the facts that have permitted it to be and to which it is subordinate. Self-assertion, the assertion of individual social power, submits to the prevailing rules of social hierarchies and freedoms. The individual's scope for influence is limited to its social, sometimes merely familial context. Since the function of the self is to serve the self-interests of the individual within the environmental niche that has allowed it to be, the narrative of the self that emerges over time naturally and inevitably unfolds in the terms and terminology of its time and place. The idea of the self, of 'who' I am, is the idea of the person at the core of my being in a particular time and place, and my self-concern is how that idea of myself will assert itself sufficiently to succeed in its life – to continue its work cycle and its lifecycle – or at least to endure it.

To define one's self is not to describe a singular subjective point. It is to assemble a series of attributes that add nothing to the essential fact of self-consciousness itself. In constructing myself I compose a set of social fictions, and in this flimsy disguise I must learn to deal with the fact of being that confronts me, the 'me' hidden behind the mask that is always in danger of being unmasked – to reveal what? Perhaps my real fear is that there is no one to be discovered.

I am, in social terms, not only what I appear to be to myself – a body with its physical characteristics and its sensations, a mind with its thoughts, feelings, anxieties and uncertainties, both of which are 'mine' but neither of which, I soon discover, are entirely under my control – but what I do. Who are you? someone asks. A name answers, a status, a function, a history, an occupation – never a bundle of sensations and uncertainties. Doing is so closely tied to being because no creature manages the continuity of its existence except through work and activity, the completion of endlessly repeated work cycles – the bird feeding, the lion hunting, the hyena scavenging, the man ploughing. I am, in all essentials, the same as any other living organism, a physical entity with work to do, but in a negotiated social context. I subordinate the mystery of my being to the essential fictions by which I define and locate myself as a person in relation to other enterprising selves with whom I co-operate or contend in the same biological and social space.

This self of mine, this person, persona, personality, ego, this fellow traveller of the body, this fiery and contentious, alert and armed protagonist and defender of its self-mythology, this self that is nothing else but the 'self' of 'self-interest' that is the manifestation of the will in nature – not only does it assume in self-consciousness the role of the representative of the total organism in nature and instinct, but subsumes under its fictional title as *possessions* all that in instinct are the limitations of its fields of *action*. Thus such behavioural characteristics as group status, territoriality and sexual selection that in unconscious evolved behaviour have no relation to 'self' but have a relation only to 'interest', are in self-consciousness gathered together as the possessions of the self as the owner of those interests and consolidated with the idea of 'me' as 'mine'. I am what I say I am, I am what I do, and I am the sum of all my possessions. The self is the conscious organism's focal point of accumulated self-interests.

All that I am in *fact* is subsumed into all that I would be in *fiction*. Both body and mind, and all the mental attributes of temperament, attitudes, beliefs, interests, thoughts, feelings, opinions, etc. make up a first person narrative of the self constantly told, retold and edited. One can exhaust this catalogue of the elements of the self to the ultimate point of tedium until the more we have attributed to it the more apparent does it become that the self is made up of uncorroborated statements, impressions, memories, illusions, compromises, lies and alibis woven together and defended as the narrative order of the self and its relations to the world of its experience, not as something incontrovertibly so but as something sufficient. The more closely we examine the self the more we find nothing contained within it but the continuous formulation and reformulation of its own interests and the negotiation and renegotiation of its relationship to the world, and nothing beyond its fictions but the pure subjectivity of being and knowing.

In whatever ways I fabricate the narrative of the self I seem always to be testing the limits of my power as an individual, advancing or retreating in order to secure a place at the dinner table – if not this one, then that one. In evolution, change and adaptation are the processes by which organisms and populations sustain their optimum forms of stability. We change in order to remain the same. The self that is the representative of the individual organic unit, and the selves that represent social groups and populations, are constantly manoeuvring to balance their competing interests. Stability is achieved through constant adjustment and adaptation to circumstances and constraints, both biologically and socially. We cannot know ourselves because what we know can never be more than the cumulative fictions of our personal narratives. We are not able to be true to ourselves because we do not know what the truth of the self is. We are sufficient to ourselves, and that sufficiency is a habit of mind that is inherently limited. It is both socially and perceptually constrained – there are boundaries to what it can do and to what it can know – and, like all self-organised systems, its present constellation is dependent on what has preceded it.

VII

Everything added to the Self is a burden as well as a pride. William James, *Principles of Psychology*

A day can't be known until it repeats itself, and even then it does not exist in experience but only as a temporal addendum to experience. I think words work in a similar recursive way. They contain nothing of themselves, nothing that can be fixed by them, defined by them, but by repetition the arc of an original idea becomes suspended in space and time like the sun across the sky. What we understand is not really related to the utterance of words but to their return to an idea, the same sort of wordless idea that is expressed in the flight of birds.

I appear to live at the frontier of time, where each unfolding moment promises to reveal something new. But the episodic nature of experience means that I can have no knowledge of the recurring present without reference to the past. As the moment unfolds it merely extends the encroachment of the past, like colonising filaments of algae. I cannot draw my perceptions from the present. I must rely on the past to tell me what I see. Thus the day that dawns is a new day only because I am already familiar with the way that days go by. If in my waking moment I thank God for the new day, I am only able do so because other days have been, and what I am in fact grateful for is not the day but its recurrence. To be grateful itself requires the transfer of a learned social obligation to an abstract principle codified in the word 'God', about which or about whom I have no direct experience beyond the history of an inherited idea. I live in the past, with what has been given. Every moment is imbued with the presence of the past. The tree is as it is because last year's growth permits it to be so. Bricks and mortar stand firmly on foundations. Nothing that is, minute by minute, can be what it is except by permission of the past. The self is permanently locked into the past, tied to its own history, memories and habits. Its continuity is a sustained fiction. The self, as the formal representative of the organism, strives to retain its integrity, as the body itself does. Body, mind and self form a continuum of self-organising stability, each interdependent and reliant on each other to fulfil their functions.

Disease of the body, dysfunction of the mind, and the disruption of the personal narrative of the self are, for man, his three destroyers.

The death of the body, the destruction of the organism with its unity of body and brain, is the absolute annihilation of the self and the persona that has arisen in it. The pathology of the brain will, through disease, accident or decay, determine the pathology of the personality, both in its external presentation of the self to the world and in its self-perception. What 'I' am is dependent on the good enough integrity of the brain, which, like many complex mechanisms with failsafe and feedback functions, props up at least some durable form of the person so long as consciousness persists. We are what we have been. In dementia, the selective, arbitrary destruction of the past renders the present experience more episodic, setting the sense of one's own person adrift between the fragmented moment and the continuity of some other, selective recollection of one's history. Thus mother, in her decline, senses the sea of loneliness upon which she drifts, abandoned and betrayed, she thinks, but by whom she is uncertain, lost, anxious to return to a house that is a composite of other memories. She mistakes her daughter for her mother, angry, burdened by a hard-wired bitter resentment whose origins are hidden behind the mist that invades all the places and the faces to which she turns her attention. Her subjectivity remains, but who she is or was, as mother, wife or daughter, is now held together by a single sad repetitive refrain that she has never been a trouble to anyone but herself, the words themselves easy to retrieve, but the life they represent unravelling like a pulled thread that leaves a smaller and smaller patch of fabric with no discernable pattern that belongs to the whole garment.

Why couldn't I, as my only legitimate narrator and self-creator, choose to be anyone I wanted to be? What if I decide one day, consciously or against my will, to make myself up from a different skein, for surely the material of the self lies all about me merely waiting to be assembled? Why should I obey the rules of habit to remake myself each day in the same predictable mould? Do I not have enough experience and recollection of my own past as well as the stories of other lives with which to fabricate a second self and then a third? Do I not already have a weekday self and a weekend self, a workday self with its own particular purposive allegiances and a freer, social self and also a more private 'real me' parading as the social self, and yet another backwoods, daydreaming unreal self that would like to be free entirely of its other selves and their responsibilities? Do I not have stored up in me a mix of good and bad impulses, certainties and doubts, beliefs and scepticism and areas of darkness unknown to me yet, to be as many people as I wish? And, at some extreme point of crisis, do I not have the capacity to become someone not of 'my' choosing but a stranger given to be me, become me, as me, out of control, irrational, inconsolable, pathetic, pathological, insane?

That artificial recreation of the *same* person, each day condemned merely to repeat itself, remembering only who I *was* with no idea at all of who I *am*, gives one some sort of organic stability, but at a cost – of never being able to discover the world as new, of being bored by the endless repetitive pointlessness of everything, of being defined as something from which I can never be free.

The assembly of the self is subject to the same rules that govern the forms of other self-organised structures from fractals to cells, from clouds of starlings in flight to the functioning of global economies. All organised structures are constrained by and get their stability from the immediately adjacent possible opportunity for change that does not disrupt the integrity of the whole. Sudden changes in condition, crises in matter in the way water becomes ice, or steam or snowflakes, are not bursts of freedom from constraint but the direct consequences of constraint. Everything must be something, but nothing can be anything. That pivotal, transformational point of constraint that, in physics, is described as a phase change, is bounded by a necessary non-negotiable state of matter in the way that at the top of a mountain the way up must become the way down without an intermediate state that is neither one nor the other. Since the organism cannot choose to be other than what it is, and its nervous system and brain cannot choose but to serve the organism of which they are integral and intrinsic parts, it is equally unlikely that the self, which is the evanescence of both, is somehow able to free itself from that which nurtured it and be anything it wanted to be, any more than a butterfly could choose to emerge from the pupa as a moth or a frog. The Queen of Spain fritillary can't be the Queen of Spain. It can only be pretty much what it is allowed to be by being at all. That is not to say the self does not have scope – scope to grow and develop and transform itself – only that its scope is limited and constrained in some way, that the self is not an abstract metaphysical phenomenon, but describable or definable in terms of a functionality that is never without its context. It is not set up to be the judge or arbiter of what is. It is the judge of how to deal with what is in relation to itself and its own interests.

The constraints that create the forms of the self are multiple and unfathomable. From the first moments of conception through gestation, the individual that develops in embryo, asserts itself in childhood, matures into stolid adulthood, unravels in dementia and death, learns only the art of the possible. By the time of the baby's first squall the self that will discover itself in due course is already sketched out by an unseen hand. Sex is determined. Of course, being human is determined, excluding thereby all other possible forms of being, other ways of knowing, inheriting, newly formed, most of what it has already been. We are born into the past. The self must grow from within the inherited form wrapped in a blanket, the formal template of the species modified by the local colour of genetic consanguinity. So much is already given by the time the child has the ability to recognise itself that what it sees in its 'I am I' reflection is nothing of its own making. The will, of course, asserts itself, the blind will cries out and makes its demands of an incomprehensible world in which internalities and externalities are still one. How those demands are met, denied, suppressed, cajoled, deceived, submitted to, and all the subtle nuances of love and tenderness, clumsiness and indifference, responsiveness and resentment, proximity and absence, darkness and light and the passing of time, will contribute in contingent and unpredictable ways to the psychology of the internalities that will become the self and shape the understanding of the self's relationship to the external.

During the first months of life, and over a lifetime, the billions of neuronal connections and pathways that tangle themselves around every incident and encounter, every experience and perception, every desire, slight, error, every emotion ever felt, every word ever heard, every confused dream – all expunged or consolidated, reiterated and retold, lost or rediscovered, all darkly dendritally rooted in the humus of the past – are beyond analysis and beyond our powers to describe in anything but broad categories of types and conditions of the personality and the simplifications of remembering and forgetting. Beneath the overt, conscious narrative of the self lies a seething mass of conflictions and contradictions that continually feed the personality and its motivations, whose intrusions are most obviously apparent when the coherent and credible story of the self is checked or thwarted. For the will is behind this. It is the will that acts and the self that is the mask.

The self, even when clothed in the pomp and ceremony of power, is a poor rag. It is a tired, secondhand thing from the beginning, not a stitch of its clothing that does not conform to the fashion of the day, not a word of its speech that has not already been spoken, used and abused, not an idea in its head that has not been passed on to it like loose coins worn thin with constant exchange. No one is an original. No one is born fully formed like an angel dropped to earth from the realm of pure spirit, a pure unconditioned and unconditional being. As mere babes we are incapable of self-determination – we can't feed ourselves, or walk, or keep ourselves warm, or understand one single thing entirely out of our inborn inner resources. We are dependants. Our dependency precedes us. I doubt that all the determinants of my character are given at birth, but I am sure that my genetic inheritance sets limits to both my physical and mental capacities and potential. Add to this that, for so long as I remain the dependant of another for my basic necessities, the everyday interaction between my demands for attention and how those are met, hour by hour, decide for me the formation of at least some part of my brain's neuronal network and, through repetition, the consolidation of what pleases and satisfies me, what provokes me, what comforts me, into the formulation of who I am. And so, hour by hour, day by day, year by year, I cannot choose either who I am or what I am to become. Once I reach a point of some degree of independence and I begin to test the extent of my own power, I discover that a joke has been played on me. I'm already done for. Not only have I been dressed and washed, combed and consoled, and sent out into the world armed with some elementary rules of behaviour and understanding and conversation, but my need for self-determination itself has already been decided by the adequacy or inadequacy of all my experiences up to that point, and all that my anger and resentment and rebellion is capable of expressing can only be expressed in the language I have been lent and within the limitations of the beliefs and habits and orthodoxies I have been given and against which I kick. All my attempts at independence, every effort to establish a clearing for myself that shall be mine alone, free, unique, individual, are mere gestures, degrees of conformity or non-conformity to conditions already given, to which I am bound, from which I cannot escape.

The self is unique only to the extent that it is attached to an individual organism as its mental representative, and lives and dies with it. The ultimate physiological form of the human species has been determined by its environment and constrained by the self-organising principles of its molecular biology. It is the way it is because that's the way its biology works. Its psychology, that is, the formal presentation of the self, is defined by the inherited limitations of the capacity and potential of its biology, and by the effects of the social and cultural environment into which it is born. The social world into which it is born is, for the mind and its ego, the equivalent of the biosphere in which the mindless biological organism must make a living. Its psychology is subject to the same rules as the biology that limits its self-assembly to the material available to it and it cannot make itself up from some abstract and eternal substance to which it has unlimited access. For so long as the self acts on behalf of the will of the organism – the will to live – so long will the narrative order of the self, however diverse and attenuated, wise or clever and individually differentiated, serve only its own interests and its status among the forms of power it must come to terms with.

I am an assembly of conscious and unconscious attributes, of deeply pre-figured necessities and superficial choices that will always manifest themselves in the language and cultural expression of *someone other than myself.* I cannot be simply pure ego. I am also a social microcosm of the strictly human world, tainted, marked, wounded by past events. Even alone, I have no resources that I do not owe to others, known or unknown to me. I will never stand entirely on my own feet. It is impossible. I am obliged to strangers who perpetually crowd in on me, to their words, their thoughts, their history, their crimes.

If the self is an instrument of the body and brain, arising in it by degrees over time (over both evolutionary time in terms of its emergence as an apparatus of consciousness, and somatic time in terms of the emergence of the sense of self) then the self in the mind is subject in its development to the same constraints as those that determine the body in its skin and the brain in its skull. It is self-organising and, as such, can only be what it is permitted to be by the rules of order that govern the emergence of all self-organising systems. The template functionality of mind must be given in much the same way as metabolism is given, as the aortal system is given. But there are relative, and relatively minor, variations in design and capacity, resilience and capability, that are both the accidents and the inevitabilities of being born that will ultimately characterise aspects of the self. I am, from the outset, at once the accident of the moment and the accumulated inevitabilities of past lives and a lost lineage. In the beginning I am, if no worse, this unique embryo brought to term and not another embryo in the lunar cycle of aborted possibilities. I am to all appearances new, yet I carry genetic dispositions and inadequacies inherited from others. The first cry that clears my lungs is ancient. I would need to cast far back in evolutionary time to discover its origins, and likewise for the neurology of my struggling bipedal movements, and the fact of my opposable thumbs that will allow me to grasp the world as an object, and for the first emergence of the waking consciousness that will name the world's objects and create the story of the self as one object among them. That story must begin, as all stories do, with the characteristic biases and dispositions of the narrator who will tell the story, who is someone in particular but also someone in general, an archetype of the human who invents small variations on a theme already given, like a skeleton playing tunes on a bone flute.

The human animal has very little internal resource from which to construct the self. It has its subjective awareness of the world, but in isolation from human society, like a wild child, it has no idea of the self that will adopt it. Its direct experience will serve to differentiate the internality of its needs and desires from the external sources of their fulfilment, but it will not function in any recognisably human way unless that experience is mediated by others, by other individuals, families, groups – by other selves – by socially, culturally and linguistically filtered encounters with the world. It is not enough, in becoming human, to stand upright, to forage for food, to run off ready-made into the wild like other animals, to accommodate its actions, like other primate species, to the instinctively acquired rules of herd and group behaviour. It is the self, not the animal that gave birth to the self, that must conduct these negotiations with other selves. It must negotiate in the language of the herd, and within its social and moral frame of reference. If it cannot construct a self adequate to its needs, it will falter and fail. The self cannot emerge from within, of its own volition. It is a reflexive construction nurtured and mediated by those who have preceded it and now surround it. It must be welcomed into its unoriginality. The self is not of and by itself an original, or even an individual, but a social element added to and partaking of already composed material. The self cannot choose to be, it can only accept or reject having been chosen.

We are, then, not originals but reflections. Our originality lies only in the extent to which we succeed or fail in the development of a coherent narrative of the self, and how that narrative serves to establish the self's position of power in relation to other selves. We may, in the course of the construction of that narrative, reject any number of external impositions, but of course those acts of rejection are themselves confirmations of the constraints that determine the emergence of the personality. We are what we cannot help being. The more I strive to escape myself the more I confirm myself in who I am.

The story of a life is a story of hurts and offences, injustices and resentments, insults and injuries, of affections and antipathies, hopes and expectations, failures and defeats. The way in which I act and plan to act, how I explain myself to myself and how I represent myself to other selves, takes the form of a continuously edited personal narrative, drawn from experience and confined by the limits of the conventions of knowledge, language, culture, society.

The coherence of the self requires neither intelligence nor insight into its own workings. The self is neither reasonable nor unreasonable, and capable of almost any accommodation with ignorance. All the self needs is the means to defend its chosen narrative, rational or irrational. The self is sustained on materials as basic as sticks and stones gathered from the bush, on myth as well as reason, on megaliths as much as mathematics. To expect everyone to conform to a single model of rationality is to miss the point of selfhood, which is to defend its sphere of power, influence and advantage through its personal forms of justification. About the original self there is nothing to be said. The original self is an illusion, a transformative mode of consciousness – the subjectivity of consciousness bound to one of its objects.

The making and continual remaking of the self is fraught with difficulties, disasters and fatalities. How can the self be other than fragile when it has no basis in reality but is reliant on mere words to sustain it? The primacy of a language in which the self can assert itself is explicit in the concept of 'self-expression'. There can be no self if the self does not find the form of its expression. The self is naturally contentious. It protects itself in the shell of its personal narrative. The self that develops incompletely is either defeated from the beginning or finds other contingent ways in which to assert itself. The self that fails to acquire the means and the art of negotiation may assert itself primitively, violently, in the pursuit of its desires and the defence of its limited personal narrative of power. As an order of the personality it may be internally entirely coherent, but its inarticulate, and therefore non-negotiable form of expression, confines it socially to the pathological substratum of selfhood. Clinically, personality disorders are those orders of the personality that are not socially and linguistically negotiated but are simply asserted. They are characterised by the incoherence and failure of the relational role of the self in securing and sustaining its own interests. In that disordered world the self is no longer the complexly constructed, consciously managed, socially tailored persona adapted to moving about adeptly in a jungle of human societal and personal relationships, but a fierce animal, a cornered and hunted, abused and haunted singularity that has few recourses to help itself beyond its emotions, and generally a single dominant strategy for self-assertion, self-preservation and self-belief. The ego may never develop a narrative that will accommodate its inchoate experiences beyond a gesture towards a social fiction. The essential nature of those hindered, pathological personalities that seem impervious to reason or motive is summarised in a statement Truman Capote quotes in his book *In Cold Blood*: 'In general, these individuals are predisposed to severe lapses in ego-control which makes possible the open expression of primitive violence, born out of previous, and now unconscious, traumatic experiences.'

Narratives of power do not all belong to the powerful. There are other, more subtle degrees of power that look like failure, weakness, surrender, that are in fact the obverse narratives of the exercise of overt power. The good and the obedient, the self-deprecating and self-sacrificing find their profitable niches. The weak, too, have their strategies of power and wait on their opportunities. There is a particular insidiousness in the survival strategies of the weak. They are the Uriah Heeps, the shape-shifting personas of the virtuous in a world of dissemblers, the good hysterics whose ends are gained not by the advancement of themselves but by falling back until their designs come to meet them.

The idea of failure, of the failed life, belongs to the narrative of the self. Failure is the collapse of the fictions by which the self is sustained. Life itself cannot fail. Living and dying is a continuum, one thing only, not two things one of which is the negation of the other. Death is, of course, the curtailment of a fiction also. No other creature but man takes its own life. No animal takes its own life to escape the burden of the impressions it has accumulated to represent its life. It possesses no illusions and therefore no causes for regret, no aims, no vanities, nothing from which it can fall short. Without conscious reflection it has no story to participate in and no disillusionment with its self-made narrative to be the cause of grief, no life to lose since it has no life to own, only the act of living, lived out in the continuous present. In the absence of consciousness the ghost of the self, too, is absent. It is not life that defeats the suicide and urges him towards death. It is not even the weight of consciousness itself that defeats him. It would take an exceptionally sensitive soul, conscious of more than we are permitted to know, to give up simply because it can no longer bear the continual *din* of consciousness. More commonly, the suicide is impelled to escape the suspension of time and the horror of endless boredom that ensues when the narrative of the self stalls and begins to unravel. In many instances, what defeats him is the strain of supporting the illusion of the self and what it believes it needs to do and to be in order to maintain its position at the centre of events. When it can no longer control its own experiences by integrating them into its life narrative, when the self fails by the measure of its own rules for being the idea of itself, when it can no longer believe in its own fictions and believes instead that it has somehow spoiled its life, it wishes then to expunge that failure, to tear out the blotted page, to no longer have to bear witness to its own inadequacy. It may see its absence as a form of redemption, and a sort of justice or revenge on life, for, since it cannot experience its own absence but only imagine it as a cessation of its troubles, the last illusion of the self's fiction is to include death itself as the blank page that closes its failed narrative. The self's assessment of the adequacy of its own story is what makes up the psychology of the individual, and the reconciliation of the fiction of the self with the reality of experience, its feeble triumphs and its perceived failures, is the source of all our pain and anxiety.

All narratives of the self ultimately fail. They fail because they are incapable of translating all the effort of being into anything more than the effort itself. They fail because they are nothing more than convenient fictions. They fail, in the end, by the very pointlessness of being to which the narrative of the self appears to lend some meaning. We are defeated by our own fatality, by life itself. The narrative of the self is the will to live working through us. Those individual narratives can't be rescued from their inherited fatality. They serve their purpose, but they are unable to sustain any other purpose beyond the contingency of being. In this sense the significance of the self by which we set so much store is purely practical, utilitarian, pragmatic in so far as it serves to support a life without, as we have said, any intrinsic worth, and as an instrument of that life is itself inescapably meaningless.

Hard though it is to say, and more difficult still to do, we should give up our selves. They are the instruments of life only, and are therefore of no greater intrinsic worth than life itself. Nature, life and self are all one agency of blind perpetuation. To know oneself, as we, *homo sapiens*, alone can, is to know only the condition of being born. If we inherit only the blind will to perpetuate ourselves and, in order not to fail, devote our lives to shoring up the illusion of the self, and never discover the tragic sense of life which is the point from which we may begin to part from our illusions, then never will the value of being reveal itself. Not only does the self fail, inevitably, but it must fail, it must be allowed to fail, we must give it up.

Because I am the subject, I am not as blind as fate, nor blind as life is. The sense of being in the world transcends the imperfect instrument of self-consciousness that makes being possible. We worry too much about living, but it is being not living that counts for us. We could not fear losing our lives if we remained unaware that we lived. What we fear losing is the absolute subjectivity of being to which life is subordinate, the 'soul' that lies at the centre of being when we release ourselves from the artifice of the self that is an instrument of life and not the essence of being. The removal of my 'self' from 'myself' is perhaps one's life's task.

But the self, that insistent survivor, is afraid of losing itself. Only the realisation that it has nothing to lose, because it never was more than it was required to be through necessity, can set it free to be what it really is – at once nothing and everything.

In striving to become my best rather than my most honest self, in losing my way by being afraid of getting lost, in playing safe when the very nature of life ultimately denies me that safety, by conserving my life instead of expending it, I have found myself in another place far from my soul's habitation.

It seems to me that life has always held out the possibility of overcoming itself, that I can, in fact, cut myself free of the conventions of the marionette theatre and the invisible threads by which I am manipulated. Must there be a plot that works itself out, a hero through whose eyes it unfolds, a striving to succeed and a tragedy of failure? Could I not remain lyrical, as the world is in essence, and deny not only life and labour, but deny the labourer, the ego itself? If I give up caring about living, I still live. If I deny myself, I am myself despite myself. If I abandon my purposeful intentions, hopes and ambitions and surrender my interest in things and my attachment to the names and shapes of them a something necessary, the world continues as it is. Being does not cease, and knowledge does not end. But I am free of the will to be, and free from the acts of the will, with nothing any longer incumbent on me to do but celebrate the lyrical flow of my individual sense of being in the materials of self-realisation available to me. I can make myself up from anything to hand, since I am no longer inventing myself for any purpose. I may go further, and step out into the unknown region of the silence of self-emptiness and try for a life that Pessoa, the poet of many selves, defined as 'a life in which the only thing that happens is its own consciousness of itself'.

It is a life fraught with danger – but only to the illusion of the self. For I will have given up the power base of the self as ego and embraced the self as the subjective awareness of the universality of the human condition. By creating a new life uncertain of the sources of its power I place my day-to-day encounters with other selves on a different footing, where we may each accept both our shared fatality and the inadequacy of the self to explain life to itself in terms of its successes and failures, and in the midst of the struggles that divide us we may learn to recognise each other's fictions and to share their common truths.

The Supreme Uncertainty

I keep repeating myself
like a crazy old man.
Do I offend you,
always telling things as they are?

Crossing over to death
you'll wonder what all
these words were for

and what kept you. Han Shan

I

...the thinking and feeling portions of our life seem little more than half-way houses towards behaviour. William James, *What the Will Effects*

The mind is a natural object. It does not stand apart, outside nature, when it attempts to weigh up its own observations. No matter how seemingly objective the mind's assessment of its own certainty and the reality of the world it observes, its reflections are self-reflections within a self-contained system of thinking outside of which there is only not thinking, not observing and not knowing, with no further ground on which what the conscious mind perceives the self and the world to be can be independently established.

By being confined in this way to thought and actual experience, we can only speak of the reality of experience and not the reality of something of which we have no knowledge. The natural architecture of the mind permits what it permits. It is clear from its attempts to establish the grounds of reality and truth outside itself that the mind struggles with its own categories and is frustrated by its failure to break through them or break out of them. Since we can't be free of them but must remain irremediably dependent upon the actual structure of thinking to think anything at all, whatever we end up thinking about thinking must of necessity (and once and for all) concern itself with the natural history of the mind and its place among other natural objects.

We are inevitably brought back to the fact that mind is the manifestation of the will, that is, of natural history, and reason an aspect of the phenomenology of mind and nothing else. There appears, therefore, to be no escape from the will and no freedom of thought that is not already determined by the formal nature of thinking and the formal basis of the understanding for the instrumental ends of thought itself.

That fact does not in itself militate against the freedom to think whatever we like, just as we are free to walk where we like and choose our own direction, but since thinking and reasoning, like walking and breathing, are fundamentally biology and not metaphysics, it is only reasonable in turn to expect that the mental disposition of the mind that thinks is organically structured on the pattern of other effective physiological organic functions. We have a neurology of limb movement for walking and an autonomic system for breathing and a complex neuronal network in the brain that governs thinking. But walking and breathing are not things that have an independent existence apart from that which walks and breathes, and thought does not exist apart from the thinker. Walking and breathing as actions are contained by the limits of the physiology of the organism as thinking is contained within the active functioning of the brain's neuronal and synaptic linkages. The idea of walking and the idea of breathing abstracted from the functions performed by a living organism and considered separately are by their nature incapable of throwing off their physical origins but remain tied to their original actions. Similarly, thinking, and the conclusions and judgments of thought, in the abstract, are not free and independent but equally remain attached to actions performed by the organism as a whole. Reason, free and unattached, is no more a viable quantity than walking and breathing separated from the person who walks and breathes. The order of the mind has at its root the order of the body. We may assert with truth that the grounds of reason provide the authority for abstract thinking, and that the *a priori* categories of the understanding for the perception of space, time and causality provide the authority for the order of the understanding that represents the phenomena of the self and the world as things subject to reason, but neither reason nor understanding have any transcendental existence as the absolute grounds of judgment, but are merely the contingent forms of judgment subject to the organic function of the body and the will.

Mind is different from brain only in so far as walking is different from the locomotion of the limbs and breathing different from the inhalation and exhalation of the lungs. Each is not the other, but one permits the other. What is permitted is tied to what permits, and what permits itself functions within the constraints of its origins. So, limbs themselves have evolved to support a body mass absolutely limited and constrained by the earth's gravity, and lungs have developed only as a transfer mechanism to carry oxygen from the atmosphere into the blood stream and return it as carbon dioxide. They are particular and peculiar things, strange and curious considered *sub specie aeternitatis*. The limits of the possible allow them to be what they are. Walking proceeds step by step, living one breath at a time. Their functions are constrained by time and space and subordinated to the integrity of the interests of the organism as a whole, which has come into being readymade and adequate for a performance that it had no part in willing upon itself.

Mind as a natural object has, as it were, its own arms and legs. It is not itself a physical or a physiological entity, but being the ephemeral construction of a physiologically constrained organism it is a thing that reflects its physiological origins and dependencies. Mind has its own skeletal order to support its body of thinking, tied to the functional organisation of the brain as an organ of the whole organism. The evolved instrumentality of *both* body and mind are equally the outcomes of iterative and adaptive natural processes, and the refined and ethereal nature of one is not sufficient ground for divorcing it from the vulgar materiality of the other.

The foundations of thinking and reasoning are given reflexively as the counterparts in second order representation of the first order persistence of self-organised behaviour.

For their purposes the bee's dance and the chimpanzee's grooming habits, though *having* an effective purpose, are effective in so far as they have consolidated a sequence of behavioural imperatives as something that *does* work and not as something that was intended to work prior to and in anticipation of the eventual outcome. These forms of behaviour can be said to have a purpose and to be instrumental in favouring the interests of individual organisms, populations and species. But they cannot be said to be purposive, still less the instrument of something, whereas the instrumentality of mind, in all its dimensions and ramifications, lies in the linking together of the objects of interest with an intention towards them. Up until this point, the point at which mind emerged, 'intention towards' was (and remains, outside consciousness) an expression of instinctive appetite.

The instrumentality of mind is to a considerable and insufficiently recognised degree an extension of handedness. It separates and sorts things out, assesses their character and their physical extension, counts them, works out their usefulness, ascribes value to them, analyses their components, uncovers their relationships and, in particular, the relationship of the object to the self's own interests. The original hand, the hand without its reflexive representation in the mind, operates purely at a functional level on that plane of integrated actions where seeing berries, picking berries and eating berries are the non-conscious, undetained events of inherited primate behaviour. The difference, in describing the hand as functional and the mind as instrumental, is that the hand is not in itself purposive, only effective. Nature has no purposes in its actions, there are only effective consequences of those actions. Nature cannot produce intention unless it can first bring about the representation of an object of intention and a subject to which the object of interest relates – in other words, by means of the intuitive understanding of causality. Intentionality is an abstracted relationship between things that already have precursor symbiotic relationships to which neither a subject nor an object adheres. The hand, at the instinctive behavioural level, may grasp an object in actuality, but the actor and the action are not separate things, and the subject and the object are undifferentiated. The distinction made between that which acts, the action itself and that which is acted upon is a matter for mind and its newly discovered second order representation of relation that will permit intention. The reconstruction of integral actions as the relationship between subject, verb and object, *ex post facto*, is purely instrumental. We act first, in evolutionary terms, and think later.

Action has never required a preliminary understanding of the causes, motivations and outcomes of action. There is an adequate systemic sufficiency in the integrity of beak and claw, the optical nerve and the olfactory gland, internal appetites and external stimuli, and the evolutionary mechanisms of inheritance and adaptation to maintain the balance of hostility between the organism and its environment. The success of species has not been based upon thoughtful assessment and estimation of its chances and the long term planning for survival. Even thinking, as we have discovered, cannot guarantee a successful outcome, but concerns itself mostly with immediate self-interest and short term advantages. Yet at some point a transition has been made from the wholly instinctive life to the superfluously intuitive. That which, as pure instinct, was once a sufficiency of relation between appetite and its fulfilment, interest and the object of interest, attention and judgment, judgment and action that proved effectual without being purposeful, historically has made an orderly transition to what might adequately be called the sympathetic system of the brain. Orderly – because whatever came to be represented in consciousness naturally reflected the implicit relationships of its original unconscious but effective order. Thus we arrive at the subject as the interested party, at the object as the object of interest, and at the action of one upon the other phenomenally represented in consciousness as causal relationships. For once the mind has been set up with the representative conceptual distinctions of subject and object with extension in space and duration in time, the relationship created is of the intention of one towards the other, for that is the only evolutionary benefit to separating them out of their already proven adequate integrity. Understanding is our mode of reintegrating what has been set apart for purely functional necessity. Pure understanding cannot be.

This is the trick that blind, purposeless, self-organising nature has performed: it has unintentionally succeeded in creating intention by setting up the fiction of the self as the locus of self-interest. In terms of evolutionary value, the balance between the benefit of reiterated binding patterns of behaviour whose value is proven by their very persistence from generation to generation, and the value of a freedom of the will that follows from the concept of the self enabled to act in its own interests at the risk of fatally mistaking where its interests lie, has in time weighed down decisively in favour of mentality. The mind has not only proved its effectiveness for the survival of the species, but has been the essential instrument of social development that has led to what we now like to describe as civilisations and cultures. But the tendentious implications of the word 'development' are to be avoided. We must stick to our guns by asserting that nature is blind and purposeless, and complexity the algorithmic result of its insistence. Organic life sustains itself for no other reason than that it must, and since we do not know why it must we give, with historical precedent, the name of the will to that which must account for it.

The mind is an instrument to serve the organism, and the formal structure of consciousness that is the mind is the formal nature of its instrumentality, originating in the organism and belonging resolutely to it.

The instrumentality of the self is evident if we consider that the total imperative of being is self-interest, and that the internal representation of a self to which those interests inviolably relate more formally advances those interests.

The efficacious self, armed with intentionality donated to it by the will, is a component of a self-contained system for connecting the internal needs of the organism to external conditions and events. To that extent the self is the teleological form of the will. It is the subjective element of a mental construction whose other components are the objects of experience represented in their subject/object relationships. The actions of the subject towards the object are full of intention, purpose and meaning, causally connected to effective consequences. The formal order of perception, representation, thinking and reasoning as a proprietary sensory process patterned for the species can make no inroads into the thing-in-itself beyond what it represents thereby. Its teleology is for itself: this is the way I shape things for me, not the way things are shaped for me. I can't re-impose purpose on the world simply because it has blindly led to purposiveness in me. All questions of meaning and purpose arise in the mind as functions of mind. They can only ever be resolved there.

Since the mind, with its thoughts and its reasoning, is a self-contained system, an extension of human biology and a result of adaptive evolution, one is entitled to expect that it not only has its ground rules for functionality like everything else, but that those rules should themselves be grounded somewhere in the natural history of sensory perception out of which ideas of order have arisen. We may be able to separate ideas from the body to which they belong in order to talk about them, but they must ultimately be recognised as the property of the body and not as things conceivable in its absence or existing ideally elsewhere. The grounds of sufficient reason can be established in abstract terms, but the grounds themselves must be founded on the sufficiency of order in actual experience, which in turn must have its support in the neurobiology of the organ of the brain in which it is all entirely suspended.

In the abstract order of reasoning that we apply, for example, to algebraic formulae and geometrical figures in order to prove a proposition, we do not require a proof of the proof, or a proof that the method of arriving at a proof needs substantiating by some other order of reasoning. We are content to start with a premise that cannot be challenged, that is intuitively known *a priori* as the unchallengeable ground of reason. Yet it must have a prior dependency on something else since the logical relation between abstract quantities is not something we have ever encountered in experience. Neither the quantities nor the relationships, nor the things they are intended to represent, exist in themselves or by themselves, either in experience or ideally outside experience. They are creative representations of the mind and its self-contained rules, premises and sufficiencies. That *all* our experience of reality, not just abstract reasoning, should have a prior dependency on the mind's internal structural functionality *for* the representation of reality, comes as a surprise every time we rediscover it. Reality is omnipresent without any effort on our part to conjure it into being, too self-evident to doubt and too important to us to wait on its corroboration by some other standard, and, though intrusive and oppressive, too much with us to permit for long that sense of release from reality that comes with the realisation that we are its prisoners or to sustain the occasional recognition that the mind which is the guardian of reality also holds the key to freedom from it.

Objects of experience would have no representation in reality were the mind unable to locate them in space and detain them in time. The objects of representation would flow away as the mere flux of sense impressions unrelated to their perceiver, even while the perceiver participated in them. Space and time, in the Kantian explanatory model, are the two fundamental *a priori* categories of the understanding given prior to any subsequent mental content and on which that content depends for its reality in experience. That is, the objects of experience must be represented and experienced *as* something, but the data of experience do not present themselves readymade as anything unless the mind has an *a priori* capability of assigning a place to them in space and conferring on them duration in time. Space and time are not anything directly experienced themselves, but the conditions in which objects of experience are suspended and from which all other figures, shapes, quantities, qualities and relations ensue.

None the less we must assume that, just as objects in their full configuration and extension, duration and relation, do not, as Schopenhauer says, 'walk into our brain readymade', the categories of mental representation that make up the network of the mind that *does* support them, have not sprung up miraculously or arbitrarily but in turn, from the perspective of evolutionary biology, have arrived naturally in intuition as an extension of patterns of behaviour laid down in instinct in their more primitive forms in unconscious and unselfconscious organisms. They are primitive only in the sense that they are earlier and primary: they remain complex and successful adaptations in organisms unconscious of how they navigate through space and time, something that in our eyes is the essence of being but in theirs is simply the unfolding of effective processes with no conceptual framework needed within which to operate to achieve their end results. I have tried to sketch elsewhere (*Ideas of Order*, 2009), in an unscientific way, how those natural expressions of behaviour might have served as the foundation for mental categories and the cerebral construction of reality. A bird, for example, has a natural spatial relationship to the tree in which it is nesting. It has a natural relationship to time in the diurnal rhythms created by the rotation of the earth and the hormonal release of nesting behaviour arising and subsiding over time, time being the experience of seasonal changes that the earth's revolution around the sun has been producing since the world began and under which the conditions for life, and the rules for life, emerged. It need have no prior mentally founded architecture for the perception of space, time or relation in order to fly through space and occupy space. Organisms display 'towards' and 'away from' behaviour that implies an adaptive awareness of space without the need for any *explicit* knowledge of space. Time exists implicitly for the bird by virtue of changes in behaviour over time whose passing it does not itself perceive. There is in this competency for the management of its interests within space and time a sort of elementary form of navigation through both, given in instinct, that works without troubling itself over a secondary ordering of things in space and time to which it might have some relation or intention. We, too, do not directly perceive either space or time purely as space or time, but perceive only things in space and time where space and time are the prior conditions essential for their production in relation to us. Some sort of *categorical competency* exists in instinct as an underlying condition for the eventual emergence of the representation of relation in intuition that has allowed formal, categorical understanding to arise.

In the example of bird behaviour, nesting activity is of course related to the bird itself as the performer of these actions. All its behaviour relates exclusively to its own interests. But it needs no sense of self, or of the existence in space and time of that which relates to it, or any sense of *possessing* the interests to which those objects relate in order to conduct its life. Yet we can see that if intentionality of mind has proven its worth it has done so on the basis of having been able to represent its interests in the shape of the self to which those interests relate, in the objects of interest as things existing in space and time, and in the active or causal relationships between the two. Reason must serve some use beyond what we are capable of achieving without it, since life clearly manages without reason and understanding, without purpose and meaning, and is always able to act without thinking. The understanding has not emerged from nothing, but from categorical competencies in patterns of behaviour which, until reason's coming to fruition, had served the living organism well enough. Reason is founded in instinct, and instinct is only how we describe what we cannot avoid deferring to – the irreducible actions of self-organised sustainable life forms.

II

For the merely speculative proof has never been able to exercise any influence upon the common reason of men. Immanuel Kant, *Critique of Pure Reason*

The fundamentally functional nature of reason, rather than the subsequent status to which it was elevated, first by Aristotle, as the proof of everything and the founding principle of a rationally ordered universe on which it may pronounce entirely on its own authority, can be more clearly seen if we keep in mind at all times its origins in instinct.

The competence of mind to guide us better than instinct is marginal, certainly when it strays from the safety of the habituated behaviour that nurtured it. George Santayana writes in *Reason and Common Sense*:

> If consciousness could ever have the function of guiding conduct better than instinct can, in the beginning it would be most incompetent for that office. Only the routine and equilibrium

which healthy instinct involves keeps thought and will at all within the limits of sanity.

Reason, in its abstract form, is not a distinct faculty of mind divorced from the more general role of the mind in forming an understanding of its own experiences. Reason, of course, has its grounds of reason, but they are hardly independent of the grounds of understanding in general, of the grounds upon which the mind has been able to establish things as objects with extension, duration and relation to something else as subject to which that subject gives attention, towards which it potentially has intention, and about which it can make or speculate on any number of connections between phenomena as might conceivably interest it. You can't observe causality as something experienced. You can only note sequential events in time, that remain unique events in time to any observing eye not connected to a reasoning faculty for reinventing randomly received data as a schema of something of real interest.

As for the birds, there are, of course, to our observation and from our superior cognitive perch, causal connections between the bird's repetitive journey to and fro gathering twigs and straw, between its reiterative head shaking and incidental weaving, and the creation of a regularly ordered nest not consciously connected in the bird brain. Sooner or later, habituated behaviour whereby an action initiated in one time and place results in a changed state in another time and place, will have a pay off in the mind, resolutely linked to the hand, in the representation of causal connections as a means to model its actions to its intentions across a whole range of variables in time and space unpractised by the bird confined to the effective limits of instinct.

While abstract reasoning can be treated on its own ground, on the basis of the rules of the game without which there is no game as such, it is not entirely free to state its own case. Just as the rules for tennis and the game of Go are never free of the framework imposed by the construction of the human body and the borders of the court or the board on which the games are played to stand on their own abstract merits, reason's seemingly infinite dexterity is tied to its instinctive organic origins, no matter how far from practical interests its speculations have now wandered. The *a priori* faculty for establishing causal connections between temporal phenomena has, by reflecting on its own reflective processes, laid down the rules of reason, of abstract thinking, symbolic representation, logic and mathematics, by which reason judges and by which it is judged. When we speak of true judgment, of the truth of reason, we mean the judgment of true causes, the reason why, judged by the rules and grounds of reason. We can't by reason alone pronounce on transcendental truths beyond the limits of experience within which reason has emerged and to which it is bound. Reason has no legitimacy as first or final cause or principle. If there are reasons in the world that are not my own, but are absolutely given, then the universe and all that is manifest in it is truly only a game played in the mind of a supreme Master of Go.

By establishing the true causes of events that happen in the physical, material universe that we inhabit, and which in essence have nothing whatever to do with us, we uncover the way things work and ultimately make them work for our own interests, inventing, as Schopenhauer says, 'machines for prosperity and perdition'. But in human affairs and conduct true causes are actually only ever sufficient causes. That is, the motivation for action is a sufficient cause and can't be reduced to a true cause as though the event belonged to the same class of events as a chemical reaction. True causes are different from sufficient causes yet nonetheless share a common ancestry and perform a related service: they both serve self-interest, one by being true and therefore reliable and predictable for all practical purposes, the other directly related to our own interests and therefore not subject to final analysis but a contingent, sufficient cause – even, and often, a false and merely convenient cause or reason – to behave in a particular way that appears to serve our ends.

If I take an axe to a log I can split the log and splinter it further into firewood and I can make a fire and keep myself warm. That same mind, by continually breaking down the chain of cause and effect to true causes can create heat from electricity, power from the nuclear forces that bind atoms together. But I cannot reduce my own behaviour to true causes beyond the sufficient cause of provoked or self-determined, self-interested motivation. I can riot in the street to claim my right to freedom, or the right to employment, but I can't predict in what way freedom will make itself palpably felt or how the economic infrastructure I want to undermine will subsequently provide me with a livelihood. My motives are none the less rational: if I am oppressed I will fight my oppressor and the causes of repression. Here, reason, as motivation, remains close to instinct, and mass movements and revolutions may not have any more predictable or beneficial effects than mass displacements or extinctions in nature until we see what sort of equilibrium – that other form of balanced self-interest – reasserts itself.

Ignorance and reason have never proved incompatible. Ignorance is not a state of suspended belief or permanent puzzlement. On the contrary, it is more often than not a heavily defended hinterland of the mind very able to resist invasion by more sophisticated external ideas founded on more disciplined and analytical forms of reason from true causes. The mind is not an instrument for the disinterested pursuit of knowledge and objective understanding. It is a self-interested organ of the body in which reason and understanding remain close to instinctive grasping. Life is a series of dramatic episodes containing very few long evenings of contemplation. Reason soon exhausts its episodic usefulness. The beginning of action marks the true limit of reason, for the sufficiency of reason is the sufficiency of its judgment for action.

Each individual mind is equipped with the faculty for understanding the world and the self and the relationship between the attentive subject and the object of interest. But that comprehension does not begin over again on each occasion by applying itself disinterestedly to the phenomenal world around it – people, horses, beds, furniture, churches, schools, stars, clouds, sun, rain, words, names – and constructing a perfect understanding of what things are and what they are for simply by observation, as though the world were a parade that explained itself as it marched by. Nothing is explicable without prejudice. Only the faculty for formal understanding is given *a priori*. The materials and means of understanding are given contingently, so that every individual picture of the world and every construction of the self is coloured and contrasted by direct experience, and experience is always contingent: socially, temporally, linguistically, culturally constrained and conformed to. The uncovering of the true causes of *everything* will gradually shift our inherited understanding further towards the integration of more reasonable facts into our relationship with *things*, with the phenomena of experience. But there are no true causes in human behaviour other than the singular cause of motivation. From time to time Utopian thinkers have imagined some governing system intended to be more objectively rational than inadequate and error-prone human reasoning, including a sort of United Nations computer program that would be able to manipulate all available information about any situation and come up with the most rational solution that, being rational, everyone will agree to abide by. There is no doubt that if programs can be devised to establish true causes for complex effects, such as the role of genes in inherited diseases, then we could program our own oracle, wiser than we are, or at least free of prejudice, more rational, more logical. But in the conduct of human affairs we do not seek truth, we seek power, and power displaces the truth of reason with reasons of its own.

Reason serves the organism. Set loose to follow its own devices as a sort of aberrant form of abstract contemplation unhitched from the necessity of its work, like the hand meant to guide the plough forever gesticulating abstractedly to the air, it will inevitably reveal the futility of exceeding its remit. It cannot establish itself either as the first cause or the ultimate end to which the world is formed. Reason abstracted from the sufficiency of reason is merely an aesthetic phenomenon of consciousness, much appreciated as such but with no authority on any other ground than the right of the creative mind to possess its ideas of order.

If the social order has become more reasonable over time, its progress has run parallel to the progress of technology and the creation of wealth. Reason, science and the application of technology from true causes, have, in broad social and historical terms, served the self-interest of individuals by meeting the needs of populations for food, shelter and material goods. (The fact that some populations suffer poverty, deprivation and starvation in spite of rational progress merely underlines the fact that reason and technology essentially serve the self-interest of groups, nations and populations, and the primal motivations of power and partiality by which they are sustained.) We have built a wonderful, if precarious, edifice on enlightened self-interest. But it is self-interest, not enlightenment, that rules. Reason prevails so long as it serves the prevailing balance of power, as it does in institutional democracies. But ignorance serves equally well if it has enough subscribers, and madmen, too, have their reasons.

Abstract, conceptual reasoning at its highest levels is essentially empty, not just because, in its daring high wire act, the mind is juggling with concepts removed from the representation of things known to it from experience, but because abstract reasoning can neither fulfil the instrumental purposes of the mind that require it to remain close to earth and loyal to its earthbound instincts, nor justify our earthly labours with the nourishment of conclusions and proofs that turn out to be nothing more than a sort of intellectual ambrosia or alphabet soup.

Practical reason, reasoning that stays close to instinct, has practical benefits that enhance the effectiveness of instinct acting unguided and unrestrained. Instinct works by consolidating habituated actions into patterns of behaviour that, while not guaranteed to work, work on all occasions when it matters by having eliminated over time, through death and destruction, the behavioural traits that don't work. In the animal, those residual, established patterns of behaviour make up the totality of its survival and defence mechanisms. Those settled sets of active and reactive behaviour that are integral to the creature's conduct of its lifecycle are, at the same time, unknown to it and therefore not a matter of choice or discretion on its part. They work because their effectiveness lies in the fact of their not being negotiable or variable, but habitually proven. Such defences are vulnerable only to a predator whose own instincts (equally unknown to itself) towards the object of interest as prey have co-evolved in the same biosphere where, at least so long as the balance of species survival is maintained, the balance of hostility between prey and predator has some sort of adequate stability. But an organism's defences are also vulnerable, disruptively so, to any animal capable of representing its prey as an object of interest whose interests towards it can be mapped in abstraction in time and space, where the causal connections between the patterns of behaviour of the potential prey as object and the self-interests of the predator as subject become evident and therefore calculable.

This practical business of connecting objects of representation in the mind for practical ends facilitates the asking and answering of all our what, when, where and why questions – which clearly, as conceptual categories, potentially have a life and world of their own capable of running parallel to the world of experience and practical reason. The 'why' question, as any parent knows, is a receding series that only stops at some end point of sufficiency that will content the questioner. Whether that end can be called 'true' is a matter of whether the causes established in the receding series are true causes (on the grounds of sufficient reason) or merely sufficient causes that are enough to satisfy the motivations of the questioner. We ask questions in order to arrive at a point where we can make practical judgments for action or potential action. In the chain of 'why' reasoning, there is no 'reason why' reason should stop at any particular conclusion, if there is no practical reason for it to stop, and no mechanism of mind that shuts down the process at a failsafe point labelled 'of no possible further practical interest to you', for of course there is no natural practical limit to our interests: disinterested investigations in atomic theory ultimately and unpredictably produced practical results central to self-interest, national group interest and the exercise of power, establishing a balance of hostility between peoples not dissimilar to that which prevails in animal populations on the basis of instinct alone. Reason does not take us far from the roots of reason.

The ever-receding theoretical why, in quest of a true first cause, ultimately succumbs merely to a sufficient cause in the mind of the questioner. There is no end, nor will there be an end, to the multiplicity of sufficient causes parading as true causes, for the deep fund of human motivation will always model reason to justify its own ends and reasons within the limits of its understanding.

Final causes, first causes, necessary causes and the whole slop bucket of truth, purpose, meaning, intention, direction, salvation, justification and divine or natural or providential or rational teleology all arise from the receding chain of thinking in concepts, all of which reigns solely in the mind and has no jurisdiction outside it in experience.

When I was a child, one Sunday morning a young man in a brown suit came and stood in the square where we lived, holding a bible and shouting admonitions at everyone. Some people came to their windows to see the source of the disturbance. Some closed their windows against it, thus confirming their deafness to the truths the man in the brown suit came to reveal to them. He told us we were all going to die. Sooner or later we will all die. The urgency of finding some reason for being that would cancel out that ominous fact was something that exercised my mind. How could we all live, day by day, unconscious of the certainty of death that bordered life, like the black frame around photos of dead relatives that stood on the mantelpiece, without a reason to be? The man in the brown suit seemed also to have given some thought to the problem, and the urgency of the solution he had found was clearly sufficient cause for him to be able to overlook any sense of the ridiculous in his sudden appearance here as a lonely preacher without an audience. When you die, do you all want to go to hell? Or do you want to be saved? You are all going to die, and you are all going to hell. It seemed hard on everyone. Yet the solution was a simple one. All you had to do was believe the same thing the man in the brown suit believed. Believe this thing, this formula that could be expressed in a few words and easily learned, and be saved and have your life and labour justified. Fail to believe, and be eternally condemned for the very same life lived and laboured over. It seemed to me unlikely that a truth externally given, a truth for all time and in all places, should in the first place be given into this man's keeping and, secondly, turn out to be such a dull and dismal and ill thought through thing, and not something that could extend one's brightly lit uncertainty into some larger illuminated vision of life that would diminish death. It was clear that, however truth was to be defined, it would always reveal itself as a self-contained product of thinking, and the more it shouted its incontrovertibility the more it would confirm itself as just that thing.

Life is one thing, that just goes on and on, but the life of the mind is another, running divergently in its own course and coming to conclusions that life itself can't come to. There are no verifiable true causes for life and existence on which to build the justification for being. There are only the sufficiencies and satisfactions of the connections the mind makes between abstract concepts. It is a question of inner harmony, worth listening to or not, like a tune hard to get out of one's head that, like music itself, is not the world but what we have substituted for it.

Schopenhauer, in *The Fourfold Root of the Principle of Sufficient Reason*, was at pains to distinguish the faculty of reasoning with abstract concepts and what constitutes the legitimate grounds of reason and explanation, from the faculty of the understanding itself, by which things present themselves in a real and connected way to the mind that perceives them. In this sense the understanding, in the seamless and intuitive possession of its own perceptions, has nothing to do with reasoning about the true nature or true causes of what it holds to be the self-evident existence of itself as the subject that perceives and all the objects of its perception. Wise men, idiots and madmen have this in common – that they wake in the morning and know it is morning and that the birds are singing, without finding it necessary to know the true cosmological causes for the rising of the sun or the hidden motivations that the birds may have for making their noise.

Nothing can be understood except as mental representations given in intuition *a priori* by the categories of the understanding, those categories being principally the mental structure for the perception of space, time and causality. Because we use the word causality usually in the sense of worked out, that is, reasoned causes that are susceptible to empirical investigation, it is less easy to see how causality can be given in intuition in the way that space can be given in order for an object to have extension and time can be given as the necessary condition for the representation of an object in duration. But it is not possible for something to exist for us represented simply in space and time as an object unless that object is connected to us as an object of our intention towards it. It might seem that an object ought to exist by virtue of its material substance alone, but we cannot represent it solely as matter since pure matter itself can't be represented by the understanding, but must be represented *as* something, and that something can't be the thing-in-itself but only the represented thing towards which we have some interest.

The understanding is not a matter for metaphysics, but for biology, or at least the psychology of biology. A caterpillar on a leaf does not need a mental representation of the leaf. Its relationship to the leaf does not exist anywhere in conceptual terms. Neither subject nor object are involved, only the caterpillar and the leaf. If we were to suppose it capable of mentally representing the leaf as something existing in space and time the leaf still could have no substantial existence for it as an object unless the caterpillar mind also possessed the innate capacity to relate that dimly perceived something as an object cut out of miscellaneous sense impressions and causally connected to it. It would remain, as it indeed does, just another meaningless and unreal sense impression to which the caterpillar responds instinctively. Nothing in general can be understood as something in particular until it is represented a such, and in this case 'as such' means becoming the object to which the subject's attention, interest, intention and actions relate. The fact of an object presupposes the fact of a subject to which the object relates. Life is all action. Only the mind differentiates one thing from another.

In reason, causality is the reason why, but in intuition causality is simply the reason why anything appears to be the thing it is, the 'objective correlative' of the understanding. The mind cannot represent pure matter, just as it cannot represent pure action. Pure matter and pure action can't be perceived, only conceived, 'added in thought to every reality as the basis thereof', as Schopenhauer says. Matter is always perceived *as* something and action perceived as the motion or motivation of something accomplished in time and space, e.g. the caterpillar is eating the leaf. Take away the subject and the object, the caterpillar and the leaf, as phenomenal representations, and you are left with pure action and no differentiation between that which acts and that which is acted upon. The undifferentiated world of caterpillar/leaf is pure action lacking either subject or object, which are merely quantities in mental representation. There is no 'reason why' things exist as phenomenal representations for the understanding except as the subject and object of action. Hence matter itself does not exist for the mind, only the substantial forms of matter exist for it, and those forms take the shape of our actions or potential actions as the causal 'reason why' they exist phenomenally and do not remain hidden from us as something we are among but which have no relation to us. The difference between action in instinct and action in intuition is that in instinct we have undifferentiated integrity of action, and in intuition differentiation in the understanding between subject and object and the representation of the interests, intentions and actions of one towards the other as things having substantial existence in time and space as the phenomena of experience.

All this is conducted of itself and by itself without first being subjected to reason or conscious analysis. Rather, it is the foundation of reason and analysis and the necessary condition of consciousness and knowledge. In this respect, arguing about it and explaining it can only be done on its own terms. The intuitive understanding that gives rise to the reality of experience is framed for that purpose and is never much in the mood, nor should it be, to discount reality as something peculiar to it rather than something already laid out for it, to be comprehended and validated. Things appear to be what they are of their own volition, presenting themselves for inspection, yet they are under no obligation to draw attention to themselves. They are what they are only by virtue of the necessity of the mind to represent them as objects of action, that is, as the concrete manifestation of the mind's interests or intentions, on behalf of the organism itself which lives among them. If we could detach ourselves entirely from them as the representational forms of our interest, we would no longer be able to differentiate phenomena from pure action, like caterpillars among leaves.

Do things cease to be, cease to be what they are, when we cease to have any intention towards them, when they no longer sit in the mind as objects full of our potential for action? Surprisingly, they do. But it should not be so surprising. When we are dead, all phenomena die with us. Deprived of sensory input, deprived of sleep, the mind soon becomes delirious, the world hallucinatory. Reality and the images of reality are fragile. What we perceive things to be, the words with which we represent those things, our understanding of their relationship to us, our ability to recognise them, our memories and recollections of them, are all tentative and, as we know from the extensive literature on aphasia, stroke and brain damage, their functional failure in the brain will expunge whole areas of that sense of reality we take to be inviolable. Asleep, the daylight connections, forms, shapes, sequences, purposes, motivations that create the ordered world of our senses that we confidently define as the 'real' world, reorder themselves in dreams where the borders of time and place in which they are fixed in experience and memory no longer contain them. In my dreams I travel roads overlaid one on another, arriving at different places simultaneously, all familiar to me but composed into a single encounter, impossible in reality, since nothing can be in two places at the same time, but clearly possible for me in my dream experience where the past is a multi-layered presence, as though I were walking on leaf mould in a wood, aware of all the past years as something always present, arriving home and opening the door of one house and finding myself in another. I dream and I remember, and since I am not awake, there is nothing to pay attention to, and whatever arises in my dream experience, though it has its origin in my waking experience, is deprived of the coherence of interest and intentionality that previously accompanied it, disporting itself purely as a mental fantasy behind my closed eyelids. Dream and reality occupy the same space. Only the necessity to act determines wakefulness, attention and thus the coherence of reality.

Surrealism juxtaposes dreamlike images in a new, disinterested form of order that makes no sense, for the reason that the depicted scenarios no longer contain our intentions, and are connected only by association, by the fact of their arising together, released from the urgency of the real and the limitations of time and space by which the real is confined.

III

The Great Argument does not require words. Chuang-tzu

From the beginning, from the first hours of waking life, it is movement, action, that captures our attention. But the first words that are handed to us are words for things, so that the movement that first appears to us is interpreted for us as something that moves, and the world of our perceptions is soon crowded with nouns. The species that shares a language of communication and explanation by which it fixes the order of its perceptions has long since decided – has had decided for it by the fundamental nature of the understanding in which the categories of space, time and causality are already fixed – that the indefiniteness and continuous *flux* of the world and our sensations of it shall be brought under control in the forms of subject and predicate in language as well as in experience. Language reinforces, heavily marks with indelible pencil the formal order of the understanding that precedes it. So things are quite definitely the things they are and are exemplified by the names we give them. I am I and I observe that that is that. Subject and object. I act and the objects of perception act in relation to me by making use of the verbs assigned to their actions, prepositionally in space and adverbially in time, with bundles of adjectives cascading from them, all the richer if the vocabulary I have so far learned can distinguish crimson from vermilion, ochre from the sad brown colour of a ploughed potato field, all plucked from the immediate present and consigned in experience to the continuous past.

It seems an arbitrary way to deal with the data of experience, forcing a largely pre-constructed formal order upon matter and movement. But that, of course, is the necessary instrumental order of mind that has taken over the role performed unknowingly by instinct to guide the organism in its contentious struggle to maintain its self-organised coherence in the process of coming into and going out of existence. It does not wipe out or subdue the chaotic swarming of motion and matter, but merely overlays it with the forms of our interests. The withdrawal of that essential interest, by accident or by design, begins to unravel the unconsciously agreed conventions of language and thought by which order is sustained. The reality of the world can't be made to disappear from our experience of it, for it is given in the very nature of experience, but the surreal exists alongside the real, and the absurd co-exists with reason. Words which are the symbolic representations of realities that are themselves representations speak of order and nothing else. They are the very idea of order. Once we challenge the rule of words by which all our interests and relationships to the world are articulated, the words that actually *say* what the world is and who we ourselves are, we reveal a world of experience both wordless and disinterested. For the practical, social being such an adventure will take him to the edge of chaos and panic. For the thinker, it is the beginning of the end of the rule of the will, the refusal of interestedness for the sake of and in exchange for pure knowing and pure being. It is a sort of great, all-encompassing sympathy that contains within it the seeds of every form of mysticism and the disillusionment with the power of words to represent things as themselves and not things as the objects of our thoughts. It becomes more natural for us, in this frame of mind, to speak of a different order of thinking, to speak of the 'heart' rather than the 'mind', as Hugo von Hofmannsthal does in his famous and revealing *Lord Chandos Letter*, to speak of some kind of renewed, intuitive apprehension of things in their first light as though 'we could enter into a new, intuitive relationship with the whole universe, if we began to think with our hearts'. Hofmannsthal speaks of things 'present, fully and exaltedly present' in a language 'of which I do not know even one word, a language in which dumb things speak to me' that calls to mind the visionary meditations of Thomas Traherne, where what is thus recovered is what has been blotted out by the everyday ways of the world, by self-interest and other distracting worldly interests: the knowledge of things uncorrupted by words in the primal innocence of their wordless being, 'the first light,' Traherne says, 'which shined in my infancy in its primitive and innocent clarity.'

Language creates a self-referential world that masks what it pretends to elucidate. One day, in the course of explaining something, Hugo von Hofmannsthal discovered that 'those abstractions which the tongue has to pronounce in making any judgment fell apart like rotten mushrooms in my mouth'. Not only literature, but arguing from principles and concepts is suddenly revealed as the artificial construction of the intellect for which only the heart can make amends, forcing one to think again about what the true relationship might be between the mind and the world, the subject and its object, when devoid of its interests and intentions.

There are moments of realisation in which the artificial structure of language and concepts that sustains the rational relationship of ourselves to the world no longer holds. Things seen without language, without words attached to them, begin to shed their meaning, become strange, if strangely familiar. The concept of space by which things are kept apart, when challenged, returns things to their original undifferentiated state, and time, without our concern for it, restores everything to the present moment. Though everything stays the same to all appearances, one world is lost and another gained, the difference between them measured by degrees of attachment. The process of detachment from the conventional, concept and language bound interpretation of experience begins with the realisation that everything to which we grant reality, without needing to think about it, is real only because we *do* think about it. Were the world a matter of complete indifference to us, as we are to it, then it would pass by us without pausing to assume any form or shape by which we might recognise it or seize upon it as something worth troubling about.

All our troubles begin with our own thoughts, as Marcus Aurelius so long ago made clear:

> The things themselves that affect us, they stand without doors, neither knowing anything themselves nor able to utter anything unto others concerning themselves. What then is it, that passeth verdict on them? The understanding.

We suffer nothing simply by allowing the images of things, or ideas themselves, to arise in the mind, but only from our attachment to them and engagement with them as aspects of the self, the self being the very essence of attachment.

The later Stoics, like the more thoroughgoing Cynics before them, were practical rather than metaphysical in their rejection of the attachments that disturb the equanimity of mind which, rightly, they saw as the only end and aim of philosophy. For what else can philosophy propose but the resolution of all its proposals – 'the mind at rest', as Charles Peirce defines it, as the end point and finality of its enquiries.

Marcus Aurelius again, in Casaubon's eloquent translation:

> The things themselves (which either to get or to avoid thou art put to so much trouble) come not unto thee themselves; but thou in a manner goest unto them. Let then thine own judgment and opinion concerning those things be at rest; and as for the things themselves, they stand still and quiet, without any noise or stir at all; and so shall all pursuing and flying cease.

Thus the Stoics sought their *apatheia* and the Sceptics their *ataraxia*, a tranquil and undisturbed heart and mind, and Paul advised the Christians that by caring for nothing 'the peace of God, that passeth all understanding, shall keep your hearts and minds', and the Buddhists attain to 'nirvana' through detachment and the extinguishing of the self that is the summation of all attachments and bring an end to the endless wheel of recurrence.

The Stoics, according to Zeller, ran into the problem that any mind encounters once it has determined to leave behind one's worldly attachments and follow 'nature' – or, more specifically, one's 'own' nature – namely, what part of one's nature one should follow, since it is in our nature to follow self-interest and selfishness, wickedness, deceit and venality, which are all part and parcel of the means by which we achieve our ends. The sleight of hand that put them back on course to allow 'nature' to stand exclusively for our moral nature (which the Taoists also accomplished) was to assert that virtue, through the rational pursuit of 'right knowledge' and 'right understanding', is the highest portion of man's nature. So what, we must ask, if this is granted, is to become of those lower, those more immediately gratifying portions of his nature? The temptation is to admit some things, by degrees, as naturally less wicked or detrimental to our natural virtue, such as the legitimacy of physical health, a sufficiency of wealth or reputation or such things as might be said to nurture virtue. But in reality there can be no compromise with the harsh resolve to be detached from the ordinary comforts of ordinary 'foolish' men in order to be wise. It is all or nothing, in or out, sudden not gradual or partial, either wise or foolish and not something in between. The will of man for the Stoics and the will of Heaven for the Taoists were an alternative way of power ('virtue') to the promptings of our natural instinct to seek power through the assertion of the self against the world, one that will make its own unhindered way like water flowing in its natural course. Detached, we follow *some* way of nature, but a nature that is more akin to the nature of the wind that blows through the pines and 'the hollow places of the earth', as Chuang-tzu says, making first one sound and then another, which is all that our important words and habits of differentiation amount to. It is another way of hearing and another way of seeing, untrammelled by our illusions and our interests, that precedes another way of acting that can be considered 'natural' in the sense that, since we are never outside nature, we are free, like the water and the wind, the fish in the ocean and the leaf in the storm, to be indifferent to it.

The idea of nature contains within it a contradiction that is never quite resolved. Nature is not benign. It is merely orderly in the way competing interests naturally find their equilibrium in the world. Poisons are as natural as medicines. Doing good disturbs the peace as much as the unbridled pursuit of evil. Our moral dilemma of how to decide which of our sexual impulses are natural and which unnatural can't be solved by turning to nature for an answer. A 'natural' moral order does not arise from nature. It was a problem for the Stoics who sought a moral imperative by which to live, for Kant horrified by his own sexuality, and for Chuang-tzu who said the wise man follows the way of Heaven but also said that the wise man 'hates' Heaven – for nature, in essence, is the will, and the will manifests itself as the ego and its attachments and self-interests.

The thought that the mind might be a net of illusions and not an infallible guide to truth and certainty is as old as thought itself. Once you begin to reflect on the place of the mind in the world beyond its spontaneous and immediate intuition of the reality of the world before your eyes, you are caught up in a net of uncertainties in which the idea of certainty itself is no more than one of the many chimerical images the mind creates of what *ought* to be – truth, reality, certainty – and what *must* be – self, thought, reason. Since action has always preceded thought, action has no prior dependency on reason or conceptual thinking. To abandon thought is to opt for action purely and simply – or non-action, like a cat asleep in the sun – spontaneous, careless, paradoxical.

Contraries, contradictions, opposites are bundles of concepts that don't belong to the thing itself and ultimately resolve themselves into action. The apothegm of Heraclitus, 'the way up and the way down are one and the same', is problematic only for Aristotelian logic, and not for experience.

The objections to the sceptical position that denies all dogmatic assertions of the certainty of knowledge come down precisely to a temperament that cannot find peace living among uncertainties and doubts. It must have its principles in order to govern its actions. The very definition of doubt demands its removal. As darkness is defined by the absence of light, uncertainty is an interim state that awaits a reason for certainty. For philosophy it is merely a matter of pronouncing on it in this fashion: 'If no statement is certain, your statement that nothing is certain is also uncertain', and having uttered this magic spell moves on to ever more juggling with words and concepts in search of finality in a perpetually unfinished world. But for those with the stomach for it, the uncertain, the unfinished, the unresolved, the open, the surprising, the irreconcilable make up the geography of this floating life. In any event, as Montaigne says in defence of the Pyrrhonian Sceptics, 'there is no school of philosophy which is not obliged to permit its sage to follow many things neither comprehended nor discerned, nor agreed upon, if he desires to live.'

The one thing that, of course, is always true about dogmatic statements is that the truth never amount to more than one of those statements, to anything other than contending voices amongst which we choose whatever, in the light of our own powers of reason, or through personal temperament, through loyalty or prejudice or preference, will in a formulaic way provide the principle for our actions. All assertions, including my own, are the confessions of an individual state of mind. All we can know is what it is for the mind to be at work in the world, saying, pronouncing, surmising, observing – and always within the limits of what it is possible to say.

To imagine the absence of mind in the world is at once to recognise that only the mind can act out this scenario, so it is never absent but contains within it all that it can imagine, including its own absence as something merely imaginary. The world outside the mind has no formal definition and everything in the world remains undifferentiated, neither matter nor non-matter, neither one thing nor another, for differentiation is a mechanism of mind. It is without substance, form, extension, utterly unmanifested as anything causally connected to mind and the idea of being. It is one thing that is both everything and nothing. It is without mind in its essence and at the same time only mind as its only essence as the knowable. It is, in Buddhist philosophy, both no-mind and mind-only and, in Kantian terminology, noumenon and phenomenon, thing-in-itself and things in representation.

Formally, the phenomenal world presents itself to the subjective mind as a set of relationships conformable to the interests and potential actions of the subject. The subject is perpetually present as observer, as the 'I', the self, as resolutely attached to the phenomenal world as a limpet to a rock. To prise oneself free, to lose one's grip, to let go of all that seems to sustain rationality, sanity, the sense of self and of oneself in the world as the one thing we value above all, as we value life above death and being above non-being, and simply to fall *into* the world, as it were, *without* ourselves, is an act of fearful recklessness contrary to common sense and the common sense practicality of getting on with life in the real world. Yet, by accident or by an effort of the will or by long discipline, the prepared mind can suddenly lose the self without abandoning consciousness. The effect of this is to experience the whole of the phenomenal world as timeless, unbounded and undifferentiated, in which self and other, subject and object, are one and the same. The self for the moment is annihilated, without the annihilation of subjective consciousness which, of course, contains this new experience. In the absence of the self to which this experience relates, the entire world appears as one eternal moment illuminated from within, without limit and without end, into which the self is absorbed and resolved. Peace and equanimity prevail. Although such experiences are beyond words and concepts and free of any intellectual content – all of which belong to the world of the self and its relations, to the mind and its understanding – since they are always the experiences of people with particular temperaments, sentiments and habits of thought, they find their expression in the only subliminal terminology available to them: God, the Godhead, Christ, Spirit, the Absolute, Atman, the World Soul. The word that can be made to stand objectively for all these experiences is 'one', the sense of all things experienced as 'one'. There is no separation of the self from the world, none between myself and God, between subject and object, between all contraries and all forms of differentiation that are the province of the practical mind and the reasoning, intellectual mind. The mystical experience is in essence a forgetting of the self, a state of consciousness with the controlling self suppressed. Similar states of mind, 'alternative' forms of consciousness, have, of course, often been induced experimentally by hallucinogenic drugs, and throughout history sacred drinks and psychoactive plants have featured in the generation of 'mystical' mental states. In William James's time there was a lot of excitement generated by the experimental use of nitrous oxide and cases of patients recovering from nitrous oxide anaesthesia who reported states of mind parallel to religious mystical experiences in those moments before the body recollected the self to which it could relate its own mental experiences, the so called 'anaesthetic revelation'.

In spite of the historical persistence and the strength of the mystical tradition as a species of thought, it does not quite go far enough to deconstruct or unravel the fiction of the self and the web of conceptual thoughts in which it is caught up. It is less a thoroughgoing cleansing of the illusions that beset the mind than a place of refuge from them in another. Chuang-tzu, in that critical chapter of his writings known as 'The sorting which evens things out', will have none of it. The unity of all things may be so, but it's best not to introduce the idea, since the one and the mention of it make two, from which all multiplicity follows. We must dispense with the one as much as with the many. In this respect we may recast the idea of 'oneness' as 'sameness', as in the expression 'it's all one', and shift our perspective from union with the sublime through the abandonment of the self and its attachments, to the detachment from all forms of discrimination and conceptualisation, from all words and statements, out of which the world and the self with all its commentary arise.

We can't depend on what we don't know to establish the certainty of what we do know, as first Chuang-Tzu and then Kant, in another frame of mind, made clear. We have nowhere to stand, we can never escape, nor should we try to escape what Chuang-Tzu has called 'the supreme uncertainty', the coexistence of alternatives, the *what is* that exists alongside the *what is not*, the whole, as it were, of *what is so*. Things 'are as they are, and as what they are make up everything'.

The intrusion of mind into emptiness fills the void with a world of phenomena in which we are perpetually immersed.

Yet there is no escape from the fact of the void and no refuge from it by choosing one thing over another out of my mental constructions to stand as the 'it', the solving idea or word to make real and concrete – hard, narrow, done, finished – the unrealised, the unborn, the unfinished, the indefinite, the uncertain, the endlessly possible.

The deconstructed mind can have no settled position, only a clear insight into its own nature. The mental discipline of Zen, undermining the distinctions of words and concepts separated from action, allows the mind to discover its original emptiness. In asserting the unity or sameness of things and in denying the certainty of all mental concepts that differentiate between phenomena, between things and their causal connections, what cannot be denied, and in Zen never is, is consciousness itself and with it the conventional, non-negotiable forms of consciously perceived phenomena as things presented to the mind in representation, but with no claim that what are thereby represented are things in themselves free of mental content. There is no access to, and never can be access to, the thing-in-itself. Hence in Zen, the words used to describe experience in the journey from illusion to enlightenment are the same at the end as they were at the beginning – for nothing has changed, nor can be changed, in the way that things are presented to the mind as the potential forms of our actions in their causal relation to us, though we have emptied our minds of all our connections to them. Things are not reduced to meaningless sensory data as they would be in the absence of mind, nor lost in a cloud of mystical 'oneness' that is one of the interim illusions encountered along the way. This is how the Zen practitioner has often described the experience:

Thirty years ago, before I practised Zen, I saw mountains as mountains and rivers as rivers. Once I was well into studying Zen, I saw mountains no longer as mountains and rivers no longer as rivers. But now that I have come to rest here, mountains are once more mountains, rivers are once more rivers.

The world of appearances is given *a priori* by the categories of the understanding through which it is manifest, and does not disappear from the mind for so long as the body and the brain coexist in their given natures. What the mind succeeds in banishing is its pretence to be anything other than phenomenal, by perceiving the world of appearances finally detached from its conceptions of the real.

Every problem, once solved, remains a mystery. Problems and solutions, questions and answers, ideas of self and other that give rise to the question in the first place, have only an illusory, mind-only foundation. Answers are made of the same mind stuff as questions. 'For mere logic every question contains its own answer – we simply fill the hole with the dirt we dug out,' wrote Xenos Clark in a letter to William James. Life ultimately remains a paradox: we can free ourselves from our illusions, but we can't free ourselves from that condition of being in which those illusions arise. Any attempt to deny our nature will remain subject to it. We have no way to resolve this paradox by becoming something other. But if we can undo the bonds that tie us to the condition of being born, if we can free ourselves from the imperative of the will to live and, in a manner, remain unborn, conscious only of the essential emptiness of all that is not yet resolved into emptiness, as one and the same, and embrace the supreme uncertainty as the nature of being, then we finally do arrive at the justification of being without a reason to be, without a principle or a dogma or a reassurance. Since we are, to be, and yet to be unborn and free of the will that gave birth to the self and its attachments – to know without any need to know, to realise that subjectivity alone gives life legitimacy and that the will is entirely subordinate to it – is the most that any mind can achieve in reconciling itself to the awareness imposed upon it.

The Freedom to Be Tragic

That I myself am the centre I owe to nothing more than a certain geometry of the abyss. Fernando Pessoa, *The Book of Disquiet*

We know a great deal about ourselves; on the other hand we are nothing. Compensating for our failure of naivety, of spontaneity, hope and stupidity, the 'psychological sense' that is our greatest acquisition has transformed us into spectators of ourselves. E M Cioran, *Beyond the Novel*

To be brief, I am a poet and a destroyer... Giovanni Papini, *Un Uomo Finito*

Somehow or other, order, once it reaches a certain stage, calls for bloodshed. Robert Musil, *The Man Without Qualities*

I

People love life more than freedom and hate death more than labour. The wise man, in his wisdom, took freedom and death from them and gave them labour and life. Su Hsun, *Discourse on the Book of Changes*

Since I possess the faculty to reflect on the fact of my existence I am entitled to ask what the point is of all this coming and going, of this confectionary arrangement of cells that struggles into existence only to go out like a light after a few orbits around the sun, and why the evolution of specific functional nodes and nerve endings in one species should suddenly introduce the problem of meaning into the inexorable ordering of matter of its own accord. We are forever in despair of finding an answer so long as we persist in confusing the stuff of the mind with the stuff of cosmology. The mind, complex as it is in terms of both brain neurology and human psychology, is simply the disposition of the species to solve the problems of living in social groups. Beyond that functional effectiveness, what else actually matters to me matters only as a bothersome phenomenon of mind and not as something to be settled by application to the outer universe, since all that the universe can offer is its complete indifference to everything it brings forth.

Everything in the world that actually matters to me is in fact wholly the matter of mind and belongs exclusively to it. It can hardly matter at all if it is not in some way presented as the matter of mind, where it takes on a more anxious form of existence. Neither the world nor the life the world sustains has any intrinsic value in itself and on its own objective ground of being. It has value only in the form of its representation as a phenomenon of mind. The test of this is to imagine being given the chance to live for ever on the condition that you remain without any conscious knowledge that you live, and then trying to work out in what respect such a life would have any value. Eternal life, in fact, is given and requires no effort on our part to achieve. Eternal life, after all, is in a manner given to all life forms through the act of reproduction. Absent the ego and we have immortality. Even the diversity of species is only another way of guaranteeing the reproduction of life in general by spreading its bets across every environmental contingency. This self-sufficient continuum is disturbed only by the entry of mind into it, unable to reconcile what it knows with what it does not know and adding value to life through a self-conscious awareness of it and the egoistical mental possession of it. Life doesn't seem to matter to life itself as something that continues in a self-organising mechanistic way, and when we wish for our own continuity as individuals what we really wish for is not life as it actually is and as we are actually held and guaranteed by it, but a timeless consciousness of being and the perpetuation of the illusion of being in possession of it.

Without mind, life and the universe go on uselessly, pointlessly, indifferently – usefulness, meaning and interest are all conditions of the mind's attendance on matter, and not prior conditions of matter. If we knew nothing of life, why would we, how could we, choose to live? Life is simply lived for us. Suppose also that we were offered another form of immortality, a sort of absorption into a universal soul in exchange for our individual subjective existences. We should object: what is the point of that? I can neither add to nor subtract from the whole since I would never know that I was in it, having lost sight of my self as that which knows. I would perhaps finally know what it is like to be God, but I would not know that it was I who knew it. No. Only my individual consciousness is real, and all that matters to me is this inner space that is my sense of unique subjectivity that has always, from the beginning of self-consciousness, been called the 'soul' – that which I am even when I imagine myself shorn of all that I am as ego, person, the self and its possessions, its qualities and attributes, anxieties and alibis – that which I am and continue to be even when faced with the evidence that the soul has no definite objective existence at all. The extraordinary consequence of salvaging subjectivity from the actuality of a world that exists in its own right is that what does not exist anywhere in the universe is everything, and what does exist is nothing – except as something of interest to the subject.

Everything is mediated by the subject. All that is not mediated by the subject is nothing. The certainty of the existence of something in the absence of the subject is something known only to the subject, for something that is not known is nothing. What the subject can know about the world is mediated by the subject and the subject's representation of the world and its objects, which includes the object of the self that knows. The objective and the subjective are two separate realms intimately connected in this way: that the objective gave rise to the subjective as the cause of its being subjective and to which the subjective must ever refer, and that for the objective to be something and not nothing it must be mediated by the subject to which it must henceforth always defer as the true cause of all values. For the subject to defer to the object and ask it to reveal its secret meaning and an intrinsic truth that it cannot posses is not only a mistaken use of the subject's powers of reason, but it is to behave like a slave or serf who, having been granted his freedom, asks to be taken back into bondage because he loves labour more than liberty, because he would rather be a slave and know where he stands than a free man who must therefore be forced to take the responsibility for his freedom into his own hands.

To remain objective is to remain a slave, a dependant, a labourer. Labour is the essence of life. At its most basic level, the life of an organism is a thermodynamic system, sustaining its integrity through the exchange of energy and the completion of work cycles until, like everything else, it runs down. Work, and how its cycles of work get accomplished, defines the nature of the organism. Work defines its organic structure. Beaks, mouths, tongues, claws, hands, lungs, stomachs, digestive systems are all elements of a dynamic process to sustain systemic integrity for labour. We work in order to live in order to continue working. Death is the breakdown of the order of work. The social order is the collective organisation of work. Society has no other foundation than collective welfare based on work and the division of labour. Since the self-interest of the individual in society is the only motivation for work, the struggle to assert the interests of the self is the same as the struggle to individualise the self as the proponent of its own interests. Work, more than anything, defines the identity of the self in relation to other selves. It is the basis and the limits of its power. Work, wealth and power are the sources of the individual's status, purpose and value in the struggle for life. But labour is an act of necessity not of freedom, and the self, too, is not free but complicit in the necessity of labour.

Labour – the necessity of labour, the organisation of society based upon the economic value of labour and the creation of the personality that bears the labour of living – has kept us close to nature and to the earth and has conditioned us to think of freedom from labour in the language and imagery of labour. Labour must be rewarded, so the labour of living should also have its reward. The reward of labour and life is rest. And the ultimate purpose of the labour of living is known only to Him under whose direction we labour, and perhaps not even, finally, to Him, since He also is a labourer, a mover of mountains, a mason and a carpenter, the supreme workman who built this folly.

The individual is the whole. There is nothing to which he

can aspire that is greater than that which he already possesses. Yet his existence is not the product of his own willing, but the production of something else of which he has no knowledge. Most immediately he is the product of his species as the means of its reproduction and in this respect has no individuality as an expendable and soon to be expended consequence of the sexual imperatives of the species. The social order is the natural, evolved order of the species. The individual has no say in the prior arrangement of the social order he finds himself born into, any more than he has a say in the forces of nature that led to his existence. The individual, as the locus of subjective consciousness, contains the whole and the whole of the mind's interests, which are 'wider than the sky', but the interests of the social order are confined to the necessities of the species *en masse*, that is to say, to sex and economics.

The first necessity of life is reproduction through division. If life had been arranged in the form of a single indivisible, self-sustaining, continuously metamorphosing entity, the entropy inherent in any system would have seen its eventual demise, or in its setting forth as a giant over the earth it would soon have fallen into a pit and died or, as nothing more than a microscopic formation, simply drowned or dried out or evaporated. What else can a singular entity do to preserve itself than become many? And what else can the many become but variations of a singularity that can never again be singular but must always be at any given moment a stage in the cycle of reproduction?

Asexual reproduction should in theory be perfectly adequate to maintain the status quo of the individual from generation to generation in a largely static and inanimate environment where minor accidental variations in structure over time enable it to adapt to minor, arbitrary variations in conditions. But survival is not simply about adaptation to external conditions, it is also about life at war with itself, about interspecies rivalry to find the route to continuity, about the appropriation of resources, including other life forms, as sources of nourishment. It is only through uncompromising ruthlessness that life finds its balance of power and some sort of equilibrium that looks like peace. In the struggle for life what struggles is life itself, life as a continuous process of becoming where species are the aggregates of that self-organising process and individuals the foot-soldiers fighting in the mist for a grandeur of order to which they are blind.

If winning in life's lottery is down to chance, then the random variations of sexual generation increase the chances of winning and of being in a position to consolidate the wealth accrued to a chance advantage.

...in competition for such local prizes, asexual reproduction simply duplicates a ticket number, and so gives no extra chance of winning. W D Hamilton, *Gamblers since life began: barnacles, aphids, elms*

The division into male and female is a division of labour in which two surviving halves of what otherwise would be merely an increasingly decrepit and decaying singularity unite again in one offspring that takes from each its most optimistic chances of survival (by the simple fact of having got this far), in turn to become one half of another. Nothing in everyday experience exemplifies better the division of labour in a single organism than the metamorphosis of the caterpillar into butterfly. The butterfly is the sexual and reproductive form and function of the caterpillar, and the caterpillar the gestation stage of the means of the butterfly's self-reproduction. The possibility of individuation escapes it completely, for at any point in its life cycle it is in the process of becoming without ever becoming itself. The diversity of species is an extension of the division of the labour of life over time. Sexuality defines species – the cells of cellular division cut off from any possibility of reintegration into one as everything falls away from the centre to the periphery, the one forever becoming many. Sexuality divides species as they drift farther apart. If we think of life as a whole, as one thing that has got itself into an increasingly complex self-maintaining system, the unity of life lies not in reproduction, by which it continues to diversify into novel and interrelated forms, but in consumption. Taken as a whole, it consumes what it produces. Life does not cross the species barrier to effect its reproduction, but each species competes to improve its chances and by doing so increase the certainty of the continuity of life in some form or other. From its redoubt, one species raids the borders of the other to consume what it cannot itself reproduce in a cycle of energy exchange that ultimately serves the accumulated mass of the whole by first producing and then consuming its parts.

The social order is organised to cope with and regulate the consequences of sexual activity by providing coherent and mutually dependent economic structures for the maintenance of populations – the second necessity of life, after reproduction, being the balancing of work cycles and energy exchange to sustain the integrity of the organic unit long enough, on average, to achieve the first necessity of reproduction. The self-regulation of economic constraints on reproduction is effected largely through sexual selection rituals pervasive among most species. The determination of fitness through elaborate displays of prowess or the seizing of sexual opportunities as an entitlement of power in the social hierarchy are not without their parallels in human social behaviour. The ubiquity and randomness of the sexual impulse may appear to be the least amenable to regulation, but, since it has consequences, it has become constrained and channelled to optimise the economic stability of the population as a whole. Whether ritualised by money, property, power, by gifts, dowries, matchmakers, interviews with prospective in-laws or bank managers, by the possession of camels or goats, by the assets of good teeth, shapely ankles, clothes, jewellery, fast cars, suntans – or, indeed, the absence of all of these – male and female sexual behaviour has an economic basis in society and in the social hierarchy. To the individual, these may all seem to be matters of choice and self-determination, for it has always been the essential illusion permitted the ego that in its construction as the agent of the organic unit in the pursuit of its interests and its relative power, it acts of its own free will.

The machinery of society has designed itself to nurture the individual only insofar as the individual contributes to its design. That a few here and there manage to detach themselves from society is of no matter to the general interest of society, and society soon expunges or accommodates its non-conformists. No individual is ever completely self-reliant but remains a product of society, its language and mores, and the defiant, the rebellious and the disaffected can only manoeuvre in and around and between the pistons and wheels and pulleys of the social machine, hating but never free of their dependencies.

Freedom is the coincidence of self-interest with self-determination. But the freedom of the individual to act in his own interests can only extend as far as the interests of society as a whole permit it. The power base of society may move around from one founded democratically in individual freedom of action and association, to its consolidation in ruling classes or factions, but in all cases the social order and its freedoms or lack of them is ruled by the need to secure the economic interests of the prevailing order. The individual adapts to, even if he does not entirely conform to, the political power structure, and where his economic interests can't be self-determined, he will give up his freedoms for the security of labour. Economic necessity and the limits of freedom it imposes perpetuate the status quo, just as the genetic inheritance of the organism and the constraints of its environment perpetuate the stability of populations. Thus, historically, kings breed princes, serfs are born into servitude and the poor continue to multiply in abject dependency. Sexual selection optimises fitness for survival, but selection is limited by opportunity and the limits of opportunity favour the continuity of the status quo. Socio-economic structures evolve, and are sometimes overthrown and turned upside down in the political equivalent of punctuated equilibrium. But the new order is the same as the old order, with changes to the order of power but no change to the adaptive order of economic interest in which groups, factions, classes, clans, families and individuals strive to balance economic self-determination with the self-interest vested in the dominant powers. Some sort of stability is maintained so long as the self-interests of one do not overstep the boundaries of the mutual interests of the whole, so there are limits to exploitation and slavery as there are limits to selfishness. The ideal of the greatest happiness of the greatest number will always be conditional on the extent to which the basis of economic self-interest is devolved to the self-determination of the individual. For happiness, in terms of the social order through which it can be achieved, is an economic commodity, a measure of the relative power of the individual to exercise the freedom to determine his own wellbeing. In no instance will we find the political and economic structure of the social order designed to nurture the freedom of the individual in such a way as to release him from his obligations to the social order as a whole and his economic role within it: that is, to teach non-conformity in the schools and to provide independence of means in exchange for ingratitude. We will find that the moral order of society is, at bottom, an aspect of production.

The individual ego, far from being a casualty of the broader economic struggle for survival and precedence, an innocent bystander caught up in events over which he has no control, is complicit in all this and its principal motive force. The ego is a composite figure, an artefact of self-consciousness that embodies the interests of the individual as a living unit performing the work cycles to which its existence commits it, and representing its interests at every point of interaction with an essentially hostile environment and a contentious social scramble for a place at the table, a voice, a role, a small victory. Self-consciousness as a phenomenon is solely the knowledge 'that' I am. 'What' I am, however much I might like to believe it the essence of my being, is an arbitrary and contingent compilation of qualities given, inherited, adopted, mimicked or learned as a result of biological, social or cultural circumstances. I can't 'be' the cumulative assortment of constantly shifting obligations, roles, identities, emotions, aversions, vanities or names that adhere to my sense of being. They are thrust upon me, overlaid on unconscious animal instincts for survival as an elaboration of them, in the process of becoming a social being, in the pupal maturation of a naïve self-consciousness into a productive and reproductive worker – the wakeful ego. The individual perceives his life as the possession of his ego. The survival of the one is the desire of the other, and from birth to death the lived life, the economic unity of the individual and its ego, its needs, wants, desires, its labours, freedoms and its fears for itself and its continuity, is the sufficiency of life, and self-consciousness adds nothing to it but anxiety for it.

The self-conscious ego, immersed in its life, has no wish to be free of the labour of living for it sees freedom from life only as death and so clings to labour and life. What it really wants is happiness, and by happiness it means freedom from the anxieties of labour and from the *insufficiency* of labour to meet its needs and desires. Happiness is relative. A man is happy if the rewards of labour are sufficient to meet his needs, but if he defines his needs not just in terms of survival but in terms of relative power or status in relation to others, that is, to the immediate social context in which he lives, labours and struggles, then his happiness is tied to the attainment of a balance of power and the freedom of action to determine his relative wellbeing. There are no limits to discontent and, as everyone knows, the limitless pursuit of power and wealth does not guarantee happiness, for happiness is not the reward of ambition but of the successful adaptation and editing of the ego to meet the limitations of its achievements.

Happiness is always bound to be relative, conditional and incomplete, the product of a partial, half-blind view of life, since happiness has no absolute ground in being but only in the temporary favourable circumstances that create a sort of bubble isolated for the moment on the surface of a deeper, darker body of water that carries it along. To be happy we must ignore unhappiness, take comfort only in our comforts, and never look down into the abyss. To pursue happiness as one's personal goal is to limit the fulfilment of life to respite from it. To work towards the happiness of the greatest number is the goal of utilitarian and enlightened ameliorative social systems based on labour and productivity. In this way we improve factory conditions, so that the rewards of the labour of living are more conducive to happiness and thereby increasingly guarantee the productivity and continuity of the system as a whole. Happiness, as the aim and end of life, is an accommodation with and a surrender to the aimless, indifferent and ultimately empty cycle of birth, labour, reproduction and death, a bauble reached for but forever out of one's grasp. If through some miracle everyone in the world were suddenly to become equally happy all at once, then life will have found its apotheosis in the total enslavement of the mind to life for the rewards of its labours.

Self-consciousness is merely incidental to the process of constructing the self as ego to perform the vital function of pursuing and defending its interests by understanding itself and its relation to the world. The primary function of mind lies in its instrumentality in serving the sensory apparatus of the organism in sustaining and perpetuating its existence. Only secondarily does self-consciousness as such and in itself – subjectivity – appear as the locus of experience, that is, as the essence of being. If the first aspect of mind contributes nothing more to life than might be achieved, after a fashion, without it, the secondary aspect of mind is a law unto itself, untouched by necessity, uncommitted to anything other than its own unique experience of being, and free from the labour of life even if body and soul, of necessity, must keep themselves together day by day in the Endless Belt and Leather Company to which everyone is apprenticed at birth (the ever-present factory imagined by Nelson Algren in *A Walk on the Wild Side*, in whose shadow the alienated bums and punks of Division Street live evasively and, like publicans and sinners, closer to redemption by virtue of their vices).

The story of life is a story of mass production. The usefulness of the individual lies solely in becoming many, in toiling for the mass and not for himself, toiling for himself only insofar as the social order permits. For the individual, death is inevitable, and his labours come to nothing, but the mass profits from his labour by not dying. Only in our literary ad filmic apocalyptic visions do we imagine the individual, the last man on earth among the ruins and devastation of cities and landscapes, as the sole representative of the whole of humanity, the last flickering flame of self-knowledge. His own death will mark the extinction of all that collective self-consciousness has created. But the end of the world is not in itself a tragedy, for we cannot be tragic *en masse*. The tragedy lies in the realisation that all knowledge of the world is to be lost, that it will go on unconscious of itself without a mind to realise it, and all that we have worked for will vanish. We are tragic as individuals but we are never tragic as a species. The species is inured to the fate of individuals. No single death disturbs the equanimity of the many, and even the death of many only serves to impel the whole to renewed vigour. The individual is subservient to the whole and has no choice as one of many producers to be also one of its many products. The desires of others produced me, the long inheritance of the species bespoke these arms and legs and brain, the others gave me thought and language, life and labour, and all that I think and say and do are things given not things created. Therefore I am nothing if not the whole, but the whole equally is nothing without me. I am always the last man on earth, a witness to the apocalypse, for whom death is tragic, the one in whom the whole world lives and for whom the whole world is lost. Life knows nothing of its own loss, and would not care if it did. The individual creature strives in vain for its own survival, succeeding only in contributing to the survival of the whole even when, like a colony of ants when its weakened infrastructure is overthrown and its population consumed by a rival colony, by failing it perpetuates the lives of strangers. Self-consciousness merely adds the instrumentality of purpose whose purposes may succeed or fail. And so in essence I am lost to life, for life is lost to itself, and I must labour for life, and life will employ the instrumentality of my self-conscious striving to succeed and not fail, but all the time I am not working to any end but the ends of life, and there is no other reward for my labour than happiness, and happiness is surrender to life and not freedom from it. I can only be free by becoming tragic. Life has no value in itself and has no sense of the tragic because it cannot lose what is already lost. Life can only be lost to me. This is my one and only and my final freedom, the freedom to be tragic.

II

It's too bad, but suffering is about the only reliable burster of the spirit's sleep. Saul Bellow, *Henderson the Rain King*

Life goes on... but since life is, as it were, a thermodynamic process, it goes on only through the process of continuous individuation, dividing itself into many, and those many, having come into existence not all at once but over long periods of time, exist in complex relationships to each other and to the conditions of the world into which they are born. A complex self-organised architecture of competition and co-operation supports the superficial appearance of chaotic swarming. The whole is an algorithmic expansion of the formulaic behaviour of the individual. For ants and humans alike, the individual is the means by which the whole subverts its mortality by delegating death to its servants. The individual isolated human consciousness-in-the-brain that tracks and internalises external phenomena, that orientates itself in the midst of its interests, that distinguishes threats from opportunities, friend from foe, its own from the alien, functions in a similar way to individual ant receptors for pheromone signals and chemical indicators in response to which its actions unwind. We may call it knowledge, the ant might call it information: it's all the same – judgments must be made, optimal judgments for action, and actions have consequences and so, whether through the evolution of consciousness or chemical signalling, the individual behaves in accordance with the habits for survival that have led to its individuation. The incidental representation of the self as the actor and the world as its field of action is a phenomenon of consciousness only. In the animal world – in the ant's universe – the individualised organism fulfils its genetically habituated role, selfish of course in the ultimate interests of the whole, but selfless also, not, as we are habituated to think, as the subjective pivot about which a world of personal experience revolves, but simply as the agent of its own nature. Consciousness considered on its own ground of phenomenological instrumentality, as phenomenal exaggeration, does not raise the human above the life dictated for it by life itself. Insomuch as the mind is earthbound, grovelling after food, social position, the sources of its power and influence, working for the satisfaction of the needs of its organic life, then despite the illumination of consciousness it is the slave of life, which itself is blind, and accomplishes no more with it than it would have done without it, as though a mole had been granted the use of a candle. What the mind reveals is nothing to life so long as life just goes on, and the individual's consciousness of self matters not at all if the illusion of the self is only an adjunct to the labour of the individual in sustaining his own life.

Now, if I ask myself, Do I value life? I cannot see how value pertains to it if my individuation represents the division of labour towards the continuance of life for its own sake, and my consciousness is the cerebral equipment that fits it for that role. If I ask myself what it is that I do value, it is not life as such because I do not know what life is as such, I only know the matter of mind presented as self and other, subject and object, that is, I only know life as a personal experience, and that is my only source of value. My subjectivity is superfluous to life for life is utterly objective and hidden. But the superfluity of the subjective is all that rescues life from the oblivion of the objective. Life goes on.... The sensory mechanisms and exchanges of energy by which it accomplishes its work cycles, its self-renewal and self-organisation of incremental complexity, are as self-effacing as the flower that blooms unseen in the desert, lost to its own reality. The many minds for whom the world is a shared reality labour to construct a parallel conceptual world of language and knowledge. But the collective enterprise of both life and knowledge is unknown to the collective mind, for there is no such thing. Subjectivity is the sole possession of one. I alone am the subject. And though life matters equally to everyone it matters only as the matter of the mind in which it is made known. I may, of course, and do, confer value on life beyond my own selfish awareness of it, but that value is itself a reflection of my subjectivity and life does not thereby acquire value on its own ground but only on the ground of the manner in which I know it. So in fact it is never true to say that I value life. I only value subjective being as the source of value, and merely acknowledge life in general as the condition of the will that allows me to be. Life has only the value that I confer on it, just as the world has no value in itself, as thing-in-itself, except as the formal representation of my interest in it. And therefore I am, on the ground of being subjective. But the world and the self are not, except as representations of my subjective being. I am at once an objective fact, a single organism that is the product of life and of the many, which exists as a matter of fact lost to itself as thing-in-itself, and the subject that bears the fact of being, of being a singularity, an existence.

Life, though unequivocally red in tooth and claw, is indifferent to itself, and indifferent to its own suffering. The symptoms of distress are descriptive. They do not by themselves indicate the presence of a subjective consciousness that experiences them. The sensory defensive order of the nervous system that, raised to consciousness, is the experience of pain, without the subject of experience remains objective, a dislocation of the objective condition but not the assumption of conscious suffering that can only be experienced by the subject. Suffering is subjective. If there is no subject to bear its suffering the threat to the destruction of the individual can never be experienced as the personal tragedy of a singularity faced with the fact of its existence and the fatal ends of being. In the absence of the locus of subjective being, nothing can suffer the apprehension of losing itself if it has never acquired itself. Life has no knowledge of either life or death except as things represented by the subject. Life remains resilient under blows and indifferent to the destructive processes that are the condition of its existence and by which it recreates itself. Even the human agent, who knows what it is to suffer pain and to suffer his fate, is unable, in deference to all those who have preceded him, suffered and died, to refuse life and say, 'It is better not to have been born,' for it is accomplished for him, without him, and he, too, lives his life indifferent to the past and oblivious of the future.

There is no basis *in* life for the judgment of life. The judgments made by life are judgments for action, and are not based on any value accrued to life but only on the criteria established for judgment on the experiential basis of having worked to the ends of effective action. Whether *all this is worthwhile* on any other foundation of judgment is an irritation that can only be resolved by the subjective consciousness to whom alone this problem belongs. All that life demands of one is to live. It has no expectations or hopes, and does not explain itself. The super-addition of mind does not change its essential and intractable nature by creating internal references to it. Mind is the instrument of the self, and the self is the abstract instrumental representation of the individual organism, which itself is the means of production and reproduction through the devolution to each of the labour of becoming many. Pain and suffering are confined to individual consciousness. They are the internal signals of frustration and defeat. As happiness is the goal of each, so the avoidance of pain, harm and unhappiness is the goad. The fatality of the individual is the regulating mechanism that guarantees the resilience of the many, and happiness and unhappiness are paired like hunger and satiety in the cycle of becoming. The self that suffers is only one of many, whose suffering matters to life only as a spur to behaviour that serves the ultimate benefit of the whole.

There is nothing at all that can be retrieved from life that can justify life on its own ground. The antlike ego and the causal connections it makes between the world of its experience and its interests are objective, cumulative, formal modes of organic behaviour unsusceptible to self-judgment and unavailable to external judgment. But the subjectivity of being has its own transcendental ground, and needs no further justification, since everything is justified by it. By standing on *this* ground we can easily see that no *other* standpoint is possible. Life has no reason for being, only efficient causes for being, and to ascribe a secret wisdom and a hidden beneficent motive to nature is to contradict nature, and to put one's faith in a first cause is a contradiction of our own reason, for a first cause can't have a reason without presupposing a further cause behind it until we arrive at no cause and no reason, which is the true state of things. There is no cause, only a condition. Only the subjectivity of being has a cause or reason for being.

Whatever is unaware of its condition is incapable of suffering its condition. The crumbling of inorganic matter happens in the void. The collapse of whole species has an impact on the balance of interdependent life but is not in itself tragic. The fish caught in a net struggles for life and suffers its death, but does not suffer its fate. Every creature that struggles in its labour of living suffers only its labour and not its existence. The human being, too, though conscious of living, is for the most part mired in the labour of life, for whom the reality of pain, suffering and death is the frustration of the rewards of happiness he has struggled to accumulate. His existential condition is incidental to his life, to be as far as possible subdued and suppressed, ignored or shrugged off, and faced only as a final encounter with the inevitable. His fatality is an obstacle, an awkwardness, a blow to his assumed condition and not the condition itself. He accepts his life and must needs accept his death. His life may be filled with suffering and misfortune, but it is not tragic (though he will commonly call his misfortunes tragedies) because, as obstacles to happiness and contentment, misfortune and suffering are secondary unwanted intrusions upon his entitlement to happiness, which he sees as the natural condition of his life if those obstacles can be removed or ameliorated. But happiness is conditional, dependent entirely on the conditions that are conducive to happiness and the absence of those conditions that intrude on it. But those conditions are never absent. Life does not know itself, but when it does awake to itself as subjective being it knows once and for all the tragic condition of being to which happiness and unhappiness are both subject. The tragic sense of life is the first principle of subjective being: not the secondary condition by which happiness is thwarted, but the primary condition in which it is justified.

The ego trammelled in its motives never escapes the attachment to its interests to rise above the role to which life assigns it. The ego, by its very nature as the body's way of representing its motivations, always of course appears to be in charge, the owner of the body itself and the possessor of all the self's qualities and attributes. It can and does assert its legitimacy to be, from its first cry as it enters the world in search of a personality to the expiration of its last breath and the loss of it. Its subjectivity merely confirms it in who it is, confirms the certainty of 'I am' as the foundation for the reality of its experience. Subjective being and the fiction of the self are one and the same to it. The ego, fully occupied with its motives, has little reason to turn from the labours of self-interest in order to devote the knowledge of itself and its powers of reason to understanding its false position and demolishing the only security it has in this world by undermining the ground on which it stands. The self's absorption in life guards it against the intrusion of unwelcome insights. And getting on with life, devoting oneself to work, preoccupying the mind and occupying time are everyone's displacement strategies for filling the empty spaces that open up into the abyss. The more one succeeds in promoting and embellishing the self and its interests and its happiness, which is what everyone means by success in life, the more unlikely are we ever to lift up our eyes beyond the gratification of the lived and laboured life if all that we can glimpse beyond it is the emptiness of the illusions we have created for ourselves.

There is no will on the part of life to require a creature to do more than accept its life. Thinking disrupts life. Life examined too closely is an unpleasant business, and it may be that only when that unpleasantness forces itself on our attention in some way that we attend to our situation and question the blind imperative to live without knowing why, or who this is who is compelled to be. Insight into its condition can happen only to the prepared mind, and only suffering its condition can awaken it to its condition from the dream of life. It often takes some great personal catastrophe to shatter the carefully constructed illusion of the self and its successes. The loss of wealth, of power, of status, of ambition may crack the foundations on which the self has been built, and the abyss then opens under it. Suffering ends the illusion of happiness as anything more than a provisional circumstance. If we ask, then, on what basis life is worth living, life, if it could, would answer, 'There is nothing in life that makes life worth living, and I do not recognise who it is that asks.' The absence of intrinsic value is not compensated for by the ant-ego's act of living, which it must perform willy-nilly. Something else is demanded of life, and demanded by that subjective sense of being, the one who dares to ask, to be retrieved from the objective indifference of the whole world. For so long as consciousness, by performing its required function, merely aids and abets life, it is just as lost to life as life is lost to itself. Subjectivity is the entirety of what is not lost, of what cannot be lost, the solitary nexus in which the world is held, and held to account, and in which the tragedy of life is revealed. Only here does the self cease its labour in the machinery of life to become the author of its own drama, for whom, finally, nothing else can matter. Our judgment in the end must be simply that life is worthwhile or it is not. Once we have understood that no affirmative answer can be given either from a cause or reason lying outside it, or by virtue of any supposed intrinsic purpose or meaning locked into its self-organised perpetuation, then the answer that subjectivity alone demands must be given by the subject that demands it, and as nothing less than the sufficiency of being the subject.

III

Is that the real tragedy, that I never shall know tragedy, never find anything but blustery complications that turn out to be a farce?
Sinclair Lewis, *Main Street*

Language is forever strange. The most familiar everyday words – stone, stream, handle, spade, net – are not themselves concrete things but abstractions of other things without names. Each word is a refinement of the history of speaking about things, a refinement of experience in conversations about things that in themselves are objects of experience and not subjects of conversation. In conversation, concrete things are filled with intention, anticipation, expectation and fear – with abstract conceptions of their relation to us. Language, when not signalling intention to act, is busy establishing the grounds for potential action – saying what things are and what qualities they possess. Everyday conversation is constantly establishing, adjusting and sorting out the groundwork of relations and all that is the case. So everyday conversations are concerned with establishing the *status* of the subject's everyday experience. If we speak about the weather, the times of the trains, what's in the newspaper, what I am going to do, where you are going, what my view of this is, what your opinion of that is, what the likelihood of this or that happening might be, we are locating ourselves in our field of action. If we exchange information about our health, our income, work, responsibilities, family, plans, ambitions, hopes, regrets, successes and failures, we are adjusting and renegotiating the social being through which our individual subjectivity operates. When we are not engaged in conversations about the immediate conditions of our actions and our field of action, the present and its futurity, then the subject of our conversation is the past, the recollection and recreation of the past status of our experiences along with the adjustment of those experiences to meet the status of things in the present. The main use of memory is to accommodate the personality to its own history.

While all these animated conversations are taking place between two bodies exchanging phonemes that are the representations of their interests abstracted from the concreteness of their experience, the individual subject whose experiences these are is present as a silent observer. When you and I speak to each other, but look beyond the words we speak and the gestures we make in the conduct of our lives – when we look into each other's eyes to find the originator of these words, we see reflected the individual subject who, though an entirely separate soul, shares a common subjective ground of being and therefore one common subject, the sense of a tragic subjectivity through which the whole world of experience is realised. It may itself be unexpressed, it may never find its expression, hidden from view behind the very words we use to project and protect our ego-selves, but it is never absent.

Our conversations, with ourselves and with each other, are

always on two levels. One is concerned with the everyday business of living, the conscious awareness that permit us to represent the grounds for our actions in concepts abstracted from concrete experience. The other takes place at the subjective foundation of experience, irrespective of the content of experience, that holds that experience to account.

At one level we are like characters in a play who, for the sake of the realism of the play, must believe they are really the persons who speak, and who must speak the lines given to them as though they had made them up on the spot and the unfolding of the drama were the result of their own actions, their individual will. In order to allow the play to unfold we must believe that the play's the thing. But on another level we know we are the actors, and while we act out our roles we are also spectators of ourselves, and it is through the division of the self into actor and spectator, persona and subject, that the real tragedy of the play is realised, for the play itself is not a tragedy, even when described as one. Life is not tragic, only our awareness of the drama being played out lends it the character of a tragedy, only the realisation of life is tragic.

Life – life that just goes on – is a self-organising thermodynamic work cycle, with or without the apparatus of consciousness that helps to feed it. For the organism, life is independent of knowledge of life and does not need the looming shadow of death to provoke it to desperate acts. There is no death in life. The various limited ranges of sensory awareness that organisms possess permit life. They do not on that account need to converge to a *point* that knows, a point that is the originator of its actions, in order to act in its own interests. Nothing and no one is watching over it. It is only when we introduce the spectator, the subject, into this business of living and being in the world that life becomes worthy of note, becomes tragic.

Because the mind is divided between the life that is destined and must be lived for its own sake and the consciousness of the tragic nature of that life, the self that is the agent merely of the will to live must rediscover itself as subject among the material of its experience, find itself again in the collective record of experience as story, history and myth.

Populations bear the act of living. The individual bears the fact of his existence. There is nowhere else where that fact may be said to exist. It can exist only as the prerogative of individual knowledge and self-awareness.

Life itself does not cease, only individual expressions of life come and go, so life is continuous and unending until the last expression of it should cease to be. The desire of the individual not to cease to be is of a different order from the desire to live. The will to live is the expression of life, it puts forth leaves on trees, pollinates the apple, propels crowds of spermatozoa along fallopian tubes and pierces the dark at 3.00 a.m. with its entrances. The individual has no desire to live. The desire to live is the expression of something else manifest in him. The struggle for existence does not ensure the survival of the individual, it ensures only that something survives (that same something, something else), for to struggle is to fail as well as to succeed. Immortality is given, despite the failure that is mortality, not for the individual but for the many, for the many possibilities of being an individual. To desire to live is only to acknowledge that one does live. To desire not to cease to be is not to desire to live for ever (the most ardent and irrational egoist eventually concedes that tedium and boredom are the only certain rewards of immortality), only not to cease to be the subject who bears the fact of his existence. The paradox of subjective existence is that I am never able to form any conception of my life without me, yet I never cease to fret over the inevitable loss of myself. Since, rationally, nothing exists for me before or after experience I ought to be able to accept the unceasing experience of being as the totality of a life that has neither beginning nor end, as something I know directly that is never nothing. But I am subjective by virtue of being in time, and while life itself forever looks outward into the open, expending itself as it goes, the subject looks backward to what it has lost and forward to emptiness. We are trapped, by the very nature of being, in the matrix of space, time and causality, in an endless cycle of questioning and examination of the condition of being whose premise is that we know we exist, we know that we will cease to exist and we know that there is no supportive causal reason for either that will satisfy the premise.

The fact of existence is the preserve of the individual and individual consciousness. Death is self-evident as a matter of observation and not as a matter of direct experience. The fact of being is a matter of direct experience without a beginning or an end despite the fact of death. The belief that death should not be, must not be, cannot be the end of being is the natural consequence of the continuous sense of being, the sense of continuous identity persevering through all the vicissitudes of the body's experience of living that becomes even more insistent as the body comes to bear its injuries, illnesses and decrepitude. That the sense of being is a temporary neurological phenomenon of the body and its brain in no way lessens the reality of the direct experience of being by its attribution to the underlying mechanism by which it becomes possible to be, just as the inheritance of genes that institutionalise particular patterns of behaviour in any way diminishes the significance of our actions by being the root cause of them.

To wish not to cease to be I must in the first instance be able to recognise the fact of death, a fact that is not available to life, which knows only the experience of living, a fact available only to the subject as the spectator of itself. By this act of self-knowledge, the individual conscious identity is promoted to the supreme arbiter of existence, as the one who alone knows he exists and knows the world exists and is inescapably aware of the tragic connection between the two. It is inconceivable for the world not to be conceivable, and equally that in my absence my conception of it should cease to be. Both being and non-being, subject and object, are inner and not outer realities. For the subject, the subject is all that there is and all that can be and thus, in this manner, we have come to the deification of our subjectivity, to God as the eternal subject through whom everything is known, and known for ever, and to whom the individual may look for confirmation of the indestructibility of his subjectivity.

The struggle of the subject with its objective condition is the struggle between spirit and flesh, between being and nothingness. We are at once what we cannot help being, creatures of the abyss who must accept our fate, the fate of having been born, and creatures of the light who refuse our fate, for the world of light is a greater thing than the night without us. That is the essence of tragedy, that we should be heroes of our own lives and undefeated by our fatality, that what appears to defeat us is not defeat at all but only the inevitable condition of being that is both accepted and refused. The ant and the ant-ego are equally slaves to their fatality and can never be heroic, and therefore can never be tragic.

Conformity with inevitability is never tragic. Neither is suffering in itself tragic. The suffering of the ant-ego lies in its failure to achieve happiness, the failure to escape its travails, in the unravelling of the narrative of the self, the evaporation of the stories one tells oneself to keep off the nightmare of non-being. To be defeated is to wish not to be the tragic deathless subject that bears the fact of its life and the sufferings of life in their seasons, but to wish only for rest, for a cessation of trouble, for the continuity of the life of the ant-ego, for more of the same life but freed from its unhappiness.

Mythologies have their roots in that wish. Mythology is essentially untragical.

> ...wherever the mythological mood prevails, tragedy is impossible.
> Joseph Campbell, *The Hero With a Thousand Faces*

That primitive undercurrent of belief in our own deathlessness that we have in childhood, and that never quite leaves us, requires a sort of magical ruse whereby the immortal world – the world that goes on without us – is appealed to, is ritually invoked or propitiated to confer benefits and advantages in this life and the continuity of it indefinitely and beneficially in another. The myth-making mind is untragical because it does not accept the fact of its life and fate. Yet myth does open up the way to the transformation of life by refusing to be defined by it. Just as we cannot escape our nightmares, we never escape our dreams.

The gods jest, of course. They cannot themselves be tragic for they have no fate. They can only amuse themselves. They are as immortal as the passions they represent. The hero can never exceed the limits of his fatefulness, and is constantly reined back by it, and this contention between his own will to be and the gods' will that his fate must be, is the theme of his tragedy and of all tragic drama. Achilles is ruled by his passions. Only when his actions are translated into Homeric hexameters and we are thereby given the power to reflect upon them is it possible for them to be seen as heroic in the face of his fatefulness.

There is nothing tragic about the squabbles of warriors over the division of the spoils of war, nothing tragic about unfairness and nothing heroic in complaining about it to mother. The accrual of wealth, the pursuit of power, the passions aroused by offence and injustice, jealousy, envy, retribution and the defence of personal reputation and status, are all familiar motivations of ordinary mortals, not heroes. They only become heroic when translated into myth and poetry, when they are abstracted from the actual and placed in the narrative context of their fatefulness, of their destined failure. The epic is not contained in the act but in the form of its telling and retelling, in the narrative of a life and not in the life itself, which simply ends, in the story that concludes by making the act of living meaningful. That is to be the meaning of art from that moment on – to find within ourselves the authority to create what is otherwise merely given and taken without question or answer.

Life itself is not tragic. It only becomes tragic in the perspective of its fatefulness, in the refusal to be defeated in spite of the inevitability of succumbing to a fate already determined. We are condemned to repeat the past. But at least we are able to rescue from it the narratives of our failures in the stories we tell ourselves, in the continuity of myth, epic narrative, poetry, song, dance, ritual and prayer, and to renew our sense of the tragic that delivers us from blind obedience to our fate. We need the acculturation of mythic layers of meaning inherited from one generation to another, without which the individual is unable to redeem his fatefulness. Confronted by our fate, we are without resource to call up from within ourselves unaided the cultural forms, the language, the articulated dreams in which the spirit is divorced from its organic shape and released from its fatefulness to become the eternally enduring subject of its own tragedy. Without an inheritance of cultural forms in which we can make our experience understandable we can make nothing of it. Simply by looking around and looking within we have nothing to seize on that will justify the consciousness of being subjective and bearing the knowledge of our fate. We are able to grasp only what has already been prepared for us – whether as ritual or reason, myth or makebelieve – sometimes merely as the untragical compensation for being and being *unhappy*, or, at a higher level, as a language of expression in which we may rediscover the universality of tragic being that the awareness of the impossibility of happiness awakens in us.

We are only truly happy when we are released from the necessity of happiness. At the most fundamental level the tragic sense of life requires neither philosophy nor theology. It requires only a capacity to realise the universality of experience in which our striving after the impossible makes up both the comedy and the tragedy of life, in which the individual sense of the continuity of subjective experience replaces the pathetic ego as the essence of being, which, as the true hero, at once accepts its fate and overcomes it.

IV

God is infinite subjectivity. Søren Kierkegaard, *Journals*

It has never been enough that life unmediated and unexamined should satisfy the act of living, that suffering, defeat and death should remain irredeemable and inescapable. Life is only ever sufficient in itself if we are inured to it by habit, as a minnow in a bowl is unconscious of the medium that sustains it, by the habit of living completely immersed in life where consciousness is simply the companion of the sensory apparatus by which we satisfy the everyday needs of living and getting, whose measure is the relative measure of happiness alongside others living in the same way, and for whom sickness and death are resented as unwanted and unexplained intrusions into its unfolding. This sort of unquestioning immersion in life is not simply to be equated with the acceptance of life on its own terms, for one who lives merely like a fish in water never faces up to those terms. To live autonomously as an individual worthy of the name we must first accept our fate and tragic being. They who live life for its own sake – healthily, robustly, cheerfully – in the light of their own understanding of their implicit fatefulness, are naturally heroic, for defeat can never come to them through external forces already accepted and admitted. We must, of course, accept our lives, but it is only the condition of living that is given from without. Since it has no intrinsic value, all values are the dispensation of the knowing subject, an inner resolve in the face of the absence of all values.

We are less afraid of life and the prospect of death than we are of casting off all attachment to life and accepting it as 'nothing'. We prefer the familiarity of labour and life to freedom and death. Life cannot offer us freedom for it is in bondage to its own condition. To be free is to be in revolt, not against life but against the slave condition of life. But it is as hard for one to face the possibility of freedom as it is to face the inevitability of death, since they both present a certain finality, the finality of escape from life, when what we want is the perpetuation of the given condition and the indefiniteness of hope. There has always been, and will always be, a choice to be made – between the questioning acceptance of life and its unquestioning refusal for the sake of something else that is everything that is not the condition. The material condition of life that is given is either the whole of it, in which we are lost, in which the ego functions like a periscope to guide the body through its lifecycle in the depths of unknowing, or it is nothing, and the realisation of that nothingness is the realisation of the self and of all values.

The perpetuation of the same, of the continuous and wearisome earthly round of birth and death, suffering and hope, labour and the reward of happiness, is what the great religions of Buddhism and Christianity have attempted to overthrow. In both, the original impetus is an inner resolve to free oneself from the condition. In both historical instances, the foundation of religion was a profound inner realisation followed by an attempt to teach what had been revealed. But profound personal experiences are not easily communicated. We can inherit only discipline and doctrine through which that same revelation might come, but there is no direct transmission of self-realisation until one is prepared to receive it. As soon as religion loses touch with the personal insight of its acknowledged originator and the striving after self-realisation, that is to say, ceases in essence to be tragic, it reverts to the untragical status of an earlier mythology, the mythology of self-perpetuation after death, of hope, of rewards for good deeds. The Buddhist Nirvana and the Christian Kingdom of Heaven, the inner location of a permanent refuge from the condition of birth and death that they confront, accepted as doctrine and belief and not as individual experience, return to the status of their mythological counterparts, happy havens of eternity and everlasting life, that very everlasting repetitiveness we should wish to be released from. In Buddhist causal reasoning, the condition we inherit from lifetime to lifetime arises of its own accord and has as its first cause not the benign will of God but deepest ignorance, in which the impetus to be, and hence consciousness and all the desires and attachments that result from consciousness, has its origin. The cause of being and the consequent destruction of being is not something we know or can know. All that we know of being therefore arises from the immediate consequence of that ignorance, from Karma, or the will to live. There is nothing that we can know that wills. The value of this idea for the subsequent development of Buddhist philosophy is that the fact of ignorance as the first cause guarantees delivery from ignorance by detaching ourselves from all its dependent causes, from desire, clinging, old age and death, from all that is the condition – nothing less, in fact, than the denial of the will identified by Schopenhauer as the will's only freedom – through ultimate enlightenment and an end to eternal recurrence. What recurs, from one life to the next, is not the Platonic notion of the individual soul but the aggregated forms of the self and the forms of its actions, and it is those forms of our being that are to be surrendered. Something, naturally, must *be* to surrender its somethingness to emptiness, to enter Nirvana free of its forms. Something remains of being. What remains is the apotheosis of subjectivity, the subject that is the denier of the will arising in ignorance and put finally to rest in the knowledge of its original emptiness. If we insist that the condition of existence does not arise out of emptiness and ignorance, but is given by God, by God's will as the first cause, then our freedom of the will would be impossible, for the will of God cannot, by definition, be denied, so that the condition also cannot be denied, but is willed to be so for ever and we can never escape it, neither by living nor by dying.

Time and time again we give up, lose faith in the supreme power vested in subjectivity, that subjectivity rescued from the abyss of emptiness, and from fear of death surrender ourselves to the objective, to the ignorance in which we trust. We become mythological and superstitious, afraid to live by our own light to which even God is subject. Both Buddhism and Christianity, in their origins, recognised that our true freedom lies in relinquishing the objective, in the conquest of all that is the condition by the will of all that is not the condition, by the will of the 'omnipotent subject' that is beyond the reach of birth and death, not of this world but excepted from it.

It is no small matter to have found a way out of the world and to have taken that fateful step to remove yourself from the lives of men, from all that ties you to life. For both the prince Sakyamuni and Jesus the Nazarene, it was impossible for such a revolt to be partial, to be merely an element of life.

That translation of oneself from the surrendered ego mired in the illusory objective world of Samsara into the undefiled, omnipotent conqueror whose kingdom is not of this world but Nirvana or the Kingdom of Heaven, the refuge of purely subjective being, is the whole of life, an alternative life. It is the utter reversal of life, and therefore can never be, to those who would follow the same path, a part-time occupation, an allegiance to a handful of compensatory ideas that make up a philosophy, a belief, a religion to fit in with this life. Religion, in essence, is an inspirational moment that each individual must rediscover through his own efforts. The teaching itself can only provide the ground, fertile for the mustard seed, but fertile also, as history and human nature attest, for reafforestation by a new mythology, a dark wood of doctrine and theology, rituals and sacrifices, in which over and over again we lose ourselves until we are able in some manner to rediscover the light that is its original subjective source.

Both religions have their obscure origins in a mendicant tradition, in a rejection of hearth and home, of the sufficiency of going through the ritual motions of appeasement and prayer, either in house or temple, as a path to redemption that clearly could only be achieved by a state of mind far removed from its earthly day-to-day obligations. The Buddha, at first a wandering ascetic, practised self-denial and self-mortification in an attempt to find release from his earthbound self to become the immortal form of himself, only to find release in the discovery of the emptiness of the self and its attachments. Life was to be accepted, and life in its social context could be accepted too on its own terms, since neither the social order nor God, and all the gods who may or may not be part of the cosmic order of things, had anything to do with individual self-realisation and enlightenment. The Judaic tradition, of course, has God at the heart of it. But every word of the teaching of Jesus is concerned with individual redemption, with the steps to be taken towards the Kingdom of Heaven, and with no suggestion that this state of grace is to be conferred on anyone who has not found his way there by his own efforts. Ritual orthodoxy was dismissed as the road to salvation. The outer form cannot deliver an inner transformation. The Sabbath is made for man, not man for the Sabbath. The approach to the Kingdom of Heaven requires the removal of obstacles in the way, divesting oneself of the things of this world – wealth, power, social and religious orthodoxy, the empty forms of ritual, of what is included and excluded from the forms of moral life – which must be exchanged for understanding and revelation. It was never going to be an easy ride for anyone, and no one was going to secure salvation by holding on and not letting go, but only by turning away from everything for the sake of another thing. In the Buddhist way, there are three steps to enlightenment. First there is the teaching and the truth embodied in the teaching, the Dharma. Then there is the discipline required to learn and to practise, hence the need for a school or Sangha. And only then can understanding follow, and enlightenment only for the mind thus prepared to receive it. The teaching of Jesus required the same steps. It is clear, from the internal evidence of the gospels alone, that there was a Judaic mendicant movement to which both John the Baptiser and the wandering Nazarene preacher belonged, and which was to continue through the creation of an order of disciples who were 'not to take anything with them for the journey, except only a staff, no bread, no bag, no coppers for the money-belt, with sandals on their feet, and no extra tunic'.

'He who has ears to hear, let him hear.' The way is open only to those who understand, but a superficial understanding is not enough. There is a lot to lose, and we must lose everything. Only a few will get through, perhaps only one, Jesus himself. He was in no doubt that his message would fall by the wayside, that there would always be those who simply did not hear. Then there are those who hear, but only hear the words and have no understanding and for whom therefore the words and the teaching have no inner authority. These are 'men of the moment' and do not stand fast. Some hear and understand, but are overwhelmed by the everyday business of living and, like the rich man in the parable, have too much to lose, are too tied to life to wish to lose it. There is only the single seed that finds its roots and grows. It is the only measure of a life. By any other measure what we do not have by *this* measure, even that will be taken from us. In the end the choice is a simple all or nothing, the inevitable outcome of the gathering momentum of right and wrong directions, towards God or away from God, away from the inner defilements of 'vile thoughts, fornications, thefts, murders, adulteries, greedy dealings, vices, trickery, laxity, the vicious eye, blasphemy, pride, wildness' towards the holy spirit. The absoluteness of the dichotomy is made clear. Your offences can be forgiven, but what cannot be forgiven is the offence against the spirit, for one is ultimately of no account, and the other is all the accounting there is. Jesus dealt with last things, the ends of earthly powers, intoxicated by the eschatology of a pure heart. After two thousand years of exegesis the essential simplicity of the man has been overlaid by the figurative Christ, a singular subjective imagination reworked as an imaginary system for salvation, the person remoulded as the body, the transformed singularity become the intercessory agent, the subjective returned to the objective, the way to Heaven turned aside from towards the slippery slope to eternity.

God exists as all that is not the objective condition, as the subjective will that makes a bonfire of this vain world, the world that will perish because it *must* perish. God is absolute subjectivity. Released from its objective condition the individual consciousness finds itself again in absolute subjectivity, in the great 'I am', the one who has overcome his demons and his enemies, the free, the undefiled, sitting at the right hand of God, who is himself nothing less than 'pure absolute subjectivity':

Christ is the omnipotence of subjectivity, the heart released from all the bonds and laws of nature... Ludwig Feuerbach, *The Essence of Christianity*

And in the words of the Buddha: 'In this world I have overcome all and am omniscient. I am defiled by nothing. I have abandoned everything. I am delivered. I am the conqueror.'

The significance of myth and religion is to be found amongst the accumulated material of our endeavours to justify our existence by attempting to redeem ourselves from the tragic condition of being. In essence they are about the overthrow of the given, inherited condition of being. In so far as we insist on returning them to the objective, returning myth, God and redemption to the will itself, to the command or grace of the other, to the external, then our imaginative creations serve only ignorance, ignorance of the wellspring of creation and the source of meaning. Religion simply as an aspect of the social order is nothing more than one of the many faces of earthly power, partisan and tribal, ameliorative and compensatory, adaptive to the condition, a manifestation of the will and not its denial. Religion must always be in revolt, and the religious in revolt against their religion. Myth reveals the face of the hero to himself. Religion pits the hero against the whole world and the temptations of his fatefulness so that he may become the eternal subject who determines to stake all on nothing and remake himself in his own image.

V

*If in some manner the voice of an individual reaches us from the
remotest distance of time, it is a timeless voice speaking about
ourselves.* Eric Hoffer, *Reflections on the Human Condition*

We are the created before we are creators, peripheral
before we are allowed to be at the centre, the product of the
will of something other than ourselves before we may become
ourselves, objects before we are subjects under whom the
objective is subsumed as that which is known only to the
subject.

All that is the world is subsumed into all that the subject
knows of the world. The limits of knowledge are set by the
limitations of the instrument of understanding which is not
subject to the individual will but is given as an attribute of the
species for practical living, and whatever facts that instrument
is able to uncover empirically in the exercise of its reason – the
reasoning that relates the order of the objective world to the
subject that perceives it – can only confirm that the order of the
world and the self is the condition given as fact.

The order of the world is whatever the order of the world
is whether we know it or not, but its known order is all that can
exist in experience. The social order in which the subject that
has knowledge of the world expends its life is whatever the social
order is capable of being as a self-sustaining and self-defensive
discrete population existing in its present, past-dependent
era. Knowledge, and the language and cultural conventions in
which that knowledge is expressed and held in common, is the
social capital of the social order and, regardless of how wide
we extend the outer margins of either the concept of society or
the body of accessible knowledge, the scope of the individual's
understanding is limited to the materials available to it. The
understanding can create nothing new from its own resources,

but only rework or rebuild its picture of the self and the world from materials already given. If it will deny what it has inherited from the past and recreate its own present, it can only do so in the face of and with the evidence of what it knows and what it can know. The times can only be addressed on their own terms. We are none of us visitors passing through, carrying a suitcase of eternal truths, but products of our time, absorbed in the present or at odds with it.

It is a mistake to believe that the accumulation of knowledge as social capital represents progress in the social order. The social order simply renews itself under changed circumstances, as organisms themselves do. If we say the social order evolves, it evolves to maintain or regain an equilibrium, as organisms and populations adapting to change and disruption create the diversity of species over time. The social order is the order of diverse populations contending internally and externally with threats to its stability and continuity. It is not a progression, any more than the evolution of species represents the linear progress towards some goal. We should not mistake increased complexity for achievement. The social order simply renews itself, for there is nowhere to progress to, no end to aim for, no escape from factory conditions by progressively improving them. Man is not evolving towards perfection, and society is not progressing towards universal peace and harmony. We are each born into the given condition and bound by its terms of engagement. We cannot save ourselves within it, we can only make use of the materials at hand to recreate, again and again, the inviolable transcendent subject dressed in the fashion of the day.

Every generation feels slightly superior to the previous one, if for no other or better reason than having left it behind. They are the past and we are the present, a step ahead of them (rather than, as the Greeks perceived time, following on their heels behind them towards the past). The past becomes something we own in the present, and that only in parts and fragments, since all that remains of it is whatever view of it we are able to possess. We may inherit the accumulated knowledge of the past but we do not acquire its experience. Who now knows the mind that built the pyramids, that hauled stones to Stonehenge, that painted in the dark in the Lascaux caves, and who has the public mind of Socrates or the faith that was Cranmer's? In any case, for the most part knowledge just lies around to be picked over and used to serve an immediate purpose. The present doesn't recapitulate the whole of the past before it decides to act in its present interests. Politicians and generals make the same mistakes they have always made. Superior technology serves the same practical and convenient ends as its primitive precursors, and the wisdom of the ages offers no restraint to the motivations of self-interest and the pursuit of power. The light that falls in the present has no more power of illumination than the light that fell in the past. It only seems so, because it shines on us, as it might seem to the clown in the spotlight at the circus, at the centre of attention for the moment. Conditions, historically, are changed, but we know them in the same way.

The light of the present is sufficient to each generation. The people who dwell in darkness are always other people, alien people, people of the past. But the dark ages were filled with light and men of the Enlightenment were yet to discover their errors, and we, who live at the end of time and must therefore know most, make ciphers of history and do nothing more with our knowledge than we did formerly with the arts we have now lost. The social order and the knowledge, culture, arts, sciences, beliefs, institutions and laws that are its accumulated social capital, serve only to preserve and promote the social order itself and the self-interest of populations at the expense of other groups who have their own territorial imperative to possess the present. The individual's will to live and will to power work within and against the self-organised will of the whole. In victory or defeat, the individual will can succeed in nothing more than bringing about a minor adjustment to the social order, to the body politic and, at most, shift the basis of its power, influence and self-interest from one foot to another. The *sort* of knowledge one possesses makes no difference, since knowledge is always sufficient to its time. Since there is nothing else to go on except what we know, only by drawing on that knowledge, on the available social and cultural capital, can the individual give expression to the insufficiency of what he has inherited from the past and find the terms in which the autonomy of individual subjectivity can be realised. It is an error, therefore, of both understanding and sympathy, to dismiss historical expressions of subjective autonomy as episodic, mere products of the ignorance of the time or the limitations of its understanding, and to deny the universality and continuity of subjective experience. The only freedom we have is the freedom to rediscover ourselves in the social order as the subjects, and not as the objects of history. History is neither cyclical nor progressive. It is simply repetitive, as life is repetitive, as seasons are, as the motivations of people and societies are. It is not the past that repeats itself, but the present.

The only way to understand the past is on its own terms, and not as a number of stations along the line to the present, put back in their place, as it were, as stages in becoming ourselves. Seen on its own terms, the past can be understood as a continuous narrative in which subjective consciousness continually reasserts itself as the absolute arbiter of the historical and determined present condition of being. What is given is given, and what is given is always the same, that is to say, the condition of being. What difference does it make that populations have a history? They are not going anywhere. They are not moving out, or moving in any particular direction, only jostling to be here, having emerged out of nothingness by the command or demand of the species, with only nothingness to look forward to. I open my eyes to circumstances that are a little changed from what they were, but I am not to know that, for my objective condition is the same, and the struggle to assert the primacy of the subjective over the objective is the same, whatever the times, from a later perspective, appear to portend.

All societies constrain the subjective interpretation of the ways in which the world can be understood. Each individual mind is born into a state of affairs not of its own making. It is immediately conditioned by the prevailing social order and the political and economic circumstances in which it finds itself as the embryo become aware of its subordination to family, society and state. It grows up within a belief system – moral, supernatural, or merely practical and useful. And its understanding is determined by the limits of reason – its own, its mental capacity, and whatever access it may have to knowledge, to both reason and unreason in the world. It has nothing else to work with, nothing it brings with it but promise and propensity, only what it can discover in the present and what it can retrieve from the past as it is represented in the present. It has nothing on which to base its efforts at self-realisation and self-determination but the awareness of its condition and its understanding of the state of affairs.

Whether or not the state of affairs is more or less enlightened from the perspective of another prevailing state of affairs is neither here nor there, and nothing can be done about it. It is hardly likely that the present moment, at the end of time for the time being, that has forgotten so much, is the flower for which the past has been mulched and composted. There never was a past.

Whatever the state of affairs, the situation of the individual is consistently the same in relation to his condition. He can, and inevitably will, accommodate himself to the social order that is given, to a role and a station in life. Even in revolt against the social order, he is a revolutionary in name only, for he is merely caught up in that order, and turning the social order upside down does not abolish it but only brings about another state of affairs to which he must accommodate himself, and in which he suffers the consequences of his actions. No course of action can undo his existential condition, and restructuring the order of the world that inevitably continues to bring about the condition of his birth and death only changes the contingent circumstances and not the facts of the matter.

This is the final dichotomy of being: I am either an object in an objective world, whose subjectivity is objectively given as the mechanism by which the self as object constructs the egocentric power base for its actions; or I am the subject, for whom the objective world, the social order, the past and the present, reason, knowledge, understanding and the fact of being are justified by my creative vision whose materials of construction these are, and by nothing else. The true revolutionary mind seeks only to escape its slavery to the objective world, seeks the freedom of absolute subjectivity. For the true revolutionary, the mind is not the slave of the world, but the world itself.

VI

And they should have begun with metaphysics, which seeks its proofs not in the external world but within the modifications of the mind of him who meditates it. Giambattista Vico, *The New Science*

What is that unreal and immaterial thing we have called the soul? That thing that is impossible and cannot be because it can't be found, as God and beauty, truth and justice can't be found but only construed from the heartless and meaningless elements which are all that can be found in the objective world? What else is the soul but the subjective mind freed from its condition?

In the West, for two thousand years the grammar of meaning has been construed from the theology of God and Christ. Outside the language of Christianity we have had only godlessness and the indecipherable blanks of the natural world and natural philosophy that can never reveal to us anything beyond what is, and what is is the fact of the matter, and the fact of the matter is always what we had already known it to be, the fact of the condition that is given.

What is given is given as fact. To uncover more facts about the given is only to understand more clearly that nothing else is to be discovered in the objective state of affairs but what is already given. By mining ever deeper into the facts of the matter to establish the '*certum*' of the world, we do not thereby reach the wellspring of the '*verum*', the truth of the matter that belongs exclusively to the subjective self and its fictions – its fictions of science and art, mathematics, reason, creativity and imagination. We only bring to the surface the material of the given. What is not given, all that is not the condition but all that is made from and made of the objective world, is not the dependency of the given (that is, 'nothing but' the material world translated into its phenomenal form) but itself determines what will become of – what, indeed, will be made of – the world that itself is entirely dependent on its *a priori* representation as the matter of mind grounded in subjective being.

The mind, being at once both the instrument of the organic unit of life and therefore inseparably a phenomenon of the objective and given world, and the subjective will to which all that is objective is subordinated, finds itself at one moment absorbed in the world, the world of doing and getting, the world of labour and relief from labour, the world of struggle, suffering, ambition – and the next moment, whether by reflection, imagination, revelation or disillusionment with all that had previously occupied it and absorbed its attention, suddenly become aware of its tragic situation and the futility of the mere animal, social and egoistical striving after *more of the same*. Whatever value life may have in the here and now, it is not to be found in the here and now of one's objective condition but in the subjective sense of both being in the world and being in possession of one's own soul. For the most part we oscillate between the two states of being, at worst blindly subservient to the will that manifests itself as ego, and at best subjugating the urges of self-interest to the tragic sense of life and the rescuing power of imagination and creativity. We recognise, in this blessed state, the truth of the words of Alexander Herzen:

> Art, and the summer lightning of individual happiness: these are the only real goods we have.

In reality, the choice between being the subject and being the object equipped with the illusion of self-determination, between the soul and the self, between God as absolute subjectivity and the world as absolutely unknowable, between heaven and earth, Nirvana and Samsara, is an either/or dichotomy. Few have ever been able to make that choice, resolutely and permanently, to give up the given in exchange for the created. You can't devote yourself to God and give up the world but, like Augustine, say to oneself, 'not yet.' You can't be half in and half out of illusion. You can't be an occasional mendicant or part-time Son of God or weekend prophet, or too sick or exhausted to be God's minister as though it were merely a choice of career. You can't come and go between man's need for redemption and the needs of the poor for better social housing like some latter day Archbishop of Canterbury trading in the difficulties of faith for liberal platitudes. To become as Christ, to become a Bodhisattva, are tasks hard to achieve and hard even to understand. There are immense difficulties involved in finding a firm foothold in order to take the first step, in knowing which direction to go in, in recognising the beginning of the journey in the condition to which we are subjected that will prompt us to look up from it.

A personal realisation does not immediately translate into a shared experience, let alone a revolution of the mind and spirit of an entire people. It is hard. It is hard to travel alone and to suffer the collision of an inner understanding with the world's will. It has to be enough for the moment that 'those are for us who are not against us', enough that the world learn to be charitable to those not of this world, enough for men to repeat a good word rather than a bad, and little by little open up the possibility that each might discover the power to recover from the endlessly recurring contingency of experience the continuity outside time of eternal and eternally subjective truths.

Only the singular subjective vision is capable of redeeming the individual from the mass, for whom the individual is the means and not the end, to become the end for which societies and civilisations are simply the means. Only madmen set out to redeem whole populations or save the world. Revolution belongs to the mass. Revelation is the province of a single mind. Christ never proposed to save mankind, only to heal the sick soul. Marilynne Robinson suggests the Greek word *sozo*, usually translated as 'saved', means 'healed' or 'restored', and that makes all the difference. Christ's healing ministry, and its extrapolation in retelling into stories of miracles, is about restoring the divided, broken soul, not to be saved from sin (for sinners, outsiders, are already closer to God) but rescued from error, released from the rule of the will and returned to life with God as the eternal subject. The Buddha's teaching, like Christ's, was for those who had ears to hear. There is no other way to enlightenment than the diligence of the soul in the achievement of its own insight.

And we should remind ourselves that God did not create Man, but a man, Adam, one man, as Traherne says, 'one alone to be the end of the world and its heir.'

If the business of the artist is to make something out of nothing, as Paul Valery proposed, then our mythologies, epics and religions are our first great artistic creations. Wherever we look in our own history our achievements have always been the things we have made to substantiate our existence, what we have created that has allowed us to translate emptiness and nothingness into a worthwhile enterprise that satisfies our subjective sense of aesthetic order that in the end is the only formal means of meaningful judgment available to us.

From the beginning the light itself has been enough, the light that alternates with its absence, the somethingness of consciousness arising from the nothingness of non-being, darkness made visible. That I should be the heir of the world that does not know itself except as it reveals itself to my individual mind is the world's original miraculous sufficiency.

> The ring enclosing all
> That stood upon this earthly ball;
> The heavenly eye,
> Much wider than the sky... Thomas Traherne

We celebrate the light and invoke it in darkness. By rushlight we have daubed ochre on walls in the recesses of the earth that mimic the unconscious regions of the mind, that we might not take for granted the world that is blind to its incarnation but continually restate our relationship to it and our responsibility for it. We are the source of its illumination as much as the sun is ours. And are there not tribes who, living in the mountains high above the world, are the first to see the sun and by invoking it each morning make themselves responsible for the light of the world? We engineer the cycle of the seasons with ritual invocations, sacrifices and sonnets. We have stepped up towards the light by creating great monumental public works that do not serve a public but rescue only a singularity, a shining pyramid where the eye of one all-seeing soul might live for ever and never depart from the all-seeing eye of the sun. We have built cathedrals so that a single soul's aspiration may be fulfilled: to be known by God for all that the soul itself knows of God.

There is no vision, no experience, that is not the sole prerogative of my subjective consciousness. Why then shouldn't the subject be elevated to the status of the creator of all this, for the objective is forever the uncreated unless it is seen by the eye and touched by the hand in the act of creation? The objective world is material unreality made real only by the subjective mind that is its formal creator, which alone is able to make something out of nothing, to transpose an eternity of emptiness into the tragic dimensions of time and space.

Science will argue that the relentless rational and theoretical pursuit of the objective, the objective truth, promises a sort of universal enlightenment that will level the cultural limitations of subjective forms of understanding. Little by little we will break free of local and tribal criteria for right judgment and adopt universal measures of objective truth. Science defines for us the new global culture of technology-based economies and a rational world-view. As a social enterprise, the promotion of the scientific method and mathematics to the supreme measure of objective truth is mankind's greatest cultural achievement. But it will always remain a *culture* of truth, a formal, rational, explanatory framework that insists that rationally arrived at explanations are, at least provisionally, 'truths' that can only be supplanted by better worked-out rational principles. But 'reasons are only reasons, they are not truths,' as Miguel de

Unamuno says.

Truths are always subjective, *'verum'* not *'certum'*. The two don't meld. A culture is defined by its cumulative self-interest. No group, tribe or population sharing a particular world-view sees itself as mired in ignorance awaiting enlightenment from outside. Its belief system is the material of its social cohesion. An individual may grasp the promise held out to him by an alien culture and a wider education, for it is the prerogative of the individual mind to make itself up from the material to hand. But cultures themselves are defined by their limitations and the constraints placed on the exercise of the individual will. Only the individual subjective mind has the capacity for enlightenment, self-examination and self-understanding. It is the function of society to limit the scope for individual self-assertion for the sake of the self-interests of the whole. Rationalism serves the ends of an open society so long as it fulfils its rational purposes. But closed societies are impervious to reasons that do not serve the principles upon which its own forms of social coherence are founded. And under stress even the most open and democratic forms of social order will subvert the freedom of the individual will to the will of a newly discerned collective purpose in defence of that freedom. The freedom of societies and the freedom of the individual have to be separately defined and are never fully reconcilable. In a rational society, science is the new priesthood. Outside the practical, technical, medical and cumulatively beneficial applications of science, at a theoretical level science is already well beyond the comprehension of the average citizen, who calls himself a 'layman' in deference to the new church. Or, put another way, the discoveries of science lack 'stickiness' – that is, they are recognised and understood to a degree, as 'information' or 'information about', but they are not fully able to supplant either our own more intuitive ways of thinking about our connectedness to the world of our self-interests, or our long since embedded need for meaning or, at least, our need for consolation.

First, no one can absorb more information than the short span of life permits, and second, the quantity and effortless ease of reception mean stupidities multiply incomparably faster than the fruits of thought that are hidden deep in the jumble of information. Anita Albus, *The Art of Arts*

The priesthood of science explicates the true nature of the universe and its operation, and explains the origins of life and attempts to explain the working of the brain, but, unlike the priests who were the interpreters of the mysteries of the universe that were working to some purpose for man at its centre – man's self-conscious need for immortality and redemption – the truth that the priesthood of science reveals is not a saving truth. It is only the truth of the nature of the unmovable and impervious seam of the given condition – reality more accurately described and its causes more rigorously analysed – that we have known all along in a more general way to be the facts in the case: there is no objective reason for being, only a subjective awareness of being that continues to raise the same unanswerable questions about itself. Science fails to establish 'truth' because all it can do is describe the truth of what are already established as the facts in the case. Surprising as it may seem to those who practise it, the work of science is as much a creative and imaginative activity of the subjective mind as any other art by which we make something out of nothing. By elaborating the objective description of the world that is known to us we are making, with the toolkit of the *a priori* categories of the understanding, an understandable phenomenal world that will conform to the measures of our understanding.

That the world should have fundamental principles by which it can be understood is as strange as (and no stranger than) the fact that it should be understandable at all. We argue that the parameters of the universe are finely tuned to allow both the existence of stars and the fundamental conditions under which it has been possible for life to arise from the concatenation of its material elements. For such an improbable set of conditions to be possible, we are forced to conclude the existence of multiple universes of equal improbability in order to make this one possible. While we may speculate that an infinity of universes is both possible and probable, we can never discover if it is so, for the really inescapable improbability of the universe is that it should be modelled on the principles of our understanding and not be entirely and wholly unknowable. Only by defining the universe as something knowable have we created one thing out of many. A multiplicity of unknowable universes is probable simply because the fundamental principles of this one are inevitably modelled on the fundamental principles of the understanding, and all that is unknown to the understanding remains infinitely unknowable. It is the finitude of our understanding that locks out the infinity of the unknown.

Science does not uncover the truth of the world, the 'verum', but its 'certum'. Truth is not what we discover but what we make. Thus science, in the pursuit of the objective, in fact serves to provide a secular revelation for one age that faith in a world made for man served for another, for the subject remains at the centre and all the wonders of the world, whether made by God or arising out of nothing of their own accord, are known only to the subjective mind, the 'ring enclosing all'. The only value the world possesses or can possess lies in our knowledge of it.

Art is the subjective recreation of the objective world on our own terms. By declaring the objective world understandable we are implicitly acting in the role of artist by asserting the supremacy of subjective knowledge as the sole judge of the nature of the objective. Science is also art. Copernicus did not remove man from the centre of the universe. Rather, by handing over the final responsibility for the nature of the universe to the intellect, he put man's understanding of it at its heart.

Before Copernicus, man was not the centre of the world; after Copernicus he was. T E Hulme, *Speculations*

Whether it declares itself for science or for art, the creative mind remains subject to the social and cultural constraints that permit it. It does not and cannot reign supreme in society, for the social organisation belongs to the objective – the subjective is the province of the individual mind only. Science is frustrated in bringing about universal enlightenment, the end of false dogmas, irrational principles and superstitious links between effects and their causes, as much as religion has been frustrated in its attempts to establish a heavenly kingdom on earth and as much as art itself has failed to lead the world towards the transfiguration of man into artist/creator as his natural destiny. The social order does not refer to the subjective vision of its component parts, but blindly and implacably pursues its self-renewal against all obstacles.

VII

...this imminence of a revelation that does not occur is, perhaps, the aesthetic phenomenon. Jorge Luis Borges, *The Wall and the Books*

The triumph of art is in having succeeded both mythology and religion as the cultural expression of man's consciousness of his tragic being. Its failure is shared with the failure of myth and religion to overcome the implacable will of the objective, and the end of hope that the expression of the creative will of the individual will initiate a new collective vision, a reason for being, that will release us from our egocentric obsession with merely practical reason and elect in its stead our dreams of being other.

Somewhere along the trajectory between Blake and Apollinaire, between Nietzsche and Berdyaev, between Beethoven and Wagner and Wagner and Scriabin, there took hold in our minds the fervid idea of the possibility of a self-transfiguration through art that at its apogee would have the power to once and for all free us from our fate as the victims of creation and the objects of elemental forces outside ourselves to become the artist-heroes of life and the creators of our own destiny. In 1810 Bettina Brentano wrote to Goethe of Beethoven that when his spirit reaches its highest perfection 'he will leave us the key to a heavenly revelation, which will bring us one stage nearer to true bliss'. To be an artist is to be always at the point of revealing what neither God nor alchemist, scientist nor professor of philosophy, astronomer nor theologian had ever been able to reveal: the true purpose of creation and being. It has been the triumph of art in the nineteenth and early twentieth centuries to have shown the people the promised land shaped by the creator's vision. Its failure is never having been able to cross over from the diurnal to the eternal, from earth to heaven, from death to Valhalla. To borrow the words from Dostoevsky that serve every revolutionary and transcendent ideal, political, social or creative, the vision of art is 'directed towards the future, towards eternal ends and absolute joy'. The nature of art is to promise what it cannot fulfil, because it is the promise that makes it art. To be finished, concluded – what is the point of that? We were *always* finished.

Ultimately art fails in its works to objectify what must and always will remain subjective acts of imagination that alone are capable of transcending experience. By sacrificing life to art we discover, as in Balzac's canvas of the 'unknown masterpiece', that there is nothing in what we have created but the imagination, and life in its inapprehensible beauty stands weeping at its loss to art and the artist. In the dominion of art, the image of life is consumed, evaporates, disappears to reappear only as another 'oval portrait', a substitute for life and not the apotheosis of life.

The promise and the failure of art have left their mark on those of us born too late to be the makers of the revolution in the realisation, like those failed millenarian cults of the final days, that the future lies in the past as a moment in history, that art is finished, along with the heroic epic, sainthood and martyrdom, that the revelation will not come. 'But what else is there?' asked Weldon Kees. As always, we are alone. We have only the material of the self, of the eternal subject, to be the work itself. One's own life must be one's art. The eschatology of art is a return to life. To be modern is to see ourselves in the mirror of the past and find ourselves wanting, wanting in everything but the self-knowledge that prevents us from forming a naive hope of rebirth. We are neither mediaeval nor renaissance men, but men of the moment, 'spectators of ourselves' and our past.

> As art sinks into paralysis, artists multiply. This anomaly ceases to be one if we realise that art, on its way to exhaustion, has become both impossible and easy. E M Cioran, *The Trouble with Being Born*

The sudden acceleration of creativity whose beginnings coincided with the French Revolution, is the revolution that failed. The rush towards self-revelation and the triumph of subjectivity ended where it must end – in the return to life and the end of art. Once awakened to the consciousness of its own power, art would never be able to recover its unselfconscious naivety and innocence, or return to what Goethe called the 'somnambulism' of creativity, of means without ends. It is awake and aware, and it celebrates its newfound consciousness of power to reveal itself in the forms of its art until those forms are exhausted. And then all that remains to it is the realisation that art can only return to life, to life that, seen merely as 'a happy episode' relegated to the material of art, had been subordinated to the will of the artist, 'thrown away', as Rubek declares in the closing moments of Ibsen's last play, until 'we dead awake' and 'we see that we have never lived'. For to do otherwise, to persist in a lost cause, is to attempt to make an epic out of exhaustion that has for its theme one's own self-consciousness of the failure of art itself.

To be modern is to be self-conscious of the artifice of art, to have lost the essential naivety of the artist able to seize on the next form of his art and instead become capable only of referring to the *last* form available to it, that last form being nothing less, of course, than the form of the dissolution of its past. *The Bridge* was an attempt to make an epic from the modern, *The Waste Land* to make exhaustion itself the new epic theme of modernism, and the *Cantos* to co-opt the memory of the cultural past to become the material of the cerebral present. The artist is left with only one thing to discover – that he is trapped in the circularity of his self-consciousness as an artist: Eliot in poetry, Becket in the novel, Duchamp in art, Webern in music, where the emptiness of expression has become the only genuine form of his despair. Thus art, since the end of art, is a footnote to all that preceded it. We are impersonators, imitators and reproducers, spectators, critics and commentators, or charlatans too afraid to admit the loss of power the past had promised us. We are all, in the bitterness of our disappointment, nostalgic for the future.

Art is the revolution that failed, as all revolutions do. In the political and social sphere, revolutions only bring about changes in the structure of the order of power. The underlying state of order itself, as order, is unchanged. Revolutions in consciousness must end where they began, with the individual subject and the material of its self-realisation, bereft of the possibility of transforming anything other than itself and adrift in its own company. We who know too much, but yet do not know ourselves, must make up ourselves in the present from the material of past times. We have no other authority to go on but the authority of the past and the irreducible certainty of our subjectivity.

It is characteristic of the brain-fever of the visionary artist or philosopher – such a one as Nietzsche – that what is thought and what is conceived in the mind should at once become possible and allow him to describe the world in the language, colours and shapes of his imagination. Once he has envisioned the transformation of the self that casts off the notion of an *a priori* moral order and embraces the purely aesthetic foundation of life, that rejects nature and remakes his nature in his own image, that sublimates the will to his own will and rises above it, then he may come to believe in the possibility of the transmutation of the whole world into its newly discovered ideality. In reality, the visionary is a dangerous lunatic and the natural order of the world and the moral order of the world and the objective will of the world ensure that his transformational vision remains locked in his head as surely as a madman was locked up in Bedlam. An idea is only useful if it can be subpoenaed by its enemies to serve the original causes of the will and its power. There is only one will, not two.

The world is what it is, and it goes on for ever in its relentless course as though it had a duty to ignore the wishes and dreams and visions that belong to thought, to trample on the fantasies and illusions of the febrile brain, deaf to the anomalous musical phrases in which the individual will expresses its contempt for the world that is not of its own making: deaf because it has no reciprocal interest in what it has unknowingly and unwittingly made.

The apocalyptic vision of art in which the power of the objective will, the will of the gods, is ceded to the subjective will, the will of the artist/creator who alone has the power to be in love with his own creation, who alone can make something in his own image capable of reciprocating his thoughts, perhaps reached its highest point in the closing drama of Wagner's *Ring* cycle. In music, which has no other terms of reference than itself, we find the reciprocation of meaning that we had hoped to find in the order of the world itself. Each time we rediscover that we ourselves are that order, we free ourselves from the manacles of labour and life as if by a magic spell. If the essence of the Wagnerian drama is the triumph of love over power, it is also, beneath that, a conflict between art and industrialisation, between the artist/hero and the forces that would keep him at work in the dark underground workshops forging the chains of his own enslavement. That surge, in the nineteenth century, towards a final transfiguration of art into life, of artist into hero, one that allowed Nietzsche to conceive of a civilisation led by the 'artist-tyrant', was propelled by its antithesis – the rise of industrial mass production and the threat of the perpetual enslavement of the soul of *homo economicus* to the power of capital. If Siegfried is the new hero of a new philosophy of art, the triumph of love and the aesthetic over power and the will of the gods, he must, like all heroes, fail at the point of his triumph. That is what the heroic is – to be, in spite of one's fate: to be that which has arisen out of the objective will, the will epitomised in the drama by the twilight of the gods whose will this is, to become one who is undaunted by fate because his destiny has been decided by his own creative will to raise love and the love of his own epic adventure in life above the fear that keeps all men enthralled to power. The hero's act of transcendence gives the world another chance. That is what our heritage of mythology, religion and art offers us: a history of failed attempts to redeem the world from the objective and the will to power from which we may recover the materials of self-renewal. Thus we are never without heroes, nor without hope.

It was Kafka, not Nietzsche, who understood the true position of the artist in society, the artist as outsider and underling and not as the prophet of the 'art of the future', as social revolution. As an individual, as a *person*, the artist is also a member of society and enjoys its protection, where, like a boisterous child, his excesses of rebellion are indulged and even, in times of crisis and self-doubt, looked to in order to refresh and recreate a spirit for the times. For the artist, too, there can be no art without society. The artist's terms of reference are always those given by and permitted by society – whether literature, painting, sculpture, opera, theatre, film or philosophy. Art needs an audience, even if only so that art can affront it. But the artist does not *count*. The aberrations of the individual will and its expression that are central to the artist are merely peripheral to society as a whole.

The artist and society are complicit. A society that naturally looks out for the interests of the individual in society, the worker, tolerates the artist so long as the artist reflects its own idea of itself. The artist may cling to his integrity as an artist, but it makes no difference – he is soon forgotten. The appropriation by society of the artist's works is its way of forgetting the artist himself.

The artist can't simply live, live as other men live for the sake of life itself, because he cannot abandon his post in order to eat and drink at the same table as others, to share the sources of nourishment that are not nourishment at all to him. So he must do without because he can't find in society what he needs. 'If I had found it,' says Kafka's fasting artist in the story, 'I would have eaten my fill like everyone else.' By his refusal he becomes the neglected, the abandoned, the unaccounted for, the disappeared.

What in general terms we refer to as 'culture' is an aspect

of social organisation. The culture of the times, more properly defined, is less the cumulative catalogue of its arts and artefacts than the totality of what the prevailing social order allows to run counter to its instincts for order and self-preservation. The culture of any society is defined by how it has accommodated all the expressions of its own insufficiency to provide any other idea of order than the social, the political, the economic. Culture in society has a similar function to the fool and jester at the courts of kings – to remind us of the essentially tragic nature of life, ambition and power, and in its stories, songs, tragedies, comedies, contradictions, affronts and ironies reduce power to hubris, and then to find itself dismissed as incidental and inessential to all that is necessary and inevitable in spite of it.

The elements of culture are the creations of individuals working within the limitations of the forms already permitted – the theatre, the symphony, the canvas, the 35mm film camera. The social order itself, and the social groups that jostle to assert their own interests within the larger social order, define its culture. No individual can be responsible for that culture. If culture in essence runs counter to the objective condition of the social order as the self-organised self-perpetuation of order, it is also, like happiness, its parallel compensation. Thus the forms of entertainment and amusement are as much the defining culture of a society as its inherited expressions of the dissension from it of the individual subjective will. The Wagnerian drama is epochal and transfiguring only as drama, as dramatic possibility. Because it could *only* exist in a permitted social context, whatever boundaries it seemed to expand beyond were imagined ones. There had to be a political, a social, a *bourgeois* element of self-reflection in which the composer and the audience were complicit.

The genius of Wagner's music, removed from the world, overcomes the world of mere existence that cannot contain it, yet, in order to be, it must be worldly, attached to the paraphernalia of performance, financial support, social compliance – it must acquire a social, political and economic dimension removed from 'art' and belonging to 'culture', a culture that is determined by the work's audience and not by its creator, who is complicit, by the need for performance – the need to be seen and heard – in the sublimation and objectification of the genius of one into the self-reflection of the many. No one attended the first performance at Bayreuth in order to accomplish the transfiguration of the self. If any such transformation took place in the hearts and souls of its audience, it would have taken on the form of a dreamlike reverie, and dreams, as we know, we keep to ourselves as not fit subjects for conversation and by no means the basis for some other revolutionary form of social cohesion. The 'spirit' of performance is social, national, racial, political, self-serving, self-fulfilling, self-regarding – revolutionary, perhaps, in its conception, but not liberating except for one who through art can become also an artist. The artist cannot live without the socialisation of his art, whose forms are social, recognised and permitted by society as a whole, or at least by one or another dominant class or faction of society.

The forms of art become the forms of power. They become adjuncts and accessories to personal and class self-interest. Art and its artefacts are expressions of an elite, the adornment and self-aggrandisement of power, the very stuff of theoretical evolutionary sociobiology – art as peacock feathers, as worldly goods, as *Rheingold*, the work not of the recreated self but the possessions of the rampant ego and its power.

Art succeeds as entertainment and as cultural possession, and *fails* as art. Art must always fail, for that is its essence – to be all that society cannot be, for art is life given up entirely to the unnecessary and the impossible.

Society can never give up life. But nor, since it is made up of self-conscious beings whose sense of self mediates all that the world is or appears to be, can it revert to a state of unreflecting self-interest. Its self-consciousness ensures a perpetual awareness of the insufficiency of the means of production, through nothing more than the continuous grinding of the machinery of work interrupted by periods of leisure, to ever satisfy ends that are greater than its work is capable of producing. Society always embodies somewhere within it the evidence of its own futility, but it will never embrace it or admit it, for that would signal its demise. Society tolerates the sense of tragedy that is bound up in the human condition, but society itself never becomes tragic. Society can have no destiny in which man himself will be transfigured. It can never be more than a battlefield or a playground in which the individual may both lose his soul and find it again.

VIII

Only as an aesthetic phenomenon can life and the world be justified eternally. Friedrich Nietzsche, *The Birth of Tragedy*

The subjective awareness of being is untranslatable. We are like islands, but islands in a vast archipelago where each rises above that flat, desolate, unbelonging, indifferent and mindless ocean of objective existence. Looking out over it, we recognise each other. Linked at the deepest geological level we share also an underground existence as ancient as the world itself. The unrelentingly flat, horizonless and, we must admit, uninhabitable and eternally unknowable world-in-itself of the objective, can never on its own account offer up the least justification for being. Society, equally, looks after its own. It nurtures the individual in so far as the individual is an essential component in the machinery of the whole, but it does not exist *in order* to nurture the individual and set him free of his obligations as a social being for the sake of all that really matters to him – the realisation of the self as observer, creator and mediator of the experience of being.

What brings us together *in spite of* society, what draws together these isolated souls that do not know the meaning of time, is the transcendent awareness of tragic being that is the sole possession of the subject that has arisen from the endlessly rocking cradle of a self-sufficient universe to become the form of its own sufficiency. In coming into possession of one's own sufficiency, all that exists is owed to the creative power of the one who knows that it is so. Thus creative power alone, the institution of the world as an aesthetic phenomenon, can be said to justify being. All other forms of power belong to the objective will that manifests itself as the self-interest of the ego and the collective interests of the social order.

Let there be no doubt: the mind is the object of the will, the representation of the world as the object of interest extended in time and space and causally connected to the interests of the self that is also the representative object of the will. Organically, the essence of mind lies in its instrumentality, and the symbolic representation of self and other only incidentally creates the consciousness of a seamlessly woven reality as the formal representation of coherent experience. None of this can be said to have any value simply as the instrument of the perpetual striving of the will to be – for no reason and possessing no *intrinsic* value. There can be no values except those the subjective sense of being creates that have value for the subject but have no absolute or intrinsic value for the will. Thus the essence of mind – *essential* mind – is without value, is only instrumental and operational, and what is incidental and *inessential* – since the aesthetic phenomenon of reality is only the *field* in which the essential mind operates – is the totality of the value of being. We can never find any value in the objective fact of existence, only mistake the fulfilment of self-interest for purpose. Until we wake up to the futility of the objective and the mind's complicity with it and discover ourselves as subject for whom the objective is only the material of self-realisation, we do not know what it means to 'be' – we only know what it is to be born into the condition of being.

We are divided between the essential and the inessential, between what has been made and what we ourselves are free to make, between the fear of freedom and the freedom to be tragic. On one side is quotidian necessity, labour, breeding, economics, power, wealth, striving, conflict, wars, nations, tribes, groups, the cult of the personality and its possessions. In this catalogue we can include the beliefs and moral principles given as the causes of and the justifications for individual and group behaviour. On the other side of the divide is simply the singularity of the self as the subject of its own experience and the imaginative creator of all values.

The task of the artist is to become himself, thus in the end there can be no difference between art and life, between the creation of representative fictions and the representation of life as the creation of the subject of experience. The conclusion that life is justified on aesthetic grounds alone arises inevitably once it is understood that all experience takes place in appearance – and that nothing whatever related to experience happens in non-appearance and the world folded in on itself.

The intractability of the objective does not give ground by lending itself to representation as phenomenon, any more than the 'real' world surrenders its essence to a painting of it. Nor will it give way to reason since its rational nature is not implicit, only discoverable in reason itself as a phenomenon of mind and causality. Even the most accurate and reasoned description of the objective, arrived at empirically, experimentally, inductively, is presented aesthetically as *order*, and only understood *as* order. The truth of any matter is not able to present itself directly to us as true. What is true is the order the mind finds in the world, and whatever satisfies the mind's idea of order satisfies its idea of the true.

In so far as we are concerned with human motivation and the interest the mind takes in the condition of being it is heir to, one idea of order can't be more true than another idea of order, only more prevalent. This may be anathema to science, but so is apostasy to the true believer.

The problem for science is that so long as it believes it is dealing with objective reality it will go on clarifying the facts of the contingency of being and assigning absolute value to the emerging ideas of order. In doing so it consigns other ideas of order to oblivion as delusions fashioned from fear of oblivion itself. Yet there are no ideas of order that are not solely aesthetic sufficiencies that have no absolute bearing on the world itself. Science, too, needs the courage of its convictions to face up to a universe devoid of meaning in which its ideas of order, too, are not truths but the aesthetically sufficient forms of its understanding.

The apparent choice between meaninglessness and some fabricated superstition (or, worse, that in the absence of meaning we must 'create our own values' through work, love, family, social institutions etc, as if these weren't also merely objective facts of the condition of being and *compensations* for being) is false. To have discovered the idea of order in appearance is the only possible justification for having also discovered the absence of any possibility of absolute objective order that would justify being. I am, because I am the subject. My understanding rescues me from the abyss of the objective and subjugates the objective to my knowledge of it. My knowledge is subjective. It belongs to me as the subject (as omniscience belongs to God). What I know and the order created by my understanding is the entirety of what the world is, not as object and thing-in-itself, but as my domain of order, understanding, recognition and, if I wish, since it lies within the power of my will, celebration – the celebration of the creative order of being that is blind to itself but is visible to me. There is only an apparent choice, a false contradiction, for knowledge itself is creative and not objectively given, and what it creates is neither moral in revealing the purpose of our actions in the action of the will, nor certain in revealing the nature of things objectively without reference to our knowledge of things subjectively in representation. It reveals the world as something worthy of being known to the subject (as the created world was found to be good by its omniscient creator) in its appearance as an aesthetic phenomenon. Neither science nor God explains the world. Only as an aesthetic phenomenon can the world contain both God and science, ourselves and our explanations, our satisfactions and dissatisfactions, our beliefs, certainties and illusions.

If life has a moral order in which our thoughts and actions have purpose and meaning, its moral order must proceed from its aesthetic order. Life must be worthwhile as a matter of perception and experience first, before we begin to hunt around for causes outside our perceptions that justify our being on any other grounds than the received fact of life and the world as an aesthetic phenomenon subject to the understanding. We must always begin with experience. To begin anywhere else is to presume that reason is embedded in the world as its own undiscovered reason for being and that that same reason for being is ultimately comprehensible to us because we are endowed, *a priori*, with a moral sense of its fitness. We can say that life has organised itself purposively from the moment it emerged in the form of self-sustaining organisms if we define purpose as the sequential and consequential actions of organisms leading to the self-organised complexity of the biosphere. The rules of behaviour that constrain what any individual organism is able to do operated before, and are able to operate without, any notes of sentiment attached to them as a result of the emergence of late onset self-consciousness in one higher primate species. How we ourselves behave is governed by rules established from the consequences of behaviour, whether that be moral in the sense of conscious choice and judgment or entirely amoral, fixed and determined by genes and gene expression in the organism. There is no intrinsically moral dimension to the rules of behaviour, only a consequential dimension for the fitness of the organism, the sustainability of populations and the resilience of the social organisation.

If the task of the subjective mind is to liberate itself from all that binds it to the objective as *will* by denying the will and creating for itself its own domain of aesthetic sufficiency, it must also free itself from the objective moral order of the will in so far as that order belongs to the same order of rules for the mindless self-organising processes of continuity and nothing else. If moral order is nothing more than what has arisen out of self-interest – the self-interest of the individual and the self-interest of the social order in the guise of absolute moral values – then that sort of moral order, too, is something to be overcome. Moral order can have no legitimacy for the subject unless the sufficiency of subjective aesthetic order contain within it all moral values.

One can exist willy-nilly, but to *be* is to be only on the basis of the aesthetic order of being. To be is to know, and to know nothing is to be nothing. One can be without acting. The only act that relates to pure being is the act of comprehending the aesthetic order of being by which we know that we exist. Thus the only value attached to being is its aesthetic value as the sum of our knowledge of being. But all that presents itself to us in appearance, as the phenomenal world and the self within it as phenomenon, presents itself *formally* in the dimensions of space, time and causality as the potentiality for *action*. So even as an aesthetic phenomenon the world is imbued, by virtue of existing in appearance at all, with our potential actions upon it and in relation to it. Those actions are not governed by anything other than our self-interests and by our interest in things as objects of attention. But as the subject to whom all appearance is subordinated I need not act, need not act in my own interests as ant-ego, either at the bidding of the will embedded in intuition or at the behest of the social organisation, but may act on the basis of a subjective aesthetic order whose formal potential for action is of my own making. I may therefore act against my own interests in one formal world of appearances in order not to relinquish the self-created values of another formal realm that supersedes it. The devil knows that Christ's execution could have been avoided if he had looked to his own interests in this world, and an accommodation with this world, instead of pursuing a kingdom not of this world in which he had his eternal being, and he would have been morally justified by society and history if he had chosen to live and to teach and add to instead of flouting the orthodoxy of religion, for the devil is in the object of desire and God is in the subject that desires only what it has made.

There is nothing to be said on the subject of good and evil in a world of appearances that presents itself to us solely as an aesthetic phenomenon. All we can say of the world of appearances in its relation to us is that it appears to us as something worthwhile and that being is to be preferred to non-being. Or else we are so disturbed, affected, horrified, nauseated by the intrusion of being into the state of non-being as a *problem* that we come to think it better not to have been born. But non-being is only an idea derived from the fact of being, and an existential despair of being can only develop out of an extraordinary degree of interest in it.

As the subject 'I am', but I do not act. My ego acts for me, and I am as much concerned with and disturbed by my actions and conduct in relation to the world as I am exercised by the nature of the world and its connections to my experience. My moral dilemma is that in having become the subject of my experience as an aesthetic phenomenon that defines my being and is *all that matters to me*, my being is only permitted by an antecedent organic existence as *something else* not in the power of my willing. *That* is the source of my existential despair, of my 'metaphysical horror' at the battle of life that I have inherited as the reality of my field of action. For I am bound to act, not because I wish to but because existence itself is the form of becoming and life the fulfilment of the laws of thermodynamics.

I am guilty of *something* the moment I am born. My existence disturbs the world's equilibrium, and that disturbance and the consequential continual balancing and rebalancing of interests and actions produces all the good and evil in the world. My original sin is to be born, and I live to exculpate myself.

It is as fruitless to look for the absolute moral order of the world to which our behaviour should conform as it is to search out its absolute truth or meaning with which we can console ourselves. And just as I can only rescue meaning from the mindless actions of the will by becoming the subject, I can only create moral order by acting in conformity with the subjective aesthetic order that justifies my being. The difficulties of untangling my actions from the actions of the will that determines them are the difficulties that must be surmounted in the act of becoming the subject, in the realisation of the self and its aesthetic order of being as the only act of self-justification open to me.

In the world of *action*, which is all that the world *is* until it becomes a subject of interest in its own right, its regulatory order does not disclose any intrinsically moral dimension. The moral dimensions of behaviour can only be supplied by the subject who finds himself horrified by the mechanistic processes that allow him to be. Moral order is the subject's judgment on its actions and might be called the *aesthetic of action* since we cannot permit ourselves, in rescuing the subjective aesthetic of being from the objective will, to surrender it again by failing to recognise that only actions motivated by the aesthetic order of being can be called moral and all other actions are acts of the will that have no objective justification for being called moral.

Nothing that does not act can possess moral qualities purely as an inherent fact of being. Moral facts are judgments made in relation to acts and the causes or motivations that give rise to actions. We are less harsh in our judgments of accidental consequences than we are of deliberately motivated acts or culpable acts of negligence or omission that produce the same consequences. We refrain from judgment of the acts of the will in nature because we believe that the natural order of behaviour is itself without any capacity for judgment. Selfishness, aggression and predation in animals is the natural order of things. It seems to us against reason to make moral judgments of behaviour that does not appear to us to be subject to the individual will. Moral behaviour is implicitly a quality of the judgment of the individual will and not a quality that can be attributed to the impulses, imperatives and motivations of the will in general in its manifestation in the patterns of behaviour that have evolved for the survival of individual organisms, species and populations. Yet judgment does take place in nature, continuously and effectively, not through any self-conscious acts of choice but through instinctive acts of discrimination. The self-interests of the organism are fulfilled in a perpetual dance, a *perpetuum mobile,* of advance and retreat whose rhythm is produced by the interaction of internally motivated appetites with the sensory information received from its immediate environment. It is a deathly struggle, and if we are appalled by the violence, destruction and bloody wastefulness of basic instincts we also recognise that, in the absence of any other form of external judgment or command, it is only by means of ruthless trial and error that sustainable patterns of self-organised behaviour have been able to emerge, and it is only thanks to the forms of life that have prevailed as a result that consciousness itself has emerged to moderate judgment and impose itself on both our internal motivations and our wider perception of the external environment with which we must contend. There is no reason to believe that in having abstracted from instinct the concept of the self and its judgments we have done more than create another dynamic in the same dance between the motivations of self-interest and the knowledge of the world to which our interests have directed us.

Selfishness is self-regulating because selfishness does not persist in isolation but defines itself in relation to others. The individual is the instrument of the many. By seeking its own interests it fulfils the interests of all. If we try to imagine the extreme of selfishness that by definition will exclude *others,* then it is this: a single creature with all its needs to hand, isolated, sterile, gross, useless, unknown, unadmired, forgotten, excluded. Selfishness in relation to others ensures inclusion. The contention between self and others, other selfish selves, refines the fitness of the group dynamic. It is the group that permits the rise to power of an individual, as it has permitted it to be in the first instance and enabled it to participate in the life it discovers for itself. To participate in life it must conform to a range of permitted actions already determined for it by history and genetic inheritance. The boundaries of self-interest have been set as factors in the survival of the species. They are not the personal remit of any individual, for the individual acts as a prescribed and already fully described component of a species or group social order that precedes individual existence and whose cumulative interests it serves.

Self-interests are best served by conformity. The natural hostility of the organism to its environment by which it achieves individuation is modified in a group social context where mutual hostility gives way to mutual self-interest. For the social or socialised creature, to strike out on its own would be an act of folly and self-destruction. Self-exposure does not aid self-interest. The strong and the weak both optimise their chances of continuing their mode of existence by following the line of least resistance (a tendency captured genetically over evolutionary time) to fall into their roles within the group that, as in all patterns of self-organised order, regulate those contiguous relationships, both spatial and behavioural, upon which the individual and the whole are dependent.

Hostilities within socially cohesive groups are limited to the jostlings for position, precedence and opportunistic advantage that readjust internal relationships but do not change the coherence of the overall order, only the connections of its parts. Order is perpetuated by the balancing of the self-interests of one with the self-interests of another – the foundation of law and justice in human societies, the necessary trade-offs of social organisms in which mutual hostility gives rise to co-operation for the fulfilment of mutual interests.

The hostility of the individual to its environment that defines its individuation defines the larger social organisation. Organisational appetite for life, for its share of time and space, is functionally generated by the appetite of the individual for survival and self-perpetuation. But an individual organism can only act by permission of the pre-existing condition that gave rise to it, itself the perpetuation of something else only existing as a matter of causality, of becoming, dependent on what preceded it. I cannot will myself to be. I am, but I am only as a dependant of what is. I could be something other than myself (as a singularity I have been everything that ever was) if being something other were the means by which all that is came to be what it is. I determine nothing for myself – my being is determined elsewhere.

The individual takes up the role defined by the organisational limits and constraints of its coming into being. Its selfishness is not within its own willing but is already willed. It lives and dies as an attribute of the whole in the mutual dependency of one and the many. By acting in its own interests it secures the stability of the whole, because the whole is the order that emerges from the self-organisation of the interests of the one and the many.

Both selfishness and co-operative behaviour serve the interests of the individual within the constraints that define the organisation as a whole as a functioning entity. Order is implicit in the limits of the possible, in the contiguity of each with each and in the fact of being something in particular and not something else. The whole wills the individual to be and the individual's willing fulfils the will of the whole. The individual cannot surrender its willing, for being *is* willing and only non-being is unwilled. But each life is expended, and each life is expendable in the inexorable course of becoming and becoming many. Some have seen a sort of natural moral order in biological altruism, in the sacrifice of the self-interests of one for the benefit of others, for the survival of many, for the continuity of the whole. But the individual cannot sacrifice the life it does not own, since it is not self-willed and did not will itself into being nor refuse the will through any act of self-conscious negation of it. It cannot give up its life for its life was only 'owned' as a means of regulating the order of the whole. If we abandon the assumption that the will to live is vested in the individual will and belongs inviolably to it as the essence of being – as though it were a matter for its own conscience and not something thrust upon it as necessary and outside its own willing – and acknowledge the individual as the *willed*, then we can see that acts of self-sacrifice cannot negate or oppose the will to live but must themselves be willed.

Colonies are older than nations, and there has been time for ants to have evolved individual heritable roles that clearly serve the colony, not as a matter of social adjustment to balance conflicting self-interests, but as encoded behaviour that permanently resolves the means by which viable order will be maintained by making that order non-negotiable. Self-interests are more demonstrably the interests of the whole and not the interests of the individual, whose appetite to live is not its own.

In an ordered society, the organism's hostility to its environment is directed outward. The individual organism is defined by its negotiated interactions with its environment, by the work cycle of its existence as a multi-cellular creature, by the continuous dance to the rhythm if its appetites and its sensory stimulation, its advances and retreats, its aggression and defensive reactions, as a process of becoming, consuming and being consumed. By behaving in this way after its fashion it does not secure anything for itself that is not already prefigured by a constitution that is guaranteed to it only because it *is* prefigured as an interest expressed before it came into being. The organism takes its place in the larger order of being where the advantages and disadvantages of being something in particular constrained by that constitution are tested against the hostility of everything that is other.

We ourselves are not yet bred to genetic servitude where our roles in the colony of others are defined irrevocably by biology, by the fact of being one thing and not another. Just the same, we work in its factories, we dig its sewers, we grow and distribute its food, we join its armies, we fight on its frontiers, and by defending the interests of our ant-egos we align our own security with that of family, kin, city, state, race and nation whose proximity of interests we share. The ant, having no choice in the matter, cannot overstep the boundaries of its usefulness because its uselessness in any other capacity has long since disappeared without trace. We are always left with what works, and choice only works for us when it is not free. Choice is the exercise of discretion in judgment, limited by the proximity of the possible. The fact of being something in particular precludes the possibility of being something other and acting otherwise. Consciousness only serves judgment, and the function of right judgment in both instinct and intuition is to determine right action – and right actions are those that serve to perpetuate the conditions under which the individual is free to act. This is a poor sort of freedom if our noblest actions in the service of others are only undertaken to preserve the order of things that permits those actions. We are as much enslaved to our condition by freedom as the ant is by necessity. Freedom of choice is freedom of discretion in judgment under conditions and circumstances from which we are unable to choose to be free.

The judgments of necessity are not judgments of conscience and cannot therefore have any moral content. But if judgments of conscience are also judgments of necessity via a different mode of discretionary judgment for the same ends – the sustaining and balancing of the order of being that permits judgment – they are only moral in the manner in which they are presented to us as something over which we are conscious of having some discretionary choice. We know what we do and we are able to estimate the consequences of what we do, which is the usefulness of discriminatory judgment. Our actions when we act without knowing what we do when we *could* act in the knowledge of what we do, since that knowledge is available to us in consciousness, are also ultimately presented to us as moral choices. Only unconscious failures of moral judgment and a pathological incapacity for moral judgment escape the criteria we apply to the morality of our actions. Morality regulates the order of judgment. It regulates the permissibility of actions and the motivations for actions. Since discrimination in judgment is what is being regulated not only the action itself but the failure of judgment in relation to the criteria for action also comes under moral constraint. Since all our actions and motivations to act are governed by the self-regulating order of what is already willed, necessary order without moral conscience and moral order only differ in their modes of judgment for action. The morality of an action is not attached to the act, or to the motivation to act, or to the one who acts. None of these can possess any intrinsic moral quality. Morality is attached only to judgments, and judgments are only moral in so far as they are discretionary judgments of conscience. They are *deemed* moral because they are judgments available to conscious knowledge. They could just as easily be unknown and non-moral judgments lacking in any qualities whatsoever and indifferently working to the same end of maintaining the order of the whole by constraining the behaviour of the component parts in relation to each other, as in all other realms of nature. But, because they are known to us as qualitative judgments in consciousness, they are no longer matters of indifference to us but matters of interest and concern for our choice of right actions. They appear to us as moral judgments within the power of our own willing, just as the self appears to us as that which wills and judges, though the representation of the self and the freedom of its judgments are no less the instruments of the will by being known.

The organisation of self-interest for mutual benefit in nature has produced settled patterns of dynamic behaviour that are not entirely driven by selfishness unmodified by the self's inevitable encounter with the selfishness of others, to which it must accommodate its own interests where it is unable to overcome opposition to its interests. The immediacy of self-interest is merely the localised constraint of the pursuit of the more distant effect of self-continuity through division and reinvention. Nothing can come into being except as a dependency of the conditions that allow it to be. Selfishness belongs to the whole condition. Were it not an element of the whole condition its separateness, its entropic isolation from the conditions in which it arises, would lead inexorably to extinction. The overall beneficiary of selfishness is not the self, which is expended as *effort* in the process of becoming, but the condition whose continuity permits it to be. The emergence of co-operative and altruistic behaviour as the micro-dynamic of self-organisation is not, *deus ex machina*, the emergence of moral order or a moral sense. We can discover in patterns of unconscious animal behaviour adumbrations of reciprocation, sympathy and even fairness, generosity and trust, whose algorithms of calculable benefits have been written into the genome aeons before the emergence of mind and its emotional and rational decision-making processes. If it seems to us that we should know right from wrong intuitively, as a matter of judgment in intuition from an *a priori* sense of the world's moral order that is as essential to mind as space, time and causality are to understanding, it is only because the modification of behaviour for our own good imprinted in instinct has resurfaced from that unknown region as the *a priori* ground of right judgment in intuition for the same good. What we see at work in nature is not moral order but the effectiveness of constrained behaviour in producing and sustaining order and viability in species and populations. We are not naturally moral, only naturally constrained by what is permissible.

In what way, then, can we describe ourselves as moral

beings, by which we distinguish ourselves from the animal, if all of our moral behaviour is already mirrored and prefigured in the animal's world of necessary actions? Right actions in nature are the cumulative effect of the sorting out of wrong actions with negative effects from right actions with positive effects on the viability of the organism in relation to its environment. What remains is what works, the residue of all that has failed to date, and what remains is 'right' for so long as that right prevails. There is no essential difference between actions that result from judgments made in instinct and actions freely chosen if the freedom to act is only a variant form of judgment constrained by the same necessity to act in the interests of the whole by acting out of self-interest. Moral judgments and necessary judgments are both designed to regulate the internal hostilities, conflicts and interests of one in relation to another, to balance the 'right' of the individual with the power of right vested in the order of the whole.

Right judgment in instinct has evolved by trial and error to be captured in the behavioural program of the organism. Its motivation to act and the sublimation of its actions rise and fall to rhythms unknown to it. It is truly a self-regulating mechanism. In the translation of judgment from instinct to intuition, if we mean by that the end of our reliance on involuntary behaviour and the introduction of a degree of volition in our actions, those judgments, being necessary judgments, must of necessity have some perceptible qualities to them to regulate the rightness of judgment. They have their own rise and fall, their origination and resolution, as something knowable and known. To recognise something as 'right' it must have the quality of 'rightness' attached to our judgment of it. If we 'know' right from wrong we must mean that we know right judgment from wrong judgment in the way an organism in instinct 'knows' when to act and when not to act. But whereas the criteria for judgment in instinct are unknown to the organism, in intuition they are known qualitatively, and hence morally, as the criteria of right and wrong judgments. In both instances, whether the judgment is made unconsciously in instinct or through conscious and rational or unconscious and emotional cognitive processes, there is a *point* at which judgment is made, and that point – where quiescence turns to action – is the point at which the organism recognises the criteria of judgment for action. It matters not for functional self-organisation that the criteria for judgment for action manifest themselves as moral imperatives in the mind's representation of reality, any more than it matters that things in themselves should appear as objects of interest in time and space full of the potential of our actions and not appear simply as sensory stimulants to action. Judgments must be made, but the mode of judgment adapts itself to the effectiveness of judgment in perpetuating the conditions that permit it.

There are limits to the freedom of judgment, for without limits there would be no freedom from error. We are free to choose, but we are only free to choose what we have chosen. We are free to act, but only so far as the consequences that follow from our actions permit the continued exercise of the freedom to act. Our freedom of judgment is fastened, as it were, to a long invisible chain whose links have been forged by necessity, from which we are never free. We are never free from necessity, only free to act within the limits imposed by necessity. We are really afraid to be free, for to be truly free is to wander off into unknown territory loosed from all the ties of moral judgment and guidance. Fear of the unknown and the unknown consequences of the absolute freedom of judgment limits the freedom of the will and chains it to the criteria of judgment for action, that is, to moral judgment and its consequence – moral order.

In a peaceable, ordered society the mutual hostility of self-interested egos is tempered by the limits of the freedom to act as anything other than a component of the whole. Any single individual's circle of influence is small and is like a single cell in an organism whose individual integrity is conditional on the integrity of the whole body and its own correct and prescribed functional role within it. If the individual cannot see clearly that his own interests are aligned with the interests of the whole, if he fails to negotiate a legitimate and legitimised role for himself in relation to the self-interests of others through a natural or learned understanding of right and wrong moral judgments and actions, a secondary level of social ordering can be brought to bear on the misaligned individual will in the form of institutionalised, contracted constraints on behaviour. The rule of law and the visibility of justice and punishments satisfy the will of the whole for order by regulating outbreaks of hostility and the invasion of the privileges and private power of one individual's self-definition by another attempting to define its own power base.

Society and its laws limit the scope for individual power and for self-aggrandisement at the expense of others. Where an individual or a faction controls a power base that is outside the moral constraints of society as a whole, sustained as an enclave by its own 'corrupt' rules, it functions outside society, as an enemy of society and the status quo, outlawed by and hostile to society and in conflict with it. But society permits the rise to power of an individual or a faction if that individual will to power reflects and represents the will of the whole for power. Kings, emperors and dictators – leaders, like pack leaders – take upon themselves the interests of the whole and are identified with the whole and by the whole as its source of power – of viability, sustainability, development, growth and, significantly, the strength to resist external hostility along with the self-confidence to initiate hostilities.

The interests of one are the interests of many, and collective judgment always has precedence. Even in quiescent situations, where each goes about his own business saying good

THE FREEDOM TO BE TRAGIC

morning and acting in accordance with his own conscience and with nothing but good will towards men, all our private and individual decisions and judgments are contributing to the order of the whole. These private and apparently voluntary acts of conformity are, in fact, collective and collectively determined decisions. Our peaceful co-operative co-existence is as much the collective will of the whole of which we are a component part as the rising up of the whole is the rising up of the will to power in one for the sake of all. When the whole does rise up it does no good to carry on with your peacetime job as though nothing had changed when all the interdependencies you rely on for stability and normality have moved off, like a flock of roosting birds rising suddenly and leaving you alone on a branch against the setting sun.

Ants are busy all day on behalf of the colony, each taking its given part. But under attack from a rival colony each takes on the role of defender. And if the ant belongs to the attacking colony it takes the part of the attacker. The same sort of transformation takes place in human societies where the moral equilibrium of normal social life and individual moral judgments give way to a collective moral imperative on behalf of the whole. What may appear to be a change of personality and a newly enforced role for the peaceable individual, a sudden and inexplicable phase change from quiescence to aggression, is just the same application of the judgment for action for self-interest. In such circumstances, where each is mobilised in the interest of the whole, and the criteria for right judgment have shifted from balancing the self-interest of individuals in their complex social interactions to the interest of power vested in the whole on which the individual is dependent, the individual who claims the integrity of his own will and conscience places himself outside the will and the interests of the whole and himself becomes an 'enemy' of society, an enclave of one among other enemies (communists, subversives, anarchists, undesirables, recidivists, anti-social

~ 297 ~

elements, dissidents, pacifists, Jews). In the act of collective self-defence and aggression, the managed internal hostilities and dissent whose tensions were diffused by the judgments of conscience, moral order and justice, are directed outward against external threats or in the pursuit of external ambitions, and directed internally against internal enemies, including the same consciences on which the social order had until then been reliant. Where once it had been an outrage to give someone a bloody nose, the same social order that has determined the criteria for moral order will arm you for mass murder (notionally accompanied by sentiments of regret at the necessity of it) and your crime now will be to refrain from giving a bloody nose, and the moral shortcomings of society will then be found in the want of fighting spirit and in the quality and quantity of its weaponry. It is not aggression itself but the insufficiency of men and armaments that is seen as a moral deficit. The first of our world wars saw the biggest mass mobilisation in history of individual souls dedicated to the vested interests of national powers and the subversion of individual moral integrity to the moral need of the whole conflict, in which women, who in normal social circumstances take on roles of loving and nurturing, spat in the street at non-combatant men because they were not dying.

For so long as there is order there are enemies of order. The fight against dissolution and the struggle to be are expressed in the terms of hostility. We are unable to resign our struggle, and even death is not resignation but the acceptance of the terms of the struggle.

Moral order is regulatory order. Moral values as such are not to be found in the instinctive behaviour that regulates the order of species, populations and societies. There is no reason to think that moral values that have subsequently arisen in conscience are not fundamentally the same constraints on behaviour acquired and learned by the promptings of approval and disapproval, guilt, remorse and self-approbation, the same necessity to possess the integrity of judgment the ant possesses, now dressed in words and uniforms.

Moral judgment is fundamental but not absolute. Where, then, shall we find the certainty of moral judgment if it is the expediency of the integrity of judgment that has determined moral order?

Despite the constant readjustment of the moral order of society for the convenience of the whole, the variability of the criteria for judgment for the advantages of power, the subordination of the will of one to the will of many, the redirection of co-operative behaviour against internal and external enemies in which the mutual recognition of the autonomy of the individual is lost, and despite all the moral justifications for our actions, the one fundamental premise for moral judgment that seems to us inviolable, even when we act contrary to it, is that when we act on behalf of or against another individual we are neither the friend nor the enemy that the moral order of society dictates we must be, but one and the same lost soul cast into the maelstrom of existence to sink or swim as the subject of our own experiences. There is comradeship in adversity as there is comradeship in war, which at one level is the necessary support of one adjacent unit of order to its immediate companion, but at another is a deeper reflection and recognition of a shared condition, the condition of being and being that thing thrust into actions not of its own willing, that is to say, the existential condition itself.

All the crimes of humanity are visited upon a single individual. There are no crimes against society, no crimes against nations or against one's enemies or against aliens, gypsies, Jews, only justifications for hostilities towards them. Only the individual is capable of suffering a crime and only an individual has the capacity to commit it. When we act morally we act within the constraints of moral order. When we act immorally we act against and outside the moral order that legitimises our actions. In both instances we do not act for ourselves even when we act out of conscience and deliberation, or from impulse or self-interest. We are acting as parts of the whole, as compliant components of the whole machine or as loose springs sprung from its internal tensions. To act for ourselves is to act neither with the sanction of moral order nor with regard to its censure. Our only freedom, our freedom from the self-sustaining self-organisation of the will whose idea of order this is, is the freedom to be the subject and for the subject to be the ground of all values, who may disregard and deny the will of the objective that is without value. The subject simply cannot take its moral direction from the external moral order of the objective of which it is unwittingly and unwillingly a part, but must insist that since the only value of being is the integrity of its subjective aesthetic awareness of being as the ground of all values, then its moral values for action must take their direction from the aesthetic value of being. Our crime is to submit to the objective and to take our moral direction from outside ourselves (as our error in understanding is to expect truth to reveal itself in the objective through speculative reason) and not from the integrity of our subjective aesthetic (whose truth this is). Our redemption from crime (sin) is to suffer, as Christianity has always understood, for it is only at this level, in the depths of the suffering soul, that we are able to realise the self's true nature as the soul saved from all the externalities of the objective order to which it is enslaved to become the eternal transcendent subject.

If the truth of Christianity lies in Christ's suffering, then that truth can be understood in this way: that in a single historical event God ceased to be the unknowable external originator of the universe and finally came into the world to be the eternal suffering subject through whom all values are mediated; that God finally came into the world to suffer on our behalf and lead us away from the world we can't possess to the possession of the soul that we cannot lose as the eternal subject in God. But we misunderstand...

We know the truth of moral judgment deep in our souls, not because it has been planted there by the evolution of the criteria for judgment in intuition, but because to know ourselves is to know ourselves as tragic, and our tragedy alone releases us from meaningless existence and the perpetuation of the condition of existence and the moral order that sustains it. Every time we lose sight of the individual and the suffering that defines him as the subject of his own experiences we lose sight of the ground of our freedom in suffering. To act on any other ground but this alone is to sacrifice my soul for the sake of the world, a world without value. To act on *this* ground, on the ground of my own tragic sense of being, is to possess my soul against the world, against the life that I shall lose that is the world's possession and not mine.

But we are afraid. We are afraid of losing ourselves in the very act of self-realisation, by denying the will, in the way an unruly child denies the will of its parent and then wonders how to manage without authority, who is not yet ready to assume authority himself and therefore does not know on what else his authority is to be founded. The fear of losing our lives keeps us attached to life by its harness, to do as it bids us do because it is life that has summoned us into being, and to cut ourselves free does not seem to us to be freedom at all but isolation and exposure on little legs that will not support this child in his wilfulness. It is easier to forgive ourselves our fears, to say that all that has gone before justifies and endorses our being as we are, and after all we are all in the same boat being carried downstream and to jump overboard and swim against the current is the most certain way to lose your life (say we all as we work the oars and sing our work songs and welcome the morning and the evening star as our guide and set the sails for oblivion). It is easier to act in our own interests, for in that way we might save our lives, and when we must act and endanger our lives we at least have a moral compass set to direct us in the storm when we can no longer see clearly, and if we fail because we cannot face our fatefulness then it is only because we are human and afraid, afraid of ourselves, of life, of fate.

It is fear not love that drives our passion for life. Fear cannot be helped, but love is within our power as the expression of the aesthetic and moral value of life for the subject. It is the faith in that judgment, in defiance of reason and the cumulative empirical understanding of the objective, in opposition to the practical and convenient, the conventional and the useful, in the denial of the ego and other, in the rejection of the will to live and the will to power, that at once overcomes life and justifies life.

In becoming a singularity I have elected to live by an elected truth, a truth the world cannot endorse. For I may wait through all eternity for the truth of the world to reveal itself but it will not come, for it is not something the world possesses, it is something only I can make. My truth is a revelation that never has been the world's mystery.

I am become one only because the many demand it. I am always one-among-many because I cannot become one unless I am first many. To become a singularity is not to deny the fact of the many or to refuse a life among the many. I cannot deny life, or the fact of life as the condition of my existence. What I deny is the sufficiency of the condition to be the ground of all values.

What I refuse is the fear of life for the sake of life. So it is true to say that in becoming a singularity I both accept and refuse my life. I accept the many as the condition of being one, but refuse the sufficiency of being one-among-many as a reason for being and as the justification of my actions.

So it is also true to say that by becoming a singularity I isolate myself from the many and in doing so elect to bear my life alone as the subject that can never concede the responsibility for its experience to the many nor justify its actions by the actions of another. For the many, becoming a singularity is a fate to be feared, for nothing is to be gained by becoming one when life is defined by being one-among-many, as though, like frightened rabbits, we were suddenly to decide, by a perverse act of the will, to leave the security of the burrow in a storm and seek out the highest point and expose ourselves to the cosmic wind. But, in truth, the experience of being one is all there is. Terrifying though it is to bear in a single consciousness the entire mystery and revelation of the world and our fate, the fear is not of what is thus made plain, which is the truth of the matter through all eternity, but of the loss of the illusion that I am justified by the many and not solely and irrevocably justified by myself to myself.

And yet I am not alone, for the condition of being is the condition of being the singular subject, and what I discover in my subjectivity is not simply the personal and ego-centred representation of the world of my interests (which belong to the objective) but the universality of subjective experience, the unbreakable thread that links one individual to another through time and space, through history and place and circumstance, links all the various and vicarious, temporal and temperamental experiences of becoming a singularity in defiance of the temptation to remain many.

Not many can resist the temptations of the sufficiency of external truths, or the contentment of labour and the rewards of happiness. Not everyone will wish to leave his observation tower to become what he has seen. Not all can walk out into the world and leave the world behind. Few will become heroes and artists of their own lives, and fewer still will sacrifice the burden of the self for the sake of the whole world. But we are all tragic, and it is the tragic sense of life that frees us from a greater tragedy – never to know ourselves because we are afraid to lose ourselves.

Lightning Source UK Ltd.
Milton Keynes UK
UKOW05f2351160813

215487UK00001B/18/P